The Chief Rabbi's Funeral

The Chief Rabbi's Funeral

The Untold Story of America's Largest Antisemitic Riot

SCOTT D. SELIGMAN

Potomac Books
AN IMPRINT OF THE UNIVERSITY OF NEBRASKA PRESS

 Potomac Books is an imprint
of the University of Nebraska Press.
Manufactured in the United States of America.

Library of Congress Control Number: 2024020283

Designed and set in Arno Pro by Scribe Inc.

CONTENTS

ILLUSTRATIONS

PREFACE

As I write this in 2024, the New York–based Anti-Defamation League (ADL) has just published its annual *Audit of Antisemitic Incidents*. This year's edition testifies to the fact that 2023 marked America's high-water mark for antisemitic assaults, harassment, and vandalism. In no year since 1979, when the ADL began counting, has the number of such incidents come anywhere near the 8,873 that occurred in 2023. Turbocharged by a surge in anti-Israel and anti-Jewish feeling associated with the Israel-Hamas war, it exceeded the tally of the three previous years combined.[1]

The 161 violent assaults in 2023—a 45 percent increase over the previous year—involved a total of 196 victims. Had the ADL been around and been counting, however, they would have exceeded that number on *just one day* in 1902. On July 30 of that year, when the Orthodox Jews of New York's Lower East Side buried their first and only chief rabbi, America experienced the single largest violent antisemitic incident in its history in terms of sheer numbers attacked and injured.

The most appalling aspect of the events of that day was not even the vicious assault on the huge crowd of Jewish mourners by blue-collar workers from a local printing press factory. That was dreadful and unprecedented in its scale, to be sure, but employees of that plant had a long history of harassing Jewish passersby. What was far more shocking was that the police themselves compounded the attack when they arrived on the scene. "They are the ones who should have arrested the aggressors," the outraged Yiddish-language daily *Forverts* (Forward) protested. "Instead, they were the ones who perpetrated violence against the peaceful Jews a hundred times over."[2]

The assault on Chief Rabbi Jacob Joseph's funeral procession was not the first such rite to be defiled by Jew haters in America. For that, one would have to go back at least to 1743, when the funeral cortege of Abraham Isaacs of Shearith Israel, the country's oldest Jewish congregation, was assaulted by a mob. As the *New York Weekly Journal* reported at the time, his corpse was "insulted . . . in such a vile manner that to mention all would shock a human ear." Isaacs's body was finally interred, but only after someone apparently attempted to subject it to a posthumous conversion to Christianity.[3]

As that example suggests, antisemitism in America is older than the United States itself, though violent attacks on Jews, at least those of any significant scale, are primarily twentieth- and twenty-first-century phenomena. This is the story of the first major one. The first one that garnered national attention. The one that ushered in a century that would, from time to time, witness more vicious attacks on America's Jews.

But it was also the one that served notice on the country that Jews were now present in sufficient numbers, and had acquired sufficient political power, to fight back. Newly a part of the New York political establishment, Jews no longer had to accept mistreatment passively or with resignation. Through their hastily established East Side Vigilance League, they would wield their newfound influence to defend their interests and push for justice.

Decades before the spate of antisemitic violence that reared its ugly head during the civil rights struggles of the 1950s through the 1970s; before New York's Crown Heights riot in 1991; and before the mass shooting at Pittsburgh's Tree of Life–Or Simcha Synagogue in 2018, which was the deadliest as of this writing and in which one of my own elementary school classmates perished, there was the brutal attack on the chief rabbi's funeral cortege. Its sole saving grace was that unlike several of the others, no one was killed in it.[4]

FBI director Christopher Wray told the ADL in late 2022 that antisemitism motivated fully 63 percent of religious hate crimes in the United States, a number that has likely risen in the wake of the Israel-Hamas war. Such offenses target an ethnic group that makes up just 2.4 percent of the population.[5] Unlike the 1902 riot, however, the modern variety of violent attacks on Jews, at least until the outbreak of the war, has usually been a premeditated strike by a lone hater. The various "crimes" these contemporary offenders attribute to Jews include support for civil rights or leftist causes, the State of Israel's policies toward Palestinians, and alleged Jewish schemes to "replace" the white supremacists who peddle that particular baseless conspiracy theory.[6]

Antisemitism remains alive and well among some in law enforcement. But although nearly all American Jews today—a poll by the advocacy group J Street put the number at 97 percent—report being concerned about Jew hatred, they do not generally expect to be at the receiving end of tear gas, tasers, or bullets from the police, at least not because they are Jewish. Not so Blacks and Hispanics. In that sense, the police role in the 1902 Grand Street riot has more in common with modern police brutality against people of color than against Jewish people.[7]

In America today, it is unfortunately not at all difficult to envision police as agents of persecution instead of protectors and defenders. The 2020 video of Minneapolis police officer Derek Chauvin snuffing the life out of a helpless George Floyd with a knee on his neck has been seared into the public consciousness. It has catapulted the issue of police brutality toward minorities, especially Blacks, into the national conversation, where it has always belonged but seldom lodged for long. In several cities, echoes of the 1902 police actions reverberated in large-scale police assaults against those who protested Floyd's killing.

Few photos of the events of July 30, 1902, on New York's Lower East Side survive, and there were no videos, nor was there social media, to inflame public passions. But, as in the murder of George Floyd, coverage of the riot nonetheless brought violent ethnic hatred front and center, for at least a short time, and forced average people to see it for what it was. The good news is that in both 1902 and 2020, it was roundly condemned—by the newspapers, by politicians, by civic and religious leaders, *and* by the general public.

This book tells three related stories: the saga of New York City's first and only chief rabbi; how his funeral gave rise to the single largest violent antisemitic incident in American history; and how, in its wake, the Jewish community organized and deftly deployed its newfound political clout to pursue justice for the victims and set a pattern for the future.

The events of 1902, although now well over a century in the past, unfortunately still resonate and continue to be relevant in our own times as we grapple with the purveyors of racism, antisemitism, anti-Muslim and anti-Asian prejudice, homophobia, and transgender phobia who act out their hatreds across the length and breadth of the land.

In 1902, New York's Jewish community found that by uniting, organizing, and building alliances, it could hold the government accountable for taking to task those who did it harm. In the more than a century since then, organizations like the ADL, the American Jewish Committee, and the American Jewish Congress, all of which were established in the wake of the 1902 riot, have done more or less the same after incidents like the murder of eleven worshippers at Pittsburgh's Tree of Life Synagogue. As they seek to leverage their political influence to combat discrimination and secure justice in modern times, they have, in effect, borrowed a page from the East Side Vigilance League's playbook.

When people speak of antisemitism, or even of racism in general, it is often accompanied by a wringing of hands. People say it has always been with us and predict that it always will be. Eradicating it is a Sisyphean task, but we must never cease trying. At the very least, we can impose a significant and deterrent cost on it when it rears its hideous head in violent expression.

In 1902 the New York Jewish community showed us how.

AUTHOR'S NOTE

As in all of my works of narrative nonfiction, the characters depicted in this book have not in any way been fictionalized. They really existed, and the events really occurred at the times indicated. All quotations that appear either between quotation marks or in block form were recorded at the time or in a memoir, though in a few instances I have condensed material or added italics to make for smoother reading. And no thoughts have been attributed to people who left no records of them, nor have feelings or motives been ascribed to them that were not made explicit by their words or actions.

The Yiddish, Hebrew, and Russian terms in this work, with minor exceptions, are Romanized according to the pronunciations favored by Lower East Side Litvak Jews—those whose families originated in present-day Lithuania, Belarus, Latvia, and northeast Poland. In a few cases these spellings may deviate from common, modern orthography.

DRAMATIS PERSONAE

East Side Vigilance League

Julius Halpern (1858–1928) Physician and president of the East Side Vigilance League

Abraham D. Levy (1864–1934) Attorney for the East Side Vigilance League

Abraham Hyman Sarasohn (1869–1940) Attorney and secretary of the East Side Vigilance League

Benjamin F. Spellman (1876–1952) Attorney for the East Side Vigilance League

Government Officials

Henry Mayer Goldfogle (1856–1929) Attorney and, between 1901 and 1915, Democratic member of the U.S. House of Representatives

William Travers Jerome (1859–1934) District attorney of New York County between 1902 and 1909

Isidor Jacob Kresel (1878–1957) Assistant district attorney of New York County between 1902 and 1909

Albert Levine (1872–?) Longtime New York City marshal

Seth Low (1850–1916) Mayor of New York City between 1902 and 1903

R. Hoe & Co.

George W. Church (1862–1934) Superintendent at R. Hoe & Co.

Robert Hoe III (1839–1909) President of R. Hoe & Co.

Herman "Harry" Serels (1882–1958) Machinist employed by R. Hoe & Co.

Mayor's Committee

William H. Baldwin Jr. (1863–1905) President of the Long Island Rail Road and member of the mayor's committee to investigate the riot

Nathan Bijur (1862–1930) Attorney and member of the mayor's committee to investigate the riot

Louis Marshall (1856–1929) Prominent Jewish attorney and publisher of *Di Yidishe Velt*; also a Republican and member of the mayor's committee to investigate the riot

Thomas Maurice Mulry (1855–1916) Businessman and philanthropist and member of the mayor's committee to investigate the riot

Edward Baldwin Whitney (1857–1911) Attorney and member of the mayor's committee to investigate the riot

New York Police Department

Charles L. Albertson (1856–1932) Captain of the Delancey Street Police Station

Theodore A. Bingham (1858–1934) New York City police commissioner between 1906 and 1909

James P. Brady (1862–1935) Sergeant at the Bureau of Information at police headquarters

Nicholas Brooks (1844–1925) Police inspector in command of the district east of Broadway on the Lower East Side

Adam Augustus Cross (1856–1934) Police inspector in temporary command of the district east of Broadway on the Lower East Side on the day of the riot

William Stephen Devery (1854–1919) Superintendent of the New York City Police Department and the department's first titular chief of police between 1898 and 1901

Henry Doupe (1870–1909) Patrolman assigned to the Delancey Street Police Station

John D. Herlihy (1856–1926) Captain at police headquarters charged with neglect of duty

James M. Jackson (1860–?) Roundsman at the Delancey Street Police Station

John McSweeney (1846–?) Sergeant at the Madison Street Police Station

John Nelson Partridge (1838–1920) New York City police commissioner during 1902

William Thompson (1844–?) Police captain in charge of the Madison Street Station

Nathaniel Blunt Thurston (1857–1917) First deputy commissioner of police during 1902

Rabbis

Bernard Drachman (1861–1945) Rabbi of the Park East Synagogue (Congregation Zichron Ephraim) and representative of the United Hebrew Community

Jacob Joseph (1840–1902) Lithuanian-born rabbi and preacher who came to America in 1888 to serve as New York City's chief rabbi

Isaac Mayer Wise (1819–1900) American Reform rabbi, editor, and author

Others

Joseph Barondess (1867–1928) Jewish labor activist responsible for the establishment of many unions

Abraham Cahan (1860–1951) Editor of the Jewish socialist daily *Forverts*

Charles Dushkind (1869–1945) President of the Hebrew American League

Organizations

Association of the American Hebrew Congregations Federation of Lower East Side Russian and Central European Orthodox congregations responsible for bringing Rabbi Jacob Joseph to America. Known colloquially as the "United Orthodox Congregations."

Central Conference of American Rabbis Principal organization of Reform rabbis in the United States, founded in 1889 by Rabbi Isaac Mayer Wise

East Side Civic Club Nonpartisan group with a clubhouse on Grand Street dedicated to the improvement of the Lower East Side

East Side Vigilance League Ad hoc group established after the Hoe riot to collect evidence and to ensure a fair investigation of the causes and instigators of the violence

Federation of Jewish Organizations Body established to deal with Jewish life issues in New York (Popularly known as the Kehillah.)

Hebrew American League Group founded in the aftermath of the Hoe riot charged with uniting local Jewish people and protecting them from discrimination

United Hebrew Charities Umbrella group of Jewish benevolent societies established in 1874

United Hebrew Community Benevolent society founded in 1901 to provide a free synagogue and burials according to Jewish law, also concerned with local issues

Jewish Newspapers

American Hebrew English-language weekly magazine published in New York beginning in 1879 (In 1902 it merged with the *Jewish Messenger.*)

Arbeiter Zeitung (Workman's newspaper) Yiddish-language organ of the Socialist Labor Party of America, edited by Louis Miller and published weekly between 1890 and 1902

Di Yidishe Velt (The Jewish world) Anti–Tammany Hall, New York–based Yiddish-language daily published beginning in 1902 by attorney Louis Marshall with backing from many German Jews

Forverts (Forward) Socialist Yiddish-language daily published in New York by Abraham Cahan beginning in 1897

Hebrew Leader Bilingual English-German weekly published in New York by Rabbi Jonas Bondi between 1865 and 1882

Hebrew Standard Orthodox English-language weekly published in New York between 1882 and 1922

Jewish Exponent Philadelphia-based English-language weekly published continuously since 1887

Jewish Herald Houston-based English-language weekly published by Edgar Goldberg beginning in 1908

Jewish Messenger English-language weekly first published in 1857 by Rabbi Samuel Myer Isaacs, initially as an anti-Reform biweekly (Became more favorable to Reform Judaism after his death in 1878. In 1902, it merged with the *American Hebrew*.)

Jewish Times and Observer San Francisco–based weekly published in English and German

Jewish Voice St. Louis–based weekly covering Jewish life in the city and the Midwest published in English and Yiddish between 1888 and 1933

Yidishe Gazeten (Jewish gazette) Yiddish-language weekly published between 1874 and 1928 by Kasriel H. Sarasohn

Yidishes Tageblatt (Jewish daily news) Orthodox Yiddish-language daily published in New York from 1885 to 1928 by Kasriel H. Sarasohn

The Chief Rabbi's Funeral

Prologue

The forecast on Wednesday, July 30, 1902, was for fair skies, and the mercury was not expected to climb above 84 degrees, both of which would make the day quite bearable for the middle of a Manhattan summer. Although it promised to be a pleasant day weatherwise, it would be a sad one for the mostly Russian and Central European Jews of New York's Lower East Side. On this day, they would bury sixty-two-year-old Jacob Joseph, who was to many the chief rabbi of the city.

Harris Rosenblum, a twenty-two-year-old fabric cutter living with his parents and four younger siblings at 128½ Monroe Street—from its fractional address, likely a converted carriage house—planned to watch the funeral procession, which was slated to wend its way through the streets of the East Side before boarding a ferry for Brooklyn. Harris, the son of a Russian-born tailor and his American-born housewife, would make the fifteen-minute trek to his workshop at 20 Broome Street today, but it would be a short workday. Most Jewish establishments would close their doors in the late morning out of respect for the late rabbi.

Harris would be one of the tens of thousands who lined the streets to watch the cortege go by. To command a good view, he would walk twenty minutes to the intersection of Grand and Sheriff Streets. What he could not know as he readied for work that morning was that before the day was out, he would be knocked to the ground and clubbed unmercifully by a New York City policeman who would then arrest him and continue to beat him in the police wagon all the way to the station house. That he would be arraigned that very afternoon on a charge of inciting a riot and jailed by a magistrate on $1,000 bail. Or that he would spend the next few months trying to secure a measure of justice by testifying against the officer who had so viciously attacked him.[1]

Adam Augustus Cross woke up that morning next to his new bride in their townhouse at 123 W. Seventieth Street. They had married only seven months earlier. Cross had been a bachelor until the age of forty-five when he wed Etta, a widow of four years. Five feet nine inches tall with brown eyes, brown hair mixed with gray, and a thick brown mustache, Cross, a heavyset man at 220 pounds, was a police inspector. The son of a wagon maker born outside of Albany, he was the scion of a Dutch family that had lived in New England and New York for several generations and was quite proud of his roots. He belonged to the Holland Society of New York and had married in the Collegiate Reform Church, home to a Dutch Reformed congregation in Manhattan that dated to 1628.

What was surely on his mind as he rose was that he would be doing double duty that day. In addition to his own Second Inspection District, which included the precincts below Fourteenth Street west of Broadway, he would also be in charge of the ones to its east normally assigned to fellow inspector Nicholas Brooks, who was on vacation. In Brooks's absence, he would be responsible for ensuring that the chief rabbi's funeral cortege received adequate police protection. What he most assuredly did *not* know as he prepared to go to work that day was that his handling of that event would sully his reputation and seriously threaten his future with the New York Police Department.[2]

Robert Hoe III was a captain of industry. He headed the foremost manufacturer of printing presses in North America, a company founded by his great-grandfather in 1805 that had always been at the cutting edge of printing technology. Nearly six feet tall, with a high forehead, blue-gray eyes, an oval face, a mustache, and a dimpled chin, Hoe was especially proud of the company's apprentice school, an institution that prepared poor neighborhood boys for jobs at the factory. But his true passion lay in his $2 million collection of rare books and manuscripts. His Gutenberg Bible and his Shakespeare First Folio were kept in the mansion he occupied with his wife, three children, a porter, and four servants at 11 E. Thirty-Sixth Street in Manhattan's tony Murray Hill neighborhood.

A man of affairs, Robert might have had any of a number of things on his mind on the morning of July 30, 1902. His work with the Metropolitan Museum of Art, which he had helped found; the next meeting of the Grolier Club, the society of bibliophiles he had established; his memberships in the Union League, the Century Club, or the Players Club; or the final editing of his *Short History of the Printing Press,* which was published that year. What certainly did *not* cross his mind as he rose that morning was the thought that those apprentices of whom he was so proud would incite a riot that would injure dozens of innocent people, smash all the windows in his iconic factory, and drag the name of his company through the mud. Or that they would make a liar of him as he defended them against accusations he knew very well were true.[3]

Forty-year-old, Russian-born Mary Greenfield and her family shared the tenement at 358 Cherry Street with nine other immigrant Jewish families. Her husband, David, a tailor, had come to America in 1885, and she had arrived three years later with their two Russian-born children. In New York she had given birth to three more. Mary helped make ends meet by working as a milliner.

Their nine-year-old son Nathan was one of five hundred Hebrew School boys invited to lead the chief rabbi's funeral procession. Mary expected to watch as well, not only to pay respects to the late Talmudist, but also to see her youngest child march in the cortege. It was less than a ten-minute walk to the intersection of Grand and Sheriff, which is where she decided to stand, on a stoop not far from the Hoe factory. What she could not know that morning was that she would see her son struck on the head with a flying iron bolt, that a good Samaritan would carry the wounded boy to safety, or that she herself would be temporarily blinded by a torrent of wastewater and beaten by a police officer, all before the day was out.[4]

Thirty-three-year-old Abraham H. Sarasohn woke up at his home at 185 E. Broadway that morning; he had already moved out of his father's house but had not yet married. Born in Russian Poland, he had immigrated with his family as a six-year-old. His father, Kasriel, was well known in New York Jewish circles as the founder of the *Yidishe Gazeten* (Jewish gazette), America's first Yiddish-language weekly, and the daily *Yidishes Tageblatt* (Jewish daily news).

Abraham had trained for the rabbinate but had changed his mind and enrolled at New York University's Law School instead. After graduating in 1889, he went into private practice and developed an expertise in criminal law. In 1892, with no political experience, he had run for the U.S. House of Representatives on the Republican ticket but lost badly to the Tammany Hall political machine–backed Democratic candidate. Since then, he had remained a public figure and a member of many Jewish social, religious, and charitable organizations.

As he made his way to his office that morning—a twenty-minute walk up Broadway to number 346—he surely knew all about the funeral of the chief rabbi and may have planned to be among the spectators. What he could not have known was that for the next several months, he would become the mouthpiece and advocate for the dozens of Jews who would be brutally attacked that morning.[5]

Emil Adams was a twenty-eight-year-old machinist employed by Robert Hoe's company. His parents, German immigrants, had had five children, only three of whom had survived to adulthood. They lived in a two-family house at 421 Grove Street in Brooklyn, a dwelling they shared with another German family. As yet unmarried, Emil was the only child still living with them.[6]

The ferry from Brooklyn to Manhattan took more than half an hour to reach the Grand Street terminal, which was, in turn, a short walk from the Hoe factory, so Emil would have had to rise early to get to work on time. He did not much care for the immigrant Jews whose homes and shops he passed every day on his way to work. What he could not know that morning was that before the day was out, he would be hauled before a magistrate at the Essex Market Police Court, accused of assault, and held on $500 bond. Or that he would have to rely on his employer to bail him out of jail before he could return home to Brooklyn that evening.

William Travers Jerome, who had assumed the office of district attorney of New York County on January 1, 1902, had made a promise while campaigning for the Jewish vote that if elected, he would relocate his family to the Lower East Side. Over the objections of his horrified wife, he had taken out a four-year lease on 8 Rutgers Street, which is where he woke up that morning.

The New York–born Jerome, a first cousin of Lady Randolph Churchill, had attended Amherst College and become an attorney. But his lofty social class notwithstanding, he had always been an unapologetic reformer. He loathed Tammany Hall and had made a career of ferreting out corruption.

Jerome could hardly have been unaware of the funeral that would soon fill the streets of his new neighborhood with mourners. But he could not anticipate being dragged into the trouble that erupted when the cortege passed the Hoe factory, whose employees had a well-known history of harassing Jews. The melee and its aftermath would occupy him for months and would accelerate his crusade to clean up the New York Police Department.

When reformer Seth Low ousted Tammany Hall and won the mayoralty in late 1901, he had turned to John Nelson Partridge, a New England Brahmin who had most recently served New York governor Theodore Roosevelt as superintendent of public works, to head the city's corrupt police department. How to bring crooked cops to justice, get rid of the bad ones, and promote the honest ones was a formidable set of tasks, made all the more difficult because the newspapers examined his daily activities under a microscope.[7]

If Partridge picked up a copy of the *New York Tribune* on his way to work on the morning of July 30, 1902, however, he might have noticed the item on page four that suggested that only seven months into his term, he might already be on his way out. Two prominent "good government" organizations, unimpressed with his performance to date, were trying to engineer his ouster. He would surely have had that on his mind as he made his way to work. He probably knew nothing about the funeral procession that would shortly be wending its way through the narrow streets of the East Side, but within a day or two he would know *all* about it. That event and its repercussions would pose the biggest threat yet to his continued tenure in office.[8]

In the coming months, the lives of all of these people would intersect in ways none of them could have imagined that morning. All would play prominent roles they neither sought nor relished in the drama that would unfold on the Lower East Side later that day.

1

"Unite the Hearts of Our Brethren"

Orthodox Judaism was under assault in America at the turn of the twentieth century, or at least that is how it appeared to some Jewish immigrants from Russia and Central Europe living on New York's Lower East Side. Their rabbis and communal leaders were especially alarmed and were convinced something needed to be done about it.

To be sure, the *goldene medine* (golden land), a popular Yiddish term for America, had conferred many blessings on the more than a million Jews who had already arrived by 1900, most from Russia, Poland, and other countries of Central Europe, and it would do the same for the close to two million more who would come by the mid-1920s. First and foremost, perhaps, was freedom from the pernicious combination of population growth and economic hardship that had made it a struggle to eke out even a basic existence in the old country. America offered those willing to work hard the prospect of deliverance from the grinding poverty that had defined their lives in their former homelands.

Then there was freedom from pogroms, the violent, antisemitic riots in which Jews were attacked, raped, and murdered and their property destroyed. That sort of thing did not happen in the United States. Though some Americans were ambivalent about Jews, antisemitism was never officially sanctioned, and Jews enjoyed freedom to choose where they wished to live, freedom from extralegal expulsion from their homes, freedom to attend school, freedom to elect the public officials who made their laws, freedom to enter the occupations of their choice, and freedom from the compulsory military service that, in czarist Russia, could claim Jewish sons and brothers for as long as twenty-five years.[1]

But where there were freedoms, there were also dangers. Judaism—or at least their traditional version of it—seemed to their community leaders to be losing ground in America. Many of the immigrant generation were content to live insular lives in the ghetto that was the Lower East Side, cheek by jowl with German, Irish, Italian, Polish, Chinese, and Black people in their crowded tenements. They were not the problem. They had little interest in adopting the habits or customs of their neighbors or of the members of the gentile establishment who lived in other parts of the city.

The younger generation, by contrast, many members of whom were American born, had begun to see things differently, and therein lay the threat. The weekly *American Hebrew* framed the challenge as "the battle which must be waged to keep the next generation faithful to Judaism in spite of educational, social and business influences." These, the paper asserted, were so powerful as "to make our sons and daughters forget their duty to the religion in which their ancestors lived, and for which those ancestors died."[2]

Not that Christian Americans were all that welcoming. The nation's founding fathers may have envisioned the United States as a land of religious tolerance, but the populace had always harbored mixed feelings about Jews. Antisemitism tended to wax during periods of social unrest and economic crisis and wane when conditions improved, and it did not always express itself in the same way. But it had always been present to some degree.

Not even the earliest Jewish arrivals, the Sephardic Jews from Brazil, Spain, and Portugal who began coming in the seventeenth century or the Germans who followed them in significant numbers beginning in the 1840s, were immune to gentile ambivalence. They were simultaneously admired *and* reviled. Praised by some as a pious and charitable people who achieved remarkable success in their new homeland, they also came in for a drubbing for their religious beliefs and, eventually, for their ostensible racial and cultural traits as well.[3]

Initially, Americans' animosity toward Jews was rooted mostly in religion. Jews' rejection of Jesus Christ, their supposed role in his demise, and canards like the blood libel, which accused them of using the blood of Christian children in their religious rituals, caused many gentiles to dislike them and wish to limit their rights and their numbers. The late nineteenth century, however, saw the addition of *social* reasons to dislike Jews. The demonic portraits Europe had been producing for centuries, like Shakespeare's Shylock and Dickens's Fagin, well known in the United States, were augmented in the 1870s and 1880s by a new crop of homegrown antisemitic literature that caricatured Jews as vain, ignorant, corrupt, moneygrubbing, ugly, dirty, and disease-ridden subhumans locked in perennial, elemental conflict with Christians. Many American gentiles had begun to decline to associate with Jews, who were banned from many hotels and clubs.

The coming of unprecedented numbers of Russian and Central European Jews in the late nineteenth and early twentieth centuries only exacerbated the social antisemitism problem. The arrival of what *Forverts* (Forward) editor Abraham Cahan, writing in 1896, described as "a seething human sea fed by streams, streamlets, and rills of immigration flowing from all the Yiddish-speaking centers of Europe," the majority of whom settled on New York's Lower East Side, occurred against a backdrop of unprecedented urbanization, industrialization, and social disorder. These newcomers provided convenient targets and scapegoats. Those who clung to old-world customs and traditional religious practices, spoke their own language, and kept to themselves were criticized for being perpetually foreign and unassimilable.[4]

For some Christians, the solution to the "Jewish question" was conversion: Jews had to be made to realize that only in Jesus Christ could true salvation be found. Not that there were forced conversions in America, as there had been from time to time in Europe; here proselytizing was mostly clothed in kindness. Free schools and settlement houses—which provided impoverished immigrants and their children with recreation, hot meals, medical and social services, and instruction in Americanization—could actually pose serious perils. Those used strategically by missionaries as vehicles to call Jewish children to Christ were the most feared and the most reviled, especially when, as was sometimes the case, the missionaries were themselves converted Jews.

"Our 'friends' the missionaries have found more ways than one of carrying on their campaign," the *American Hebrew* grumbled in 1902. The article continued,

> They have resorted to every possible device that will bring under their influence the Jewish children of the neighborhood in which their activities are centered. . . . Jewish children attending so-called nonsectarian kindergartens are taught Christian hymns and prayers and told religious stories.[5]

Christianity had a way of insinuating itself into the classrooms and assemblies of the public schools most Jewish children attended as well, though despite the way it appeared to some, there was no nefarious Board of Education–driven conspiracy to convert them. Many principals and teachers simply conflated being good Americans with being good Christians and saw no harm in causing Jewish children to witness, and sometimes to participate in, Christmas pageants. They were taught Christian hymns, made to memorize the "Lord's Prayer" from the New Testament, and led in the recitation of psalms according to the distinctly Protestant King James translation of the Hebrew Bible.

Perhaps even more vexing than Christian influences was the perceived threat from fellow Jews. Those who hailed from the German-speaking parts of Europe had largely gotten their start in America on the Lower East Side as well, but most had left it behind by the turn of the twentieth century, many for more elegant quarters uptown. These upwardly mobile German Jews guarded jealously the success and acceptance they had achieved and saw the arrival of massive numbers of poor, lower-class, and apparently unassimilable Russian Jews, with their old-fashioned ways, as a threat to their own tenuous status. For both philanthropic reasons and selfish ones—to avoid being tarred with the same brush some were using on the newcomers—they provided aid to the ghetto, establishing settlement houses of their own to accelerate the Americanization of their immigrant brethren.

Many recent immigrants may have envied their German brethren's success, but not their religious beliefs. The Germans had brought the Reform movement, a revisionist brand of Judaism, to America, where it had taken root. Reform Judaism was reviled by many on the East Side. Reform Jews rejected those traditional Jewish practices and rituals they deemed irrelevant to modern life and declined to observe many of the commandments in the Hebrew Bible. The Orthodox, by contrast, considered all of them binding, in principle if not in practice. As a result, to the deeply traditional Russian and Central European Jewish immigrants who lived in the tenements of Lower Manhattan and Brooklyn who now made up the lion's share of New York's estimated six hundred thousand Jews (out of a total population in the city of more than 3.4 million), what many German Jews practiced in their uptown temples simply did not look much like Judaism.

Their sanctuaries contained pipe organs, and at Shabbos (Sabbath) services, one could see women displaying their natural hair sitting side by side with bareheaded men. These were sights and sounds one did not generally experience on the East Side, where musical instruments were verboten in the shuls (synagogues), where men were expected to cover their heads during prayer as a sign of devotion, where women were relegated to balconies or the far side of a *mechitza*—a partition erected to prevent the mingling of sexes during worship—and where married women kept their heads covered with hats or wigs in public, lest they be viewed as immodest.

Reform Jews were still relatively few in number, but their movement was growing. In 1885, Reform leaders had articulated their progressive approach to Judaism. Their "Pittsburgh Platform," a manifesto adopted at a meeting of Reform rabbis in that city, held explicitly that "all such Mosaic and rabbinical laws as regulate diet, priestly purity and dress originated in ages and under the influence of ideas entirely foreign to our present mental and spiritual state" and thus no longer needed to be observed.[6]

To many of the Orthodox, this was nothing short of blasphemy. Some worried their children would find the laxity of Reform's approach inviting and might be lured by its siren call, especially given the strong pressure in America for immigrants to assimilate and the myriad enticements their new country offered for advancement, adventure, and romance. And that was to say nothing of other threats: the various "isms" that vied with one another in the marketplace of ideas that was the Lower East Side—atheism, socialism, anarchism, nihilism, ethical culture, and materialism—each of which had its appeal and threatened to pry Orthodox youth (and some adults) from the sacred traditions of their forebears.[7]

Finally, divisions existed within the "downtown" Jewish community itself. This was no homogenous population. Historian Moses Rischin counted five distinct "varieties" of Jews on the East Side: Hungarians; Galicians (who hailed from what is now southeastern Poland and western Ukraine); Romanians; Levantines (from the eastern Mediterranean); and the Russian, Polish, Lithuanian, Ukrainian, and Belarussian Jews, the most numerous group. He was even able to delineate their distinct neighborhoods for his readers. Their customs, lifestyles, religious practices, accents, and even language differed to some extent. These mitigated against unity not only among synagogues—there were some 130 of them on the East Side, without central leadership—but also social clubs, mutual aid societies, and even burial societies.[8]

Nor were all immigrant Jews strict in their observance of the commandments, out of either necessity or personal choice. Many men had little alternative but to work on Saturdays, the Jewish Sabbath, because their American bosses might fire them the following Monday if they failed to show up. And although Jewish law specified what could and could not be eaten by the observant, and the biblical books of Deuteronomy and Leviticus and the Talmud, the primary source of Jewish religious law, set out rules about how meals had to be prepared, not all women, who were generally in charge of their households, kept strictly kosher homes.

Nowhere were disagreements more profound than in the kosher food industry, where true chaos reigned. How and by whom an animal was slaughtered and its meat processed before it could be considered fit to eat was important to many, if not most, Lower East Side Jews. In turn-of-the-century New York, however, there was reason to be deeply suspicious of the probity of those entrusted with ensuring the sanctity of the food supply—the *mashgichim* (supervisors) and the *shoychtim* (slaughterers) as well as the local retail butchers. Some were playing fast and loose with the rules, with the result that observant Jews were sometimes being sold meat that was not, in fact, kosher.[9]

It wasn't as if there had never been fraud in the kosher meat business in the old country, but there religious life, at least in the larger *kahals*, or "Jewish communities," had generally been under the authority of a communal rabbi who was empowered, and sometimes even appointed, by the local government to certify slaughterers and supervisors, reexamine them from time to time, and punish or dismiss them for transgressions. The men had to pass qualifying examinations, and many were paid flat salaries that were pointedly *not* based on volume. In such cases, where they were not permitted to participate financially in the sale of the meat they handled, a key incentive for corruption was removed.[10]

In New York, however, where church and state were separate, civil authorities were not involved, and many rabbis asserted jurisdiction over kosher slaughter. Food processed under the supervision of a rabbi from one geographic subgroup might be considered suspect in others. Worse, some rabbis were paid by the slaughterhouses, which were only too happy to pass cheaper, nonkosher beef off as the more expensive kosher variety. Kosher meat cost more because the specially trained slaughterers and supervisors had to be paid, because the cattle had to be brought in from the Midwest on the hoof and killed locally, and because only certain parts of certain animals could easily be rendered kosher.[11]

Nor was there any likelihood of agreeing on a single authority who might assert jurisdiction over the industry as a whole in a way that would satisfy everyone. The city's Jewish community was simply too large and too balkanized for that. And where money was at stake, there were vested interests, and vested interests had a way of trumping piety.

Still, the idea of establishing an umbrella organization to bring kosher slaughter under a central authority and recruiting a chief rabbi to oversee it was a popular one. It had been discussed as early as the 1860s. Such a plan had worked in London, in part as a Jewish answer to the state-sanctioned role of the archbishop of Canterbury in Anglican life. In 1879, twenty-six New York congregations had pooled their funds and extended an offer to an eminent Talmudist who had headed congregations in Poland, Romania, Ukraine, and Germany to come to America and oversee the industry. Meir Leibush ben Yechiel Michel Wisser, known by an acronym of his Hebrew initials as the "Malbim," was deeply anti-Reform. But he was in his seventies and already in the twilight of his career, and he knew no English. Although he initially expressed interest, he ultimately refused the offer and died soon afterward.[12]

That was a setback, but the conversation continued into the 1880s. In 1882, a highly placed member of the Beis Hamidrash HaGadol, the preeminent

Russian shul on the Lower East Side, predicted that an effort would soon be launched to find another candidate. But he was pessimistic about bringing Reform congregations into any sort of coalition. Not only had they eschewed the dietary laws as antiquated and unnecessary; they were hardly likely to accept the authority of any traditionalist who would satisfy the Orthodox congregations in other religious matters. "Those who preach for the benefit of the gentile newspapers at the expense of the Hebrew community do not like us," he remarked derisively of the uptowners, adding, "We have no use for them or their very elegant liberal ideas."[13]

But if the right man were chosen for the chief rabbi position, perhaps even these people could be brought back into the fold. The man went on to opine,

> We are the true conservatives of Judaism, and are quite willing to bide our time, which is, I believe near at hand. The day has come for us to select a . . . chief rabbi, a man keenly alive to Jewish interests, one whose influence, knowledge and position will draw many recruits from that large class who have lost all faith in the mockery and shallow pretext of religion so apparent.[14]

In fact, that day would not come for several more years. It took the death of the rabbi of the Beis Hamidrash HaGadol in 1887 to jump-start the effort. That shul, which now needed a new leader for itself, took the lead in securing commitments from fourteen other congregations and a few wealthy individuals to underwrite the recruitment of someone who might preside over its membership and double as chief rabbi of the community. Funds were raised and an organization was established. The Agudas Hakehilos B'Amerika was registered under the name of the Association of the American Hebrew Congregations, but it was known colloquially as the "United Orthodox Congregations."

A job description of sorts for the new chief rabbi was prepared:

> His mission would be to remove the stumbling blocks from before our people and to unite the hearts of our brethren, the House of Israel, to serve God with one heart and soul, and to supervise with an open eye the *shoychtim* and all other matters of holiness to the House of Israel,

> which to our deep sorrow are not observed nor respected, because there is no authority nor guide revered and accepted by the whole community, and each one is an authority unto himself.

He was to be a man "noted for his scholarship and piety." Although his major task would be to rationalize the disarray in the kosher meat industry, his responsibilities were also to include overseeing and strengthening Jewish education for children and organizing and presiding over a *beis din* (religious court), which would adjudicate disagreements, supervise conversions, and opine on other religious matters. Additionally, the new *rav ha'kolel* (chief rabbi) would play an external role as ambassador to the non-Jewish world.[15]

This brief was shared with prominent European rabbis, and their recommendations were sought. In a flurry of correspondence, many names were put forward. After several false starts, the United Orthodox Congregations rejected the favorite candidate of many illustrious European rabbis and settled on forty-seven-year-old Rabbi Jacob Joseph of Vilna (Vilnius).

Joseph had been born in 1840 in Krozhe (Kražiai), a small Lithuanian town 120 miles northwest of Vilna whose Jewish community, which dated to the fifteenth century, had produced many eminent scholars. After excelling in his basic studies in cheder, an elementary school in which Hebrew and religious knowledge were taught, he was sent at age sixteen to study under two eminent Talmudists at a yeshiva (an Orthodox Jewish school) in Volozhin (Valozhyn), where, because of his keen intellect, he earned the sobriquet Yankele Charif, or "Jake the Sharp."

After a stint at a second yeshiva in Kovno (Kaunas), where he married, he assumed rabbinical positions and organized yeshivas of his own in various towns until 1883, when he relocated to Vilna, whose Jewish community had hired him as its *maggid meisharim*, or "preacher of righteousness." It was a much sought-after position that involved delivering sermons on Sabbaths and holidays, and it carried a regular salary. He also found time to write and publish *Beis Yakov*, a collection of homilies and novellas.[16]

On December 7, 1887, the association made Rabbi Joseph an offer. It read,

> During the last meeting chaired by the Association of the American Orthodox Hebrew Congregations, we discussed the issue of inviting

1. Jacob Joseph, the one and only chief rabbi of New York. Wikipedia.

> a chief rabbi to New York. It was decided by the majority that we, the committee, should invite Your Honor to accept this illustrious position. Should you decide to accept, please notify us as soon as possible and we will discuss your conditions. If they are acceptable to the majority, a *k'sav rabbonus* will follow.[17] Please reply as soon as possible, as we are anxiously awaiting a response.[18]

Rabbi Joseph replied promptly and negotiations ensued. At first he was not specific in his demands except to assert that he expected a six-year commitment and a salary in excess of his then-current compensation of 50 rubles (about $25) a week, which, he noted, was insufficient even in Vilna to "live generously," as his position required. By that, he appears to have meant being in a position to dispense charity to the needy rather than to imply that he expected to live in luxury.[19]

In the end, the two sides settled on a six-year term and an annual salary of $2,500—nearly $80,000 in purchasing power today—a king's ransom on New York's Lower East Side at the turn of the twentieth century, where a typical Jewish laborer was fortunate to bring home $12 a week. In addition, the association pledged to underwrite transportation for the rabbi himself; his wife, Esther Rochel; his teenage daughters, Chana and Nehama; and a servant girl as well as accommodations for the family commensurate with his position.[20]

There was still one sticking point, however. Rabbi Joseph also asked for a signing bonus equal to his promised annual salary to enable him to repay his substantial debts before departing for America. His creditors, aware of his plans, had threatened to block his departure unless they were paid. The sum was more than the officers of the United Orthodox Congregations—who expected to fund the rabbi's activities through dues from the constituent congregations and fees paid by the kosher butchers—could afford, and it caused great consternation. They were embarrassed to issue a public appeal, fearing criticism of the rabbi for demanding such a large sum, especially given the enormous salary he was to be paid. But word got out, and in the end, the money was raised quietly, mostly from private contributions.

Although there was now agreement on the terms of his employment, the rabbi had not signed a contract before departing Europe, nor could he have entered the United States legally if he had. In 1885, lobbied hard by labor unions who feared that a mass influx of immigrants willing to work cheaply would undermine their goals for better working conditions, Congress had passed the Alien Contract Labor Law, a measure that prohibited immigrants from accepting jobs before they had entered the country. Although it was aimed at unskilled Chinese laborers and could hardly have been less applicable to the office of a chief rabbi, the law was the law. It was later amended to exclude ministers of any religious denomination, but at the time it meant the rabbi would be free to return to Europe if he was inclined to do so.

New York Jewry—or at least much of its "downtown" contingent—was excited at the prospect of a *rav ha'kolel*, and preparations for his arrival began soon after the deal was struck. But could the chief rabbi model work in a Jewish community far larger and far more complex than any the world had ever seen before, and one in which the civil authorities did not empower the man? And if that job were doable, was Jacob Joseph the right man for it?

By the old-world model, he seemed qualified to lead New York's Orthodox Jews, if not the others. Highly intelligent, he had years of experience as a teacher, a scholar, and a spiritual leader. But although he had a command of Russian, Polish, German, Yiddish, and Hebrew, he didn't speak English. What is more, he lacked any kind of secular knowledge and did not possess even a basic understanding of life in America.[21]

These would be obstacles. How well he would overcome them would remain to be seen.

2

"An Old Fogy in Their Eyes"

The fifteen congregations that had teamed up to invite Rabbi Joseph to reign over them hoped he would be able to come before Passover, which in 1888 fell in late March. But he was not able to leave Europe until early July. Still, they began making arrangements for his arrival well in advance of that. They rented him a four-story house at 179 Henry Street, at the northwest corner of Jefferson Street, about an eight-minute walk from the Beis Hamidrash HaGadol, at a cost of $1,350 per year (about $41,000 today). The house was equipped with steam heat, a luxury in 1902. And they spent an additional $4,000 (about $120,000 today) furnishing and decorating it.[1]

The SS *Aller*, the steamship bringing the rabbi to America from Bremen, Germany, was due to arrive in Hoboken, New Jersey, just across the Hudson River from Manhattan, on July 7. The fact that it was a Saturday posed some logistical problems for the reception committee, since as Orthodox Jews, they were forbidden to travel on Shabbos. What it meant was that they would need to take the ferry to Hoboken on Friday afternoon and arrive before sundown, when the Sabbath officially began. That occurred at 7:30 p.m. that day. They would then spend the night and most of the next day waiting in New Jersey.

The prohibition against Shabbos travel did not apply to the rabbi as long as he neither embarked nor disembarked on the day of rest. So although the ship docked at 1:30 that morning, he remained on board all day. He had left his family behind and come alone; his plan was to send for them once he got settled.

When three stars appeared in the night sky, signaling the end of Shabbos, four members of the reception committee, in dark suits and fine silk top hats, emerged from the huge crowd gathered at the pier and ascended the gangplank to welcome their new leader. Representatives of the United Orthodox Congregations, the Beis Hamidrash HaGadol, the Jewish Immigrant Protective Society, and journalist Kasriel Sarasohn, editor of the *Yidishe Gazeten* and the *Yidishes Tageblatt,* were among those who escorted him to Meyer's Hotel, where other VIPs were waiting to shake his hand.[2]

After prayers, Rabbi Joseph was taken by carriage to the Hoboken terminal, where he and his escorts boarded a ferry for Barclay Street in Lower Manhattan. From there it was a short ride to his new home, where an immense crowd had gathered to catch a glimpse of him. A half dozen policemen had been dispatched from the Madison Street Station to keep order, but there were no reports of problems.

The newspapers, having now had their first sighting of the rabbi, gave their readers a full description. He was a man of medium height, rather portly in figure, with a full beard but no touch of silver in his dark hair. Dressed in robes and a skullcap, he had a pleasant smile and puffed on a cigar. The *New York Herald* judged from his manner that "he is an educated and thoughtful man and one accustomed to hold authority."[3]

The following day, from early morning to sundown with only a break for an afternoon nap, the rabbi received some two hundred members of the various congregations over which he now presided. All were men; no women were present. They called to congratulate and welcome him and to pray, taking turns sitting beside him for short conversations. It was decided he would give his first sermon at the Beis Hamidrash HaGadol on Saturday, July 21. Any earlier date would have occurred during the annual three-week mourning period preceding Tisha B'Av, the anniversary of the destruction of the First and Second Temples in Jerusalem in biblical times. Festive occasions were to be avoided during this period.[4]

The papers took the rabbi's arrival as an opportunity to explore what his tenure might mean to the Jewish community. To do this, however, the *New York Herald* didn't send a reporter to conduct man-in-the-street interviews on the Lower East Side, where his new constituents lived. Instead, it polled several "well-known Israelites," all of whom happened to represent uptown, English-speaking congregations, and discovered that although opinions of

2. The Beis Hamidrash HaGadol Synagogue on Norfolk Street, early 1900s. Wikipedia.

Joseph's mission differed, none seemed eager to place his flock under the new rabbi's jurisdiction.

The Reform rabbis made this crystal clear. Adolf L. Sanger, an officer of Fifth Avenue's Temple Emanu-El, pointed out that

> the office of Chief Rabbi . . . is not officially recognized in Judaism, and the question as to whether certain congregations put themselves under Rabbi Joseph's control lies with themselves and is entirely voluntary. It is not at all likely that any of the uptown congregations will recognize him at all, although possibly some of the more Orthodox may.

Noting that "the object of the importation of Rabbi Joseph may be to check the Reform movement," he predicted that such a check would not amount to much.

Columbia University professor Richard Gottheil, president of the American Federation of Zionists, whose father had earlier occupied the pulpit of Temple

Emanu-El, predicted that the rabbi would "be welcomed by the reformers as long as he does not attempt to be too dictatorial." But he added, "He will have no authority over the uptown congregations whatever."

The Orthodox rabbis consulted were somewhat more favorable. Dr. Bernard Drachman, of German and Austrian extraction, headed the Park East Synagogue, or Zichron Ephraim, a congregation on the Upper East Side. He supported the idea of a chief rabbi but made no commitment on the part of his own congregation to follow him. He predicted, however, that "with the Russian and Hungarian Jews, his word will be law."

And Rabbi Henry Pereira Mendes, Sephardic scion of an old Spanish and Portuguese rabbinic family, spoke on behalf of the Orthodox Congregation Shearith Israel. He hailed the coming of Rabbi Joseph, although his congregation, too, declined to place itself under his authority. A critic of the Reform movement, Mendes predicted that "most of the uptown Hebrews who may object to it are a bad lot . . . and are hardly Jews at all."[5]

On July 21, the new *rav ha'kolel* addressed local women during morning services and men in the afternoon. Well aware of both his own mission to preserve the faith and the fact that responsibility for passing traditions on to the next generation among Jews resided, for the most part, with their wives and mothers, he appealed to them to fulfill their roles:

> You who have upheld the religion of your fathers with more strictness even than your husbands and sons and brothers, I beseech to aid, encourage and induce those male members of your family to . . . keep intact the structure known as the House of Israel. That is your mission. Lift them up then also to the higher spheres of the religion which have kept forever the homes of the Israelites sacred. And may God bless you for such an undertaking.[6]

Afternoon worship was not slated to begin until 4:00 p.m., so the rabbi went home for lunch and a nap. Although the synagogue doors would not open until 3:00 p.m., an hour before that the entire block of Norfolk Street between Grand and Broome Streets, where the shul stood, was impassable. Twenty-five policemen attempted to seal off the block at both ends, but the press of flesh so alarmed the synagogue's officials, who worried for the rabbi's safety, that they asked the police for reinforcements.

When officers arrived from the Eldridge Street and Central Market stations, they pulled out their batons and began to beat heads. Many Jews, who were doing nothing more than waiting, were wounded, and six were arrested, including Benjamin Feiner, who owned a candy store at Norfolk and Hester Streets. He was charged with assaulting a police officer, although if he did, he got the worst of it, as it was *his* skull that had been cracked. Harris Hoffman, a hat dealer, and Nathan Agusky, a tailor, were locked up for interfering with Feiner's arrest.[7]

Men from each constituent congregation of the United Orthodox Congregations were placed at the doors of the synagogue, which was large enough to accommodate 1,000 people comfortably. They were to deny admission to all but their members, but even with this check, at least 1,500 men among the 2,000 or so who had amassed on the street managed to make it into the sanctuary and fill the pews, aisles, corridors, vestibule, and even the gallery, which under normal circumstances was reserved for women. In keeping with tradition, the men all kept their heads covered despite suffocating heat and humidity, a lack of ventilation, and the press of the crowd.

Escorted by several VIPs, the new chief rabbi, in a robe and a high silk hat, left his home at 3:30 to return to the synagogue. By this time all the streets along his route were lined with onlookers. When he reached Norfolk Street, the police parted the crowd and opened a corridor to the entrance to the shul.

After he ascended the pulpit, he donned his *talis*, or "prayer shawl," kissing all four corners of the garment and draping it over his shoulders as he recited the appropriate Hebrew blessing. Then he began his sermon. The good rabbi had not been blessed with a booming voice, and he was nearly inaudible in the rear of the hall, which meant that everyone pushed forward in an effort to hear him and remained standing for the entire hour he spoke.[8]

In his inspirational address, he urged congregants to be virtuous and kindhearted, to live strictly according to Jewish law, and to be a light to the nations. Sprinkled with biblical references to Abraham, Noah, and Moses, the sermon described Judaism as "the jewel we have inherited from our ancestors" and urged listeners to "wear it on our breast constantly." The goal was to inspire others to emulate their forefathers' example. Here he may well have had those uptown Reform Jews in mind. "As you have honored me with the election to stand at the helm and guide your course in religion and morality," he added, "I pray to God that your determination be to follow in the path of our ancestors, and that he may grant me the strength and the wisdom to guide you toward our destination."[9]

But was he the man to provide such guidance? The reaction to his inaugural sermon suggested a serious generational problem that he would have to overcome in order to fulfill his mission. Although his remarks delighted many of the older, immigrant Jews who found his language and ideas familiar and reassuring, they by and large fell flat with the younger congregants, especially the American born: the very youth the rabbi had been told were most in need of his message.

The first barrier was language. As the *New York Sun* pointed out, many of the young men simply could not understand Rabbi Joseph. "The remarkable jargon in which he usually expresses himself is not intelligible to them. . . . Many of these young men left the synagogue on Saturday openly expressing their disappointment." By "jargon," the paper was referring to Yiddish, a term that was not yet in common usage in America to describe the lingua franca of most Lower East Side Jewish homes. It was not as if the children of the immigrants did not understand Yiddish, but there was a big difference between the vocabulary of daily living they heard at home and that of the Torah and the Talmud.[10]

Even those young Jews conversant in Yiddish lacked, for the most part, a basic education in Jewish law. Despite the fact that New York had two yeshivas, Jewish parochial schools, almost all Jewish children were sent to public schools. Any Jewish education they received was likely in after-school Talmud Torahs—Hebrew and religion classes for primary school–age children—or from a roving tutor engaged by their parents for some ten cents a week. Many had mastered little more than the Hebrew alphabet, and their knowledge of Jewish law was superficial at best. They lacked the basic foundation that would have enabled them to comprehend the rabbi's words in any depth.[11]

But the issue ran deeper than language. It wasn't just about understanding; it was also about receptiveness to the rabbi's message. To preserve traditional values, he insisted that Jews remain a people apart. But the *Sun* pointed out that

> it is with the Jews as it is with other foreign immigrants . . . the young people want to be classed as Americans, and hence take pains to rid themselves of whatever has the foreign stamp. . . . In the schools they acquire what increases the gulf of separation between them and Rabbi Joseph.

The dilemma of remaining true to tradition on the one hand and assimilating into mainstream American culture on the other was hardly unique to the children of Jewish immigrants. But it was a major issue for the Lower East Side Jewish community at the turn of the century, and the *Sun* correctly identified it as the main challenge Rabbi Joseph faced in discharging this particular errand. Exhortation to strict obedience to Jewish law was not the message they wanted to hear.

"He is an old fogy in their eyes," the paper wrote of the new chief rabbi, "and they look with something like pity on him as a good man whom the progress of the New World has left far behind, with his jargon and his old fashioned observances and antiquated superstitions."

As proof, the paper quoted a young man who had listened to the rabbi's sermon. "This is all *wrong*," the youth told its reporter. He continued,

> We believe in *Americanizing* the Jews, and not in leading them back to the opinions of times long since dead. The need among the Orthodox Jews is not for a man such as this, but for one who will make them understand the free and liberal spirit of this country. They should . . . throw aside their exclusiveness and become American citizens before everything else.[12]

Other challenges lay ahead as well. Could the new chief rabbi organize a religious court whose decisions would be accepted as binding, given that he lacked state sanction? Could he reform the corrupt kosher meat industry, the principal job for which he had been summoned to New York? Whatever the youth may have thought of the rabbi, the elders were pleased with what they had heard. They were convinced they had made a good choice in Jacob Joseph, and his contract was executed.

But it was clear he had his work cut out for him.

3

"Protect Our Holy Faith"

In his first months in New York, Rabbi Joseph made it his business to preach in all the constituent shuls of the United Orthodox Congregations. He also did all the things expected of a defender of the faith, such as paying a visit to the Hebrew Sheltering Guardian Society Orphan Asylum, which he did together with rabbis Henry Pereira Mendes and Abraham Haim Nieto of Shearith Israel. He addressed the Jewish Immigrant Protective Society and a Talmud Torah. And he accepted election to the advisory board of the Hebrew Free School Association, which had been set up in the 1860s to counter the proselytizing efforts of Christian missionaries.[1]

He also officiated at the funeral of victims of a Bayside, Queens, fire and presided over the consecration of a new sanctuary for Congregation Tifereth Israel when it moved from modest quarters on Hester Street to a former church building on Allen Street. Moving into old church buildings was commonplace but controversial; first the facilities had to be properly transformed. That same month, he ruled that the New Mt. Sinai Congregation had to postpone the dedication of its new East Seventy-Second Street sanctuary, also a former church, until two crucifixes were removed from the building.[2]

Rabbi Joseph's message was one of honesty, kindness, and virtue; he exhorted his flock to "become a blessing to this great land of freedom." But he cautioned against using only conscience as a guide. Jewish law was perfection to him, dictated, as it was, by the Almighty, and only in following it scrupulously was true happiness to be found.[3]

The rabbi was quite conscious of the political environment in which New York's Jews lived, and he exhorted members of his flock to be patriotic, law-abiding Americans. He issued a proclamation on the one hundredth anniversary of George Washington's inauguration, for example, inviting Jews to "join heart and soul" in celebrating it.[4] And when it was brought to his attention that unnaturalized immigrants were being enticed by Tammany Hall operatives to vote illegally, he issued a circular in Yiddish condemning the practice. It read, in part,

> "The laws of the country must be observed as ordinances of religion." Thus say our sages. And for this reason we feel it to be our duty to ask all our brethren who are not legally entitled to vote to stay away from the polls. . . . Do not allow yourself to be enticed to do wrong. Especially in this, our country, which treats us Jews so well and so brotherly, we should certainly not return evil for good. Take care lest you dishonor the name of the Lord. Do not take an example from others; what is a fault in others is with a Jew a great crime.[5]

In general, however, the *rav ha'kolel* made it a point of staying out of politics. In 1892, when Republicans circulated a rumor that he had instructed the rabbis who followed him to urge their constituents to vote for Benjamin Harrison in the upcoming presidential election, he indignantly denied it. He went so far as to issue a statement averring that he confined his attention to his religious duties and abstained from interfering in political matters.[6]

That being said, however, he did opine on the issue of Jewish emigration to Palestine. He was not afraid to stake out an independent position on a controversial topic like Zionism, which was opposed by most of Eastern Europe's leading rabbis, who feared it would lead to secular nationalism and insisted that the ingathering of Jews in the Holy Land had to await the arrival of the Messiah. Together with a handful of like-minded Orthodox leaders, Rabbi Joseph issued a circular detailing the reasons Russian Jews should be helped to emigrate. And when he addressed the Lovers of Zion Society on the same subject, his speech was touted as evidence that the colonization of Palestine did not, as many maintained, necessarily need to await an act of God.[7]

The *beis din* (religious court) that the rabbi established was called on frequently to rule on mundane religious matters. It decreed, for example, that at wedding receptions in synagogue social halls—where, unlike in the sanctuaries, men and women occasionally intermingled—all women had to be seated apart from the men. It also approved the disinterment and relocation of bodies buried in the old Eighty-Eighth Street burial ground owned by Congregation Shaarai Zedek, but only those whose graves were in danger of being destroyed by the imminent collapse of a brick wall; the rest had to stay put.[8]

The body also considered the case of thirty-five-year-old Taube Kuseluk, a youthful-looking widow and mother of three who wished to marry her nephew, eleven years her junior. The newspapers insisted the rabbi had initially signaled approval of the union but ultimately—and too late for it to matter—changed his mind. He strongly denied this, and after the wedding, he felt compelled to warn others against the practice by placing a notice in a local Jewish newspaper stating that "the children that shall be borne of this union will be bastards under Jewish law."[9]

And then there was the case of Tina Weiss, a young girl whose immigrant Jewish father had parked her with his wife's aunt while he traveled on business because her mother had not yet arrived from Russia. The aunt neglected her, however, and after being found crying on the street, the girl was given over by a policeman to the American Female Guardian Society and Home for the Friendless, a Christian organization under the stewardship of do-gooder Elbridge T. Gerry. The society stubbornly refused to release her to her father after his return and actually adopted her out to a gentile couple, infuriating the local Jewish community, for whom Tina's fate became a cause célèbre.

Tina's restoration to her father was championed by the *New York World*, as it was by Rabbi Joseph, who spoke out about her case. He appealed to all local synagogues to press for the return of the child and engineer the repeal of the law under which Tina had been taken. Enough pressure was brought to bear that the girl was eventually given back.[10]

Soon after he arrived, Rabbi Joseph accepted an appointment to the seventeen-member New York Board of Jewish Ministers, a body established in 1881 that consisted of the spiritual leaders of Jewish congregations of all persuasions, many of whom disagreed profoundly with him—and one another—on important practical and theological issues. Despite his antipathy toward the Reform movement, however, he did cooperate in that forum with some of its leaders, like Columbia's Rabbi Richard Gottheil, of Prussian Jewish ancestry, and Temple Beth-El's German-born Rabbi Kaufman Kohler. They worked together on matters such as addressing the conflicts between religious and civil laws governing marriage and divorce and defining the authority of the rabbis in relation to that of the courts. Since marriages and divorces in America had to be registered with civil authorities, rabbis who certified them risked criminal charges. For this reason, Rabbi Joseph's *beis din* declined to do this.[11]

Despite occasional instances of cooperation, however, Rabbi Joseph never ceased to view the Reform movement as a profound evil, and his position on the Board of Jewish Ministers did not make him shy about speaking out against Reform Judaism's tenets and practices when he felt the situation warranted it. In 1892, for example, he engaged in a very public spat with Cincinnati-based Rabbi Isaac Mayer Wise, widely viewed as the leader of the Reform movement in America. Wise, the Bohemian-born founder of the English-language *Israelite* (later renamed the *American Israelite*) in 1854; of Hebrew Union College, America's first rabbinical seminary, in 1875; and of the Central Conference of American Rabbis (CCAR), the Reform rabbinic leadership organization, in 1889; was a firebrand and a man of deep convictions who didn't mind provoking controversy.

What sparked the squabble was that the CCAR passed a resolution in 1892 declaring circumcision optional in the case of male converts to Judaism. Many believed this particular departure from orthodoxy was personally motivated, because one of Wise's daughters had married a Catholic who was willing to convert but understandably disinclined to undergo the rite as an adult. The resolution was controversial even within the Reform movement, and it set the Orthodox rabbis' hair on fire.[12]

For Rabbi Joseph, the edict was a bridge too far. Without mentioning the circumcision issue directly or even naming names, he went at Wise and his fellow reformers with both barrels in a public statement:

> We have received the disagreeable information that certain people, who have no religion, although they profess to be Jewish rabbis, are belittling and desecrating our faith and attempting to destroy the vineyard

3. Rabbi Isaac Mayer Wise, early leader of the Reform Judaism movement in America. Wikipedia.

> of our Lord. . . . It is our holy obligation to stand at the brink of the chasm opened by our enemies, the so-called reformers, and struggle with them to prevent them from widening this chasm. We do not want to quarrel with that new sect, the reformers. We want to protect our holy faith. We do not want to criticize their action. Their deeds speak for themselves. Our object is to raise the flag of Israel, and, as did the prophets of olden times, send out through the ram's horn the call to our people to stand by it.[13]

He then called for the convening of a conclave of "worthy"—that is, Orthodox—rabbis to protest the CCAR's action, sparking dire predictions of a major split. The meeting was scheduled to begin on October 9 and run for several days, but even as some out-of-town rabbis arrived in New York, it was summarily postponed, ostensibly because of Columbus Day and the upcoming Jewish holidays, and never rescheduled. No other reason was given at the time, but it was clearly a calculated decision made to avoid a rupture.[14]

Rabbi Wise gave back as good as he got. He seized the opportunity to debunk the whole concept of a chief rabbi in America, a consistent position of the Reform movement. Maintaining that "there exists no chief rabbi of American Jews, neither here nor abroad," Wise, on behalf of the CCAR, wrote in a letter to the *New York Herald*,

> Some ten or twelve of the so-called Russian Polish societies, out of the hundred and more similar bodies formed in New York, of immigrants from Russia and adjoining countries, some few years ago united into a sort of confederation and called from Russia a certain rabbi Joseph Jacobs [*sic*] to whom they gave the title of *rav ha'kolel*, falsely translated as chief rabbi, whose authority reaches not beyond that circle of the confederation, and in it he is chiefly the inspector of the said body for its butchers, bakers of Passover bread, liquor sellers and other traffickers in eatables and ceremonial utensils, with a license to perform marriage ceremonies and write ritual bills of divorce. He also preaches occasionally for his people rabbinical discourse in their peculiar jargon, which they call sermons.[15]

The *New York Sun* criticized Wise's language as "both wrathful and scornful," but it was also at least partially inaccurate. The insults notwithstanding, Rabbi Joseph's role could hardly be reduced to that of a mere inspector of butchers and bakers. His responsibilities and challenges were much broader than that. But his attempt to regulate the kosher food industry would bring him far more in the way of brickbats than anything else, and certainly more than any missiles the Reform movement might lob in his direction.[16]

4

"A Flower Transplanted to Uncongenial Soil"

It took a month or so after the chief rabbi's arrival for him to begin to address the thorny issues related to the city's kosher meat supply. The local industry was highly decentralized, with dozens of *shoychtim* and *mashgichim* who answered, variously, to the slaughterhouses, to other rabbis, or to no one in particular and who constantly feuded with one another. There were also hundreds of retail butchers with shops spread throughout the city's Jewish neighborhoods.

The rabbi had already made his own judgment as to the reliability of the kosher food supply in New York. Shortly after his arrival, he mentioned in two letters that he was not, for the moment, eating *any* meat in America because he distrusted the local slaughterers and supervisors. Some, to be sure, were good, pious men, well schooled in religious law. But many others were unqualified, inadequately educated, or incompetent, if not corrupt.[1]

The system, under which they were generally paid by the slaughterhouses and not the Jewish community to ensure that meat was kosher, actively encouraged them to bend the rules. The result was that some of the meat people ate every day and trusted to be kosher had not, in fact, come from cattle slaughtered according to Jewish law and was actually *treyf*—that is, nonkosher. No one knew exactly how big the problem was, but even a small quantity of nonkosher meat was unacceptable to the observant. It was sinful to eat it, and some feared the fraught situation might actually be driving people away from Orthodox Judaism.

The local butchers, too, were a big problem. Some dealt in both kosher *and* nonkosher meat, and who would ever know if they substituted one for the other? As early as the late 1870s, the *Jewish Messenger* had put it this way:

"Uncleanliness, over-charges, incapacity, roguery have combined to render suspicious nearly every butcher who hangs out the sign 'kosher,' and many, in their disgust and doubt, prefer to abandon distinctive practices of Judaism."[2]

It was clear to many, and probably to the chief rabbi himself after a cursory review of this unfortunate situation, that any action he took to ameliorate it was going to spark intense controversy. But that was not about to stop him. He began with the poultry industry, notorious for employing inexperienced slaughterers with minimal training. On September 19, he sent two handpicked *mashgichim* to Jacob Fleischauer's slaughterhouse at the foot of Gouverneur Slip, a short Lower East Side street adjacent to the East River.

The pair arrived in time to witness Charles Wolf, a *shoychet,* at work, and they did not like what they saw. When they accused him of failing to follow the letter of Jewish law governing animal slaughter, he ordered them off the premises, but they refused to leave. Instead, they took it upon themselves to break a leg of each chicken they believed had been killed improperly as a sign that they—and, by proxy, the new chief rabbi—did not regard the bird as kosher. Wolf called the police and had the men arrested, though the judge at the Essex Market Police Court dismissed the case.

Rabbi Joseph then decreed that thenceforth, all fowl slaughtered under the supervision of his men be tagged with a *plombe,* a lead seal stamped with the name of the slaughterer and the date and time of the killing. The latter was important because the Torah forbids Jews to consume blood. If the meat were not soaked and salted within seventy-two hours to drain it of all lifeblood, a procedure that was generally done in the home in this era, it could no longer be rendered kosher because the blood would have coagulated. The *plombe* would serve as a signal to observant Jewish consumers that they could purchase the meat with impunity, secure in the knowledge that it had been approved by the chief rabbi. It would also let them know how much time they had to perform the final step to make it fit to eat.

The *plombe* had a second purpose: to raise money. Rabbi Joseph himself was paid by the United Orthodox Congregations, and he believed the supervisors should be as well in order to remove incentives for them to accept bribes from the slaughterhouses. But the organization balked at the additional financial burden, so he reluctantly agreed to charge the slaughterers a penny for each tag. The fee, in turn, would be passed along to consumers, who were already paying anywhere from eighteen to twenty-five cents a pound for chicken, and collected by the retail butchers who sold the fowl. The proceeds would be used to compensate the *mashgichim* appointed by Rabbi Joseph and raise revenue for the United Orthodox Congregations.

The plan backfired badly. It did not sit well with the poultry dealers, who stood to lose sales if the price of a chicken rose, even by only a cent. In the days that followed the brouhaha at Jacob Fleischauer's slaughterhouse, in fact, some women, who in most Jewish households were the principal purchasers of food, actually began shopping across the river in Jersey City and Hoboken just to avoid the levy. Concerned that they were losing business, forty-six butchers set up the Hebrew Poultry Dealers' Protective Benevolent Association to fight the new scheme. They came together on September 30 for four hours to discuss how to get the new tax rescinded.[3]

Morris Levy, who was named president of the new association, worried aloud about dealers in other jurisdictions underselling them. "Now the grand rabbi asked us to pay *one* cent for *plombes*," he said. "How do we know that in the time to come he will not ask us to pay *five* cents?"[4]

Hyman Brodsky, the rabbi of congregation Anshe Russia, asserted that it was not the chief rabbi's job to issue such a rule. He said Rabbi Joseph was to be pitied for having been hired "to blow like a trumpet for the benefit of his heelers." His implication was that those who had hired the rabbi stood to benefit from the tax and that he was being used by them. It was an accusation that would gain steam as time went on, though there was no real evidence for it.[5]

These reactions were predictable, since the poultry dealers felt it was their ox that was being gored, so to speak. And many rabbis who had played roles in kosher supervision in the past saw themselves cut out of the enterprise. The men in charge of the United Orthodox Congregations, which now counted twenty-three members, felt the heat. They asked Rabbi Joseph to respond to the criticisms, which he did in a letter that appeared in several publications, including the *New York Herald*.

In it, he chose to deal directly not with the fee issue but rather with the requirements of Jewish law governing *kashrus*. In the process, he cleverly suggested that those who opposed him had corruption on their minds. It read, in part,

> When we introduced these regulations, with a view of dispelling the doubts of our pious followers . . . we never thought that men would be found to raise objections against us. If we desire to be guided in our doings by our sacred law, what does it concern others? The very fact that the butchers object to our regulations about the kosher meat shows that they wish to sell other meat in its stead. If they were honest in this matter, what difference is it to them whether the meat prepared according to the regulations of our law is marked or not? I cannot and do not make myself responsible for the fitness of any meat or foul but that which bears the seal of the supervisors I have appointed.[6]

The fact that the rabbi's rebuttal appeared in the *Herald*, and not just in the Yiddish papers, disturbed the uptown *Jewish Messenger*, which was aghast that the downtown Jews, already sufficiently embarrassing because of their old-world ways, were now airing their dirty laundry in full view of gentile New York. "The 'Jewish question' need not be thrust so often before the reading world," it asserted in an editorial.[7]

At the end of the day, of course, the dealers would pass the additional cost on to their customers, and so the paramount question was how Jewish consumers would react to it. Unfortunately, what was intended as a fee for service did not appear that way to local housewives, who felt they were being gouged to enrich the supervisors. Immigrants found the fee for the *plombe* reminiscent of a punitive tax on kosher meat called the *karobke* that they had been forced to pay in Russia. It had been collected there by the *kahal* ostensibly to benefit the local Jewish community, but it had all too often been diverted by the government for other purposes.[8]

The honeymoon was over. The knives were now out for Rabbi Joseph, and rumors began to fly. One suggested he had told his followers not to have any dealings with shopkeepers not licensed by him whose meat did not bear a *plombe*, something he categorically denied. In truth, he had never gone any further than to refuse to certify food not inspected by his own trusted men.

Another rumor held that his detractors were considering bringing a *rival* chief rabbi over from Europe. And there were conversations on how to dilute his authority. Members of the Hebrew Poultry Dealers came up with a scheme under which they would choose three rabbis and the chief rabbi three others, and *all* the men might serve together on a board empowered to decide matters of *kashrus*. Rabbi Joseph refused even to meet with them to discuss the proposal. It was also reported that representatives of the dealers approached the district attorney's office to discuss whether a cause of action could be brought against the chief rabbi for willfully injuring the business of some butchers and poultry dealers.[9]

The *American Hebrew* didn't blame Rabbi Joseph for the problem; it cited "the officious intervention of men who would like to enact the role of the power behind the throne"—that is, the United Orthodox Congregations. It insisted that the organization find another means of funding, permitting the rabbi to be "a moral power, and not a money-making machine or tax gathering instrument."[10]

To make matters worse, two domestic rivals to Rabbi Joseph did emerge. Joseph was a Litvak—a term denoting a Jew from Lithuania or one of its neighboring regions. This did not necessarily endear him to Jews from Galicia, modern-day southeastern Poland and Ukraine, who saw Litvaks in stereotypical terms and spoke Yiddish with a different accent, and many of them were unwilling to submit to his authority. In 1892, some twenty congregations of Galicianers named Rabbi Joshua Segal, who had arrived in New York much earlier than Joseph, to lead them. They gave him the title of "Chief Rabbi of Congregations of Israel of New York" and authority over *kashrus*.[11]

The following year, Chaim Yaakov Vidrowitz, a Hasidic rabbi from Moscow who had emigrated in 1891 and taken the pulpit of a Henry Street synagogue, gathered together a handful of small Hasidic congregations and posted a sign proclaiming himself the "Chief Rabbi of America." When asked who had endowed him with such a lofty title, he replied, "The sign painter." And he added that the designation meant that it would be impossible for *all* of the Jews in America to depose him.[12]

An anonymous letter writer to the *Jewish Messenger* insisted that all the chief rabbi had done since his arrival was promote ill feeling. "He is doing absolutely nothing for the religious welfare of our brethren, but rather making a business out of his office and making the poor class suffer for the benefit of his favorites," the missive went on. "The quicker he abandons his imported Russian method of taxation, the better it will be for all concerned." The writer made the leap that many made—namely, that the businessmen who had made the rabbi's appointment possible were somehow poised to benefit personally from the *plombe*. Although there was no evidence for this, the United Orthodox Congregations did earn money from the fee. Rabbi Joseph was seen as the merchants' tool.[13]

But the "imported rabbi," who was denounced as such in a mass meeting in January 1889, did get a lifeline of sorts from the uptown Orthodox congregations. It came in a public meeting in mid-February attended by Henry Pereira Mendes, Bernard Drachman, and several other prominent rabbis and citizens organized to explore ways they might cooperate with Rabbi Joseph and make truly kosher meat more available uptown. A collection was taken up and an advertisement placed in the *Jewish Messenger* seeking retail butchers willing to open strictly kosher establishments on the Upper East or West Side. But it is not clear what, if anything, came of the effort.[14]

Although Rabbi Joseph had been forced to support the one-cent tax on poultry, he was able to convince the United Orthodox Congregations to forgo assessing it in the case of beef, which was cheaper than chicken and hence more affordable to the poor. He extended the use of the *plombe* to beef as well but insisted no additional charge be made for it. Doing this required more manpower, however, and that required more sources of income.

To earn additional revenue, he proposed assessing the retail butchers $4.00 per month (just over $100 today) for the right to display a *hechsher*—a certificate bearing his signature that testified to their adherence to the laws of *kashrus*. But he soon backed off even this in favor of assessing merchants $1.00 per barrel for inspection of the flour used for making matzoh for the Passover holiday. Like his other fees, however, it was widely viewed as a money grab to enrich his cronies. The socialist press was especially critical; it accused him of swindling the poor. And to make matters even more complicated, other rabbis began to offer the butchers *hechshers* of their own.[15]

Despite his best efforts, Rabbi Joseph made little headway in overhauling the kosher meat industry. Legally, he could not compel anyone to do anything. Because he lacked official backing from the local government, his authority stemmed entirely from his ability to convince others to follow him. And in New York, with its fractious Jewish community, that would always be an uphill battle.

The chief rabbi did rack up some successes. He managed to get close to a hundred slaughterhouses and butchers to accept his authority, which permitted him to oust some *shoychtim* who did not meet his standards and replace them with others he deemed qualified. But the forces arrayed against him proved too entrenched and too formidable. The *rav ha'kolel* model was ill-suited to New York because the office lacked government backing and, hence, any enforcement authority, and the city's Jewish community was too fractious to unite under the authority of any one rabbi. Joseph's sermons seemed irrelevant to the lives of the members of his flock, and the reforms he advocated were perceived as inspired by greed rather than purity. Also, Reform and socialist figures, and even some of the Orthodox, actively undermined him.

Rabbi Joseph was a kind and warmhearted man, but he was also a creature of the old world whose best efforts clashed catastrophically with the realities of life in America. As Abraham Cahan put it, he was "a flower transplanted to uncongenial soil." Few perceived the rabbi *himself* as corrupt; the problems were generally written off to him having been misled, or used, or manipulated by evil, avaricious associates. But he was unable to prevail in the all-important court of public opinion, and as the 1890s progressed, he ministered to a shrinking number of Jews and was heard from less and less.[16]

5

"One Solid Gang of Criminals"

Fraud and abuse in New York City were hardly limited to the kosher meat industry. Corruption at the turn of the twentieth century was a way of life. For as long as anyone could remember, the levers of government had been in the hands of the Society of St. Tammany—known by its nickname, Tammany Hall. A political machine, it had managed, with few exceptions, to ensure that Democrats of its choosing ran the city, and sometimes the state, government. In the seventy years following 1854, the Democratic machine governed the city for all but ten years.

Staying in power meant winning elections, and Tammany Hall accomplished this through a combination of shrewdness and fraud. Elections could be won outright by capturing the hearts and minds of voters—only men were eligible to cast ballots in this era—or, if that failed, they could be stolen. The former involved a combination of outreach and political patronage; the latter required bribery and the stuffing of ballot boxes. And all of it required money. Throughout its tenure, Tammany enriched itself and its bosses and enabled its own survival by shaking down contractors and businesses, extracting kickbacks, embezzling public funds, and charging hefty fees for the myriad political appointments it was empowered to make.

Tammany Hall had its tentacles deep into New York's police department. Its district bosses more or less called the shots in the precincts, and that included making appointments to the force. The law required only that police officers be U.S. citizens, New York residents for a year, and free of criminal convictions. Many of the men who joined were Irish immigrants, few of them well educated. If you were otherwise qualified, a payment of $250 to a Tammany boss was generally all that was necessary to get appointed.

The force was governed by a board of four commissioners approved by the machine and formally appointed by the mayor. The commissioners exercised broad powers over internal discipline, assignments, and promotions. They also had charge of the Bureau of Elections, which meant they had control over selecting polling places, choosing inspectors, and printing ballots. Such powers, needless to say, were extremely useful in ensuring that the machine retained its hold on political power. They remain beneficial to political parties to this day, as the disputes over recent presidential elections amply demonstrate.[1]

Positions on the police force were highly coveted, especially for the Irish and others who were excluded from many nonmenial jobs, and there were a lot of them for Tammany to hand out. In addition to the commissioners, the force consisted of 1 superintendent, 4 inspectors, 34 captains, 126 sergeants, 142 roundsmen (officers in charge of a patrol), more than 2,000 patrolmen, 73 doormen, and detectives: 25 at headquarters and 1 to 4 in each of the thirty precincts.[2]

Promotion was the only path to a raise, and Tammany also charged for advancement. It cost an officer $300 to become a roundsman and a roundsman $1,600 to be promoted to sergeant. The price to become a captain ranged from $12,000 to $15,000. To afford payments of this magnitude, most candidates shook down local merchants like gambling house bosses, saloon owners, and brothel keepers, who provided the money with the expectation of future favorable treatment. Once in office, a newly minted officer had myriad opportunities to bleed other businesses in order to pay back the loans.[3]

The police were Tammany's tools for managing and profiteering from New York's lucrative vice industries such as prostitution, gambling, and after-hours drinking. They oversaw and enforced the elaborate system of payoffs that kept the machine's coffers filled. A barkeep or a madam who failed to pay up on time could expect a raid by the local bluecoats, and it wouldn't be pretty.

The system screamed for top-to-bottom reform, and one of the first to cry out for change was Rev. Charles H. Parkhurst, the firebrand pastor of Manhattan's Madison Square Presbyterian Church. From his pulpit, Dr. Parkhurst, who had been drafted to head the Society for the Prevention of Crime, launched an unprecedented attack on Tammany politicians and their henchmen. In an 1892 sermon, he declared,

> The mayor and those associated with him are polluted harpies. Under the pretense of governing the city they are feeding day and night on its quivering vitals. They are a lying, rum-soaked and libidinous lot. While we fight iniquity they shield and patronize it; while we try to convert criminals they manufacture them; and they have a hundred dollars invested in the manufacturing business to every one invested in converting machinery. Police and criminals all stand in with each other. It is simply one solid gang of criminals, "one half in office and the other half out."[4]

Ably assisted in his mission by attorney William Travers Jerome, a Republican, a reformer, and a sworn opponent of vice, Parkhurst pushed for a full-scale investigation of police corruption. In 1893, once Republicans gained control of the state legislature, he prodded the state senate to establish a special committee to investigate the matter. Jerome was recruited as an associate counsel for the body, which was chaired by progressive Republican Senator Clarence Lexow. The damning testimony Lexow's committee heard over several months shined a light on police involvement in all manner of criminal enterprises, including extortion, election fraud, bribery, voter intimidation, and counterfeiting. It also found a raft of evidence of gratuitous police violence and brutality.

The hearings—held, ironically, in a building known as the "Tweed Courthouse," constructed under the direction of former Tammany head William M. "Boss" Tweed, who had skimmed millions of dollars off the project—were front-page news in New York. And by June of 1894, several police captains found themselves in Lexow's crosshairs. Among them were William Stephen Devery, known as "Big Bill," and Adam Augustus Cross. The two captains were good friends.

A colorful man with working-class Irish roots who started out as a Tammany district leader, Devery had joined the force in 1878, been promoted to roundsman in 1881, sergeant in 1884, and captain in 1891. He commanded the Eldridge Street Station in a Lower East Side precinct known as the red-light district. And Cross, for his part, had an unusual background for a police inspector. He had actually graduated from law school and briefly practiced as an attorney before joining the force, where he thought advancement might be easier. He became a patrolman in 1878 and moved rapidly up the departmental ladder, becoming a roundsman in 1882, a sergeant in 1884, and a captain in 1890.

The committee heard from brothel keepers who testified that the captains had blackmailed them, charging them a fee for protection from police harassment. A given establishment had to pay an "initiation fee" of anywhere between $500 and $1,000, and then a monthly fee between $25 and $100. The attendant publicity put strong pressure on the police department to investigate the captains named, and the commissioners heard testimony against them in August 1894.[5]

The cases against Devery and Cross rested mainly on the testimony of women who ran "disorderly houses" and who alleged they had paid the captains or their subordinates for the privilege of running their establishments unmolested. Devery, claiming illness, did not even appear at his trial; it went on without him, however, because the commissioners didn't believe he was really sick. And although Cross's attorney mounted a spirited defense that undermined the credibility of the witnesses arrayed against him, both men were dismissed from the force for bribery and extortion by a vote of 3–1. A grand jury, however, did not find sufficient evidence to warrant an indictment against either of them.[6]

The pair appealed their dismissals and were eventually reinstated by the courts. In the case of Cross, the witnesses against him were found to have lied under oath or changed their testimony. And the commissioners were criticized for trying Devery in absentia. Reinstatements notwithstanding, however, there is little reason to believe the men were not guilty as charged. Graft was the way the police did business, and it's doubtful that the captains, who would surely have incurred substantial debt to secure their promotions, did not partake.[7]

Nor did their reinstatements convince anyone that the police department did not need reform. The revelations of the Lexow Committee, against the backdrop of a national recession in the mid-1890s, were enough to drive voters to clean house. For the first time in memory, they kicked Tammany Hall out in the election of 1894 and voted in a social reformer named William L. Strong as their next mayor. William T. Jerome, known by his middle name of Travers, had managed his campaign. Strong was the first Republican to occupy the office in thirty-four years.

The new mayor promptly ousted the police board he inherited and appointed new members. He knew he needed a strong hand at the helm to overhaul the department, and he found it in thirty-seven-year-old Theodore Roosevelt, whose most recent position had been on the U.S. Civil Service Commission. There Roosevelt had taken aim at political patronage in the administrations of Presidents Benjamin Harrison and Grover Cleveland.

Described by the *New York Sun* as "irrepressible, belligerent and enthusiastic," Roosevelt spearheaded several important reforms in his two years on the job, from 1895 to 1897, before he returned to Washington as assistant secretary of the navy. He raised hiring and advancement standards, stripping politics and patronage from the process. This meant appointing men and women based solely on their merits. "Of the 1,600 [new policemen hired], I don't know the politics of sixteen," he told a group of social reformers in 1897. "We have appointed men of every recognized creed in the city and of no creed at all. We treat Catholic and Protestant, Jew and agnostic all alike."[8]

Indeed, many of Roosevelt's appointees to the force were Jews, and when he was approached in 1897 by members of the Jewish community to deny police protection to Hermann Ahlwardt, a Jew-hating German preacher from Berlin who was slated to give an antisemitic speech, he found a good use for some of those officers. Insisting that the proper thing to do was not to decline to protect Ahlwardt but rather to make him look ridiculous, he detailed a Jewish sergeant and "a score or two of Jew policemen" to see to his security. Looking back on the incident years later, Roosevelt called it "the most effective possible answer" he could have come up with.[9]

Roosevelt punished misconduct and ousted many career men, though the newly reinstated Devery and Cross, despite their questionable records, managed to escape his purge. He also modernized the force with innovations like police call boxes, a fingerprinting system, and bicycle patrols. But his crusade to close New York's fifteen thousand saloons on Sundays—required by law but deeply unpopular with the working class—was widely cited as a factor in Tammany's subsequent return to power.[10]

In 1894, voters had approved by a large margin the merger of all the boroughs of Greater New York into a single entity. The move, ostensibly an effort to improve efficiency and cement New York's status as the nation's economic and cultural capital, was in fact a Republican-driven effort at the state level to dilute Tammany Hall's power. The consolidation was slated to take place on January 1, 1898, and Strong chose not to run for the mayoralty of the new, and much larger, City of Greater New York. Instead, he supported anti-Tammany candidate Seth Low for the office. An avowed reformer, Low had been chosen mayor of Brooklyn in 1880 by an electorate weary of the graft and corruption of the previous Democratic administration and had gone on to a second term. In 1890, he had accepted the presidency of Columbia University.

Low was running on what was called the fusion ticket—a coalition of the progressive Citizen's Union and the Republican Party—which had united in an effort to dislodge Tammany Hall from power. But the coalition split, and his opponent, Robert A. Van Wyck, whose campaign slogan was "To hell with reform," was elected. Tammany was back, and it was back to business as usual.

"Big Bill" Devery was Tammany's choice to run the police department, now an amalgam of the eighteen individual departments that had existed in Manhattan as well as Richmond, Queens, Bronx, and Kings Counties. But he was still just a captain, which posed a problem. In a matter of months, therefore, between January and May of 1898, he was promoted with astonishing speed to inspector, deputy chief, and then acting chief of police. When the state legislature abolished that position in 1901 and whittled the Board of Police Commissioners down to a single commissioner, he was named first deputy commissioner under Commissioner Michael C. Murphy.

Throughout Devery's climb up the ladder, his good friend Adam Cross, now an inspector, was at his side, and indeed, in May of 1901, Devery announced that Murphy had named Cross acting deputy chief of the department. Although Murphy denied it, the decision had, in fact, come directly out of Tammany headquarters, and it had been made despite the fact that in the previous year, Cross had once again gotten himself into trouble. This time

4. New York police captain William Stephen Devery. Author's collection.

it was the Episcopal Diocese of New York, and several prominent Jewish leaders, who took him on.[11]

The initial complaint came from Rev. Dr. Robert L. Paddock, vicar of the pro-cathedral, who claimed to have been grossly insulted by Captain John D. Herlihy in Cross's presence.[12] In late 1899, Paddock had made common cause with other notable New York reformers, including Cornell professor Felix Adler, the German Jewish founder of the Ethical Culture movement; and Jacob Schiff, the well-known German-born Jewish banker. They launched a campaign against the "disorderly resorts"—that is, brothels—of the Lower East Side. Professor Adler led the charge. Many of these establishments were in Herlihy's precinct, so Paddock had previously dealt with the captain. But it was not a warm relationship. To the extent that the police were being paid off by the brothels, they of course had no use for reformers and saw them as a threat.[13]

In April 1900, Paddock rescued a fourteen-year-old girl who had more or less been kidnapped and forced into prostitution. But when he went to the Eldridge Police Station to swear out a complaint against her abductors, as he told the story, Herlihy had called him a liar and ordered him out of the station house. When Paddock threatened to take the matter to Inspector Cross, Herlihy allegedly told the vicar to "go and be damned."[14]

True to his word, Paddock, hell-bent for leather, stormed police headquarters on Mulberry Street to complain to Cross. Herlihy had beaten him there, however, and had already briefed his boss. As Paddock recalled later, Herlihy cursed him and shook his fist at him. And Cross suggested facetiously that when Paddock got into paradise, he would surely find something there to complain about.[15]

Knowing that the matter would probably not end there, Chief Devery quietly transferred Herlihy to the "steamboat squad," a special police unit detailed to the waterfront to crack down on the street gangs active there, to get him out of harm's way. And sure enough, Paddock raised it with Bishop Henry Codman Potter, who, in turn, took it to the Episcopal Diocesan Convention, which instructed him to begin an investigation and report his findings to Mayor Van Wyck. This turn of events, the *Tribune* reported, made the higher-ups in the police department, not to mention their Tammany overlords, extremely uneasy, because it was never good politics to feud with the clergy.

Bishop Potter raised the matter directly with the mayor, who referred it to the Board of Police Commissioners and the district attorney. Given the nature of the complaint and the identity of those doing the complaining, the commission (there were still four commissioners at this point) had no choice but to try Herlihy. But it didn't necessarily have to convict him. Although he was charged with conduct unbecoming an officer and a gentleman—but more importantly, with neglect of duty by failing to close down some 143 "disorderly houses" in his precinct—the charges were dismissed in February 1901 by a vote of 3–1, obviating the need for Cross to undergo a similar trial.

But the entire event gave Cross good reason to resent the reformers and the religious leaders among them, Jews included.[16]

6

"Disgusted with the Corrupt Methods of the Police"

The forces of corruption and those of reform continued to do battle in New York, and in November 1901, Seth Low once again ran for mayor on an anti-Tammany fusion ticket. This time Travers Jerome, who had served as a judge in the Court of Special Sessions since his time on the Lexow Committee staff, ran on the same ticket for the position of district attorney of New York County.

Tammany Hall, which had begun in the late eighteenth century as a nativist movement, had long since been forced to change with the times. By the 1870s, as New York's immigrant groups grew exponentially, it had shed its roots and become Irish dominated. Tammany ward bosses and precinct captains became adept at delivering social services to newcomers, many of whom were unemployed and destitute, in exchange for their votes. Handing out jobs and food, extending loans, finding homes, offering legal aid and protection to people otherwise unable to obtain these things, and "fixing" small fines assessed against them by the police had built strong bonds and created debts that many willingly paid back at the ballot box. So had attending weddings, funerals, wakes, baptisms—and circumcisions and bar mitzvahs.[1]

For these reasons, and because Tammany Hall sometimes supported Jewish candidates for office, appointed them to government positions, and occasionally even chose one as a district boss, Jews had often supported Tammany tickets in the past. But Seth Low, though born to a privileged New English Puritan family, offered them an attractive alternative. As a public figure, he had always been sympathetic to the poor and unfortunate, and he had long been a friend of the Jewish community.

During his tenure as mayor of Brooklyn, Low had frequently turned up at Jewish milestone celebrations, such as the laying of the cornerstone of the Hebrew Orphan Asylum and the dedications of the Jewish Theological Seminary building, the Ninety-Second Street YMHA, and Mt. Sinai Hospital. As president of Columbia University, he had supported the recruitment of Jewish professors and accommodated Jewish students unable to attend classes or take tests on the High Holy Days. He had even donated to the United Hebrew Charities.[2]

And in 1899, as one of the American delegates to the Hague Convention, which negotiated international treaties governing the laws of war and war crimes, he had been responsive to a request by Jewish groups to support the substitution of an emblem other than a red cross for use by Jewish physicians on battlefields.[3]

Most importantly, though, Low and Jerome were on the right side of several issues of high importance to the local Jewish community. One of them was the Sunday laws, which mandated the closure of businesses on the Christian Sabbath. They effectively permitted Orthodox Jews, who were already enjoined by Jewish law from working on Saturdays, only five days a week to do business. In a barn-burning campaign speech on the Lower East Side, Jerome made it clear where he stood on this issue:

> I want to tell you how I can help you, whether I am elected or not. I will help to knock out the Sunday closing law. No man should be discriminated against because of his religion. My forefathers fought for the establishment of that principle. Our laws, unintentionally perhaps, discriminate against the Jew in prohibiting him from selling merchandise on Sunday. If he be a good Jew and observes the Jewish Sabbath, a Hebrew has only five days in the week on which to do business. I am an American and I have no feeling against any race, nationality or religion. If elected, I will go to Albany and ask what is fair and right and can get it.[4]

Other matters of concern to Jews revolved around the police force. Police beatings had become standard operating procedure during the garment industry strikes New York had witnessed over the previous decade. These attacks had engendered a good deal of resentment on the part of the Jewish community, since Jews were the backbone of the industry's labor force.[5]

To be fair, the New York police were equal opportunity head bashers. When they saw large crowds of people on the street, whatever their ethnicity, pulling out their billy clubs to disperse them was an automatic response. In 1874, for example, police officers brutally assaulted unemployed workers who had gathered in Tompkins Square Park for a march on city hall to demand a public works program that would create jobs for them.

In 1886, police beat hundreds of striking streetcar workers and their supporters when they attempted to block the movement of cars. And something similar occurred in Brooklyn in 1895 when streetcar workers walked off the job. In these two instances, many of the victims were of Irish descent. And in 1900, scores of Blacks were arrested and beaten by police over a two-week period following an altercation between a Black man and a white undercover policeman.

The relationship between New York's police and its Jews was never one of unmitigated antagonism, however. It was always more complex than that. To be sure, many Jews resented the heavy-handedness of the officers who abused them and shook them down. But Jews also needed the police to keep order and to prevent crime, and they knew it. They needed them for protection when they were robbed or attacked by those who wished them harm. And they sometimes even needed them for protection from one another.

On a Saturday in 1896, for example, when union and nonunion tailors were at one another's throats because of a strike, police were stationed outside the nonunion shops and at the synagogues to keep order. And on the eve of Yom Kippur in 1898, police intervened to protect nonobservant Jews from an attack by their more devout brethren. The former group, many of whom were anarchists, had ostentatiously flouted the religious duty to fast by patronizing a Division Street restaurant that had remained open.[6]

There was no denying that many in the heavily Irish police department—by 1902, Irish cops made up upward of 50 percent of the nearly eight thousand men on the force compared to only 140 Jews—nurtured a particular dislike for the Russian and Eastern European immigrant Jews. Or that they often treated them harshly.[7]

There were many reasons for Irish enmity toward Jews in turn-of-the-century New York. Although largely immigrants and the children of immigrants themselves, many of the Irish looked down on the newer arrivals, just as they themselves had been despised by many Protestants who had come before them. Jews ranked lower on the totem pole and were often desperately poor. They were clannish, and many lived in squalor. They struggled with English, and some did not seem much interested in assimilation. And they were arriving in alarming numbers.

Politically, Jews were more apt to embrace reform and even some tenets of socialism and anarchism, whereas the Irish had more at stake in preserving the system into which they had so recently ascended. Protectors of law and order, the police had a deep antipathy toward the disorder caused by union organizers, many of whom were Jews; they and their Tammany Hall overlords were far more apt to support employers. There was also rivalry caused by the press of Jewish newcomers pushing Irish workers out of jobs in the garment industry. Then, too, there was broad belief among predominantly Roman Catholic Irish in Jewish responsibility for the murder of Jesus Christ, and many subscribed to the blood libel myth, the European notion that Jews routinely engaged in the ritual murder of Christian children.[8] And it wasn't just the Irish. Many Germans, Scots, and other immigrants held similar views of Jews.

Many of New York's Jews recalled their experiences with the police in their countries of origin. Officers had often stood by without intervening as civilians harassed Jews; sometimes they themselves had been persecutors. In some ways it did not feel all that different in New York, where officers involved in altercations with Jews, no matter how egregious or illegal their actions, were seldom disciplined.

A good example was an 1894 strike by the heavily Jewish Cloak Makers' Union, whose members wanted higher wages and an end to the piecework system. Union pickets had massed in Rutgers Square. Although they were told the union had secured a permit to do so and would shortly produce it, the police didn't wait. They fell on the demonstrators with their clubs and seriously injured several. This was not merely a product of anti-Jewish feeling on the part of the police; it was Tammany Hall policy. For all of their talk of supporting the working man, Tammany politicians were deeply anti-union. Those arrested faced a hostile, Tammany-appointed judge at the Essex Market Police Court who asked each man whether he was a socialist before deciding on a fine.

Prompted by negative coverage in the papers and the threat of a lawsuit against individual officers, Irish-born Police Superintendent Thomas F. Byrnes ordered an inquiry and assigned the task to Inspector Alexander S. Williams. A twenty-eight-year member of the force, Williams had been investigated for corruption by the Lexow Committee. Known as "Clubber" because of his reputation as a formidable street fighter, he was a violent man who wielded his own nightstick freely.

If Byrnes's goal was to make the whole matter go away, he had chosen the right man. Williams, of Scottish descent, shared the prejudices of many of his Irish colleagues. He was curt and dismissive of the nearly half dozen strikers who testified against the officers, and after their captain insisted that no clubs had been used, Williams refused to take any action. As the cloak makers left the venue, he reportedly called after them, "Go home! I will not believe a Jew under oath. The officers have done their duty."[9]

Williams later denied having said that, but the cloak makers did not let the matter rest. They issued a statement that he had "acted in every way unfairly toward us and has cast a stigma on our race which he will be held accountable for." But neither he nor anyone else *was* held accountable, because Jews lacked the power to secure justice from the police department. A subsequent meeting with Byrnes yielded no action against Williams or the officers involved.[10] And although the captain who had been in charge that day was brought up before the Board of Police Commissioners, the charges against him, as usual, were dismissed.[11]

Seven years later, under "Big Bill" Devery's command, police were enabling vices like prostitution and high-stakes gambling to flourish on the East Side in order to collect protection payments, but they were blaming the Jews for it. At an anti-vice mass meeting in 1900, some eight hundred men heard Devery denounced by department store tycoon Isidor Straus, the German Jew who co-owned Macy's and Abraham & Straus, and by Professor Felix Adler. Adler quoted Devery as having remarked to him,

"Do you know who is responsible for the bad moral condition of the city? It's just you Jews."[12]

The controversial Devery's future was very much a campaign issue in 1901. He came in for a public drubbing from Jerome, who accused him of having grown wealthy from his associations with the "gambling syndicate" and called him unfit to head the police department. And at a campaign event during which he was introduced by none other than Samuel Clemens—that is, Mark Twain—Low made it crystal clear what his plans for Devery were: "I can assure you that he will *not* remain deputy police commissioner if *I* am elected."[13]

Police mistreatment of pushcart peddlers was another campaign issue, at least as far as the Jewish community was concerned. Selling merchandise from a cart on the street required minimal investment, so it was a popular occupation among poor immigrant Jews. Pushcarts were omnipresent on the Lower East Side, their vendors hawking everything from fruits and vegetables to combs, needles, scissors, knives, and other household necessities.

Peddlers were frequently shaken down by police and taxed by individual officers to avert arrest and prosecution, whether or not they were operating legally. The police also lobbied the city's aldermen to ban pushcarts from several streets; Inspector Adam Cross himself came out publicly for this measure, claiming that the peddlers "took up the time of the police" and lamenting the fact that the magistrates usually discharged any who were arrested.[14]

"If I am elected you will not have to put up with the police to get your rights," Jerome vowed. He continued,

> When oppressed come to me . . . I will see that you get fair treatment. The blackmail of the pushcart peddlers . . . and others of that ilk will not be tolerated by me. . . . That gang will be taught a few things by me, if I am elected, that they won't soon forget.[15]

The fusion ticket was also on the right side of other issues that played well with Jewish voters. Low advocated full school facilities for all children of school age, small parks and playgrounds for the city's poor, the extension of rapid transit, clean streets, and habitable tenements. The New York State

5. The Hester Street pushcart market, 1903. Wikipedia.

Tenement House Act of 1901, which mandated new standards like indoor toilets, window wells, and hall lights to make buildings safer and more livable, was being honored in the breach by Mayor Van Wyck's administration. A bribe could easily keep a building inspector away. Out of 333 new tenement buildings built between the passage of the act in April and the November election, only a paltry 15 had been constructed according to the new standards, and that was to say nothing of the upgrades that were supposed to be made to existing structures but weren't.[16]

A month before the election, the *American Hebrew*, citing Low's positions on corruption in government as well as his advocacy of more schools and cleaner streets, predicted that the candidate would get "almost the entire Hebrew vote." That, of course, was an exaggeration, since many Jews were beholden to Tammany bosses, but the reason for the paper's optimism was that Tammany Hall as a whole had become deaf to many Jewish concerns. As the November election approached, however, the machine went into full battle mode. Tammany wasn't about to give up Jewish votes without a fight. Even a dirty one.

Its operatives put the squeeze on East Side merchants who had been dependent on them for political patronage, insisting they display lithographs of Tammany-approved candidates in the windows of their establishments and threatening those who expressed support for the fusion ticket. They made it known that people who wished to vote for fusion candidates could make "any mark they liked" on their ballots, knowing full well that any mark other than an *X* would render a ballot invalid. They also put out the word that Seth Low hated Jews and that he had branded every woman who lived below Fourteenth Street "disreputable." These were, of course, bald-faced lies. Low supporters countered by issuing Yiddish-language handbills debunking them and other groundless charges Tammany men made against Low, Jerome, and other fusion candidates.[17]

"I have learned from experience that it is dangerous to come out openly against Tammany Hall," a Grand Street merchant confirmed for the *Tribune*. "Such action will result in a hundred petty annoyances, and a quiet boycott of one's business which, if it does not ruin a man, will work him a substantial financial loss."[18]

The pressure was so great, in fact, that many who supported Low kept it a well-guarded secret. A letter the candidate received from a Jewish stationer the month before the election made this crystal clear:

> I have been a lifelong resident of the East Side. I voted for you in 1897 and I intend to vote for you again. I know of many businessmen in this vicinity who will gladly vote for you but fear to come out openly, owing to possible petty persecutions. Nevertheless, they will do their utmost for your election.[19]

Several Jewish newspapers, however, were not shy about declaring support for the fusion ticket. The *American Hebrew* came out unabashedly for Low and company:

> We are tired of the persecutions of Tammany; we are disgusted with the corrupt methods of the police and the way the poor pushcart peddlers are forced to pay tribute to [Tammany Hall boss Richard] Croker and his gang of thieves. We want more schools for our children, we want our houses kept pure and the streets cleaned. The only way we can accomplish this is through the election of Seth Low and by putting an end to the rule of Tammany and Croker.[20]

In the end, the fusion ticket made a clean sweep, and Seth Low was elected mayor by just over thirty thousand votes. Travers Jerome won his race by an even wider margin. And it was clear to all that a large proportion of the votes that had put the men over the top had come from the Jewish neighborhoods of Manhattan and Brooklyn.

On January 1, 1902, Seth Low was sworn in as mayor of New York, and William Travers Jerome became district attorney. Low lost no time ousting Devery and naming Colonel John Nelson Partridge, who had headed both the police and fire departments in Brooklyn in the 1880s, as his new police commissioner. A National Guard veteran, Partridge had served most recently as superintendent of public works for the State of New York. He, in turn, announced that his choice for his first deputy would be Nathaniel B. Thurston, an inspector in the State National Guard he had known for twenty years.[21]

6. New York police commissioner John Nelson Partridge. *Empire State Notables 1914* (New York: Hartwell Stafford, 1914), 528.

Devery did not take his firing lying down, however. He did not contest his removal from the police commission, but he insisted that he remained a uniformed member of the force and therefore could not be removed from his position as chief of police. Partridge did not permit this and ultimately prevailed in the courts, but it took several months to sort it all out.[22]

The organization Partridge inherited was a thoroughly demoralized one. Corruption in the force had risen to a high art. For years under Devery, officers had had no choice but to endure what would later be described as "a direct, and almost open, alliance between the police and the criminal classes," and those in charge, who benefited most from the arrangement, had a vested interest in seeing it continued.[23] The new commissioner therefore wasted no time in making it known to the inspectors and captains under his command that major changes were afoot. He addressed them all on his first day on the job:

> As I understand the wishes of the people, as expressed on last election day, it is that politics and improper outside influences be eliminated; that the members of the force should rely on their own good record for advancement; that the collection of money for the protection of vice or for special privileges should cease, and that the police force should devote its best energies to the performance of police duty.[24]

To manage expectations, the commissioner made it clear that change wasn't going to happen overnight. He complained to the *Tribune* that "the department has been going from bad to worse for fifteen years, and has been getting still worse in the last three or four years, when Devery was the ruling spirit here." He added that Devery's influence was "still too prominent."

And yet, although Adam Cross went back to being an inspector on January 1, his stock in the department did not diminish in value. Partridge, who felt he needed Cross's help and experience to realize his plans for reorganization of the force, considered him indispensable and kept him close as his principal adviser and right-hand man. He chose to ignore the fact that Cross had a decidedly checkered record, having been accused of malfeasance in the past, and having almost certainly been guilty of the very practices Partridge had been appointed to rout out. Cross, ultimately, was a Devery man, and Devery was corrupt. What Devery had done, Cross had done.

"I look upon Inspector Cross as a capable and efficient officer," Partridge told the *Tribune* in the same interview. "He was one of the first to show a disposition to carry out the ideas I expressed to the commanding officers on January 1, and he has done so with vigor and success."[25]

Honesty was never Cross's strong suit, however, and placing his trust in Devery's cohort would ultimately prove a problematical choice for the new commissioner.

7

"So Impressive a Funeral"

Well before the turn of the twentieth century, Rabbi Joseph had ceased to be a significant factor in the religious life of the New York Jewish community. His six-year contract with the United Orthodox Congregations, the confederation of synagogues that had brought him over from Europe and paid his salary ever since, had expired, and there was no question of renewing it. Revenues from the sale of *plombes* had diminished, due in part to the emergence of other rabbis who offered butchers *plombes* of their own at a discount, and in part to the unwillingness of some Jewish consumers to foot the additional charge for his certification.

Nor was the chief rabbi nearly as popular as he had been when he arrived. He had sustained myriad battle scars in his various struggles over *kashrus*, and many butchers and housewives viewed him as a tool of Jewish businessmen and his *plombes* as brazen money grabs. Then, too, the officers of the congregations that had been paying him felt put upon; they thought it unfair that they should continue to shoulder the financial burden of a *kashrus* system that benefited the entire Orthodox community, not just their fellow congregants.[1]

There were also dissatisfactions with the chief rabbi that had nothing to do with kosher meat. He had never been able to extend his authority beyond a core group of Orthodox congregations and had been belittled not only by leaders of the Reform movement but also by many secular Jews. His ability to inspire the children of the immigrant generation had proven quite limited. Despite the fact that he had been brought over in part to promote religious education among the city's young Jews, he was, in their eyes, merely a relic of the old world.[2]

Abraham Cahan, the editor of the socialist *Forverts*, wrote later that Rabbi Joseph remained "the man of the third century he had been brought up to be," while his flock lived in the nineteenth century. He went on to write that "they looked down upon his ways as they do upon the man who has not replaced his Russian cap by a Grand Street hat."[3]

His retirement did not leave the rabbi destitute; some wholesalers were still willing to pay him to supervise their slaughterers. This, however, echoed the fraught arrangement, with its built-in incentives for corruption, that had persuaded the Orthodox congregations to seek a chief rabbi in the first place. And it did nothing to shore up confidence in the kosher meat business or in Rabbi Joseph himself.

In about 1898, a series of strokes rendered the good rabbi bedridden. Sir Jacob Epstein, the famous British sculptor who had gotten his start on New York's Lower East Side, recalled being taken as a young man to meet the chief rabbi during this period. He described him as a frail and infirm figure who had to be lifted in and out of his chair by the young men who cared for him.[4]

After that, Rabbi Joseph's only income, collected regularly by his son, came from a dwindling number of *hechshers* that continued to be issued in his name and from food producers who used him to certify that their products were strictly kosher. As late as early 1902, a sugar manufacturer introduced a new brand and advertised it as "sealed and approved by Rabbi Jacob Joseph," who in fact was no longer in any condition to seal or approve anything.[5]

Joseph had never been canny when it came to money; the many debts he had racked up in Vilna had forced him to ask for a hefty upfront payment before he could accept the position in New York. There were reports that he had given away much of what he did have to the needy. Despite the astronomical salary he had been paid during his early years in America, he had never managed to amass a nest egg, and in the 1890s he was forced to relocate to a more modest home at 263 Henry Street. By 1901 he was not only paralyzed but nearly penniless.

That such a well-regarded man should be reduced to such grievous circumstances was seen as a disgrace. In a Shabbos sermon in late January, uptown Rabbi Bernard Drachman blamed Joseph's lamentable condition on the United Orthodox Congregations' withdrawal of support. The Orthodox weekly *Hebrew Standard* also piled on:

> It has been reported that the congregations which elected him with so much pomp and gratuitous self-advertisement a few years ago have now entirely forsaken him, so that he and his family are actually in need of means to defray their living expenses and those of the necessary medical treatment. . . . If these reports are true, the facts are a disgrace of the blackest kind to alleged Russian Polish orthodoxy.[6]

The United Orthodox Congregations, feeling the heat, did issue an appeal for the rabbi and his family in 1901. How much was actually collected, however, was never made public.[7]

Although bedridden, Rabbi Joseph remained stable for the balance of the year, but by early 1902 his health deteriorated further. In mid-July, a rumor that he had died circulated on the East Side. It was not true, but less than two weeks later, on Monday, at 11:45 p.m. on July 28, with his entire family gathered at his bedside, the eminent, sixty-two-year-old Talmudist did breathe his last. The cause of death was apoplexy—a stroke—and edema of the lungs. It was almost exactly fourteen years to the day since he had sailed into New York Harbor.[8]

His body was promptly brought downstairs, where it was laid out in the rear parlor. Members of the *chevra kadisha*, the ritual burial society, were summoned, and they assumed custody of it. Orthodox Judaism forbids embalming; their job was to cleanse the corpse ritually, clothe it for burial, and then guard and pray over it in shifts until it was time for the funeral.

They sprinkled sand imported from Jerusalem into the bottom of the casket and then, after the corpse was wrapped in a plain white shroud and covered with the rabbi's prayer shawl and his phylacteries, placed it inside. More sand was then sprinkled over his eyes and his heart to signify his spiritual connection to the Holy Land. After all the mirrors were covered, another traditional custom, the doors of the home were opened and the family prepared to receive well-wishers.[9]

What happened next, however, was nothing short of astonishing.

As soon as word of the rabbi's passing got out, hundreds upon hundreds of local Jews gathered in front of his home to lament their loss. The crowds quickly grew thick and the sidewalk on Henry Street impassable. Men holding Bibles chanted psalms and prayers. Weeping women brought their children to pay their respects. Although the family did receive numerous well-wishers, far too many had come for a glimpse of the rabbi's remains, and eventually public visitation had to be curtailed. Those who could not be accommodated had to content themselves with praying for the rabbi's soul outside on Henry Street.[10]

Jacob Joseph had been humiliated during his fourteen years in New York, and never more so than in the run-up to his death, when he was left destitute and forgotten. Now, however, those who had forsaken him, perhaps guilt-ridden over their callous treatment of him, seemed intent on according him the honor in death they had denied him in life. If anyone even recalled that he had officially lost his title several years earlier, that fact was certainly not brought up now. The man New York was about to bury was no more or less than its beloved chief rabbi, the *rav ha'kolel*, not a has-been. His portraits, not seen in the Jewish quarter for several years, now adorned many store windows, tastefully draped in black mourning cloth, and were printed in the Yiddish papers.[11]

"The spiritual giant of our generation died yesterday at midnight; from a poor family grew a living encyclopedia who made a great name for himself in two worlds," gushed the *Yidishes Tageblatt*. It called on all local Jews to close their shops and mourn him properly.[12]

Jewish custom mandates burial as soon as possible after death, and funerals most often occur the very next day. But proper arrangements for the send-off of such a prominent personage required some negotiation and some time. Postponing burial for a day would permit out-of-town mourners to make the journey to New York. When the rabbis of the synagogues over which the chief rabbi had presided convened the day after his death to consult with his family about funeral arrangements, there were two points of contention. Rabbi Joseph had not left instructions as to which of the congregations he wanted to host his funeral. Nor had he specified the cemetery in which he wished to be interred.

As far as the first question was concerned, it was quite clear from the size of the throngs outside his residence that no synagogue on the East Side could possibly accommodate even a fraction of those who would wish to attend. So after deliberating, the funeral committee declared that no single congregation would host a service. Rather, the funeral cortege would traverse the streets of the Lower East Side on July 30 and would stop briefly for prayers and tributes at the entrances of six of the congregations under the rabbi's jurisdiction. This was not an improvised solution; there was precedent for it. It had been done in Europe for important figures, though this was the first time, as far as anyone could recall, that it would be done in America.[13]

As for the second issue, the honor of being the repository of the rabbi's remains for all eternity ultimately devolved on the Beis Hamidrash HaGadol, his home congregation, which owned a large tract in Union Field Cemetery in East New York. The right was secured with a pledge to pay his widow a lump sum of $1,500 (nearly $50,000 in today's currency) and a monthly stipend of $15 (nearly $500) for the remainder of her life. The costly arrangement actually turned out to be a profitable one for the shul. A Canal Street merchant immediately offered the congregation $5,000 (about $165,000 today) for rights to the plot immediately adjacent to that of the rabbi, and others happily ponied up sizable sums to reserve other nearby graves.[14]

On July 29, anticipating a large turnout the following day, Israel Levy, one of the members of the funeral committee, visited police headquarters to apply for a permit for the procession. He estimated that some twenty thousand people might turn up. Irish-born Sergeant James Brady accepted his application at the Bureau of Information. Levy had no experience with large gatherings and admitted that he did not know how many officers would be needed to manage such a crowd; he naively suggested that perhaps twenty-five might do. Brady took his suggestion at face value and did not question it, and as a result, twenty-five policemen were pledged by his supervisor, Captain John D. Herlihy—the same Captain Herlihy who had been tried for insulting an Episcopal priest and neglecting duty two years earlier.

Levy's prediction of attendance sounded to a reporter at one of the local Jewish newspapers like a gross underestimate, however, which also meant that twenty-five officers didn't seem *nearly* enough. So the man, whose identity is unclear, phoned Sergeant Brady at midnight to suggest that far more policemen would likely be needed. His warning was ignored, however, and apparently never reported to Inspector Adam Cross, who was filling in for a vacationing Inspector Nicholas Brooks and would be in charge the following morning.

By 10:00 a.m. the next day, July 30, an estimated fifty thousand people had already gathered in the vicinity of the rabbi's home in anticipation of the funeral. The air was filled with plaintive sobs and the droning of prayers. Jewish boys hawking copies of *Di Yidishe Velt* (The Jewish world), which featured a large image of the late rabbi on its front page, sold out before they got anywhere near Henry Street, which was packed from curb to curb and virtually impassable. When Irish-born Sergeant John McSweeney of the Madison Street Station gave the order to thirty patrolmen to clear the street, his officers charged the crowd. Although instructed not to use their clubs, they were nonetheless needlessly brutal. Panic ensued. Old men were knocked down and trampled, children were torn from their mothers' arms, and dozens of people were injured.[15]

It was a foretaste of far worse things to come later that day.

McSweeney's men alone were unable to disperse the crowd. That took the arrival of Captain William Thompson, also of the Madison Street Station, who brought sufficient reinforcements to clear a way for the procession. Just after 10:00 a.m. Thompson asked Inspector Cross for ten more men, and at 10:40 a.m. he asked for fifty more. The men were detailed from sixteen different precincts.[16]

At 11:30 a.m., after Rabbi Philip Klein of the Hungarian Congregation Ohab Zedek led a service in the Joseph home for relatives and visiting rabbis, it was time to depart. A loud wail arose from those assembled when the rabbi's casket, an unvarnished, unadorned pine box draped in a black pall embroidered with white Hebrew letters, was carried to the street by several distinguished rabbis. At the same time, five hundred yeshiva *bochers*—Hebrew school students—chanted psalms of David in Hebrew.

Since Judaism teaches that all are equal in death, the ornamentation of caskets is forbidden among the Orthodox, and there was nothing fancy about the one selected for the rabbi. It was unlined and constructed entirely of wood—no metal was used—so that nothing would impede prompt, natural decomposition of the body after burial. Embalming was proscribed for

The Jewish World.

דיא אידישע וועלט

Office, 9 Rutgers Street. אפפיס: 9 ראטגערס סטריט.

Price One Cent. VOL. I, No. 28. New York, Wednesday, July 30th, 1902. נױ יארק, מיטװאך, פ׳ מ״ס, כה תמוז, תרס״ב. פרייז 1 סענט.

דיא גרױסע לױה פון גאון.

אנגעצונדען ליכט אין אללע שולען.

אלע אידישע שוהלען, סאסייעטיס, לאדזשען און חברות װעלען זיין פערטראטען ביי דער לױה פון דעם גרעסטען אידישען חריף. דער קבר איף יוניאן פיעלד סעמעטרי, ברוקלין. דער בית המדרש הגדול געװינט דיא דין תורה. לױה אום 10 אוהר.

איז דיא אלמנה װירקליך פערזארגט?

קריגונג װידער א נדחה?

קרבנות פון דינאמיט.

װידער א שטורם אין קאליפארניא.

7. The front page of *Di Yidishe Velt*, July 30, 1902.

8. A scene from the chief rabbi's funeral procession. *American Monthly Review of Reviews,* September 1902.

the same reason. As the casket was loaded into the hearse, many mourners closed in, surging past the police in an attempt to touch it as an act of veneration. Those who could not reach it contented themselves with touching the garments of others who could.[17]

The cortege that began on Henry Street was a sight to behold. The East Side had never seen anything quite like it. Captain Thompson and a now augmented squad of policemen led the way, followed by the singing yeshiva boys. Next came the hearse, and then somewhere between two and five hundred carriages (estimates varied wildly) carrying two hundred prominent rabbis from the city, nearly sixty from out of town who happened to be in New York for an important meeting; presidents of congregations; officers of other Jewish groups; and relatives and friends of the Joseph family. The names of the organizations were displayed on the windows of the carriages. The horse-drawn buggies of the VIPs were followed on foot by an estimated thirty thousand congregants from nearly all of New York's East Side synagogues.[18]

The dignitaries were far outnumbered by average people. Those who took part, the *Brooklyn Times Union* pointed out, "were not the financial magnates and merchant princes whose energy and enterprise and business capacity have placed the race of Israel in the front rank in every financial center in the world." They were, instead, "the children of the ghetto, uncouth, unlettered, and strangers alike to the language, the laws and the customs of the land in which they are sojourners."

Street traffic was suspended, and hundreds of Jewish-owned businesses in the quarter closed their doors as the cortege left Henry Street and began a circuitous, three-mile trek through Montgomery Street, Clinton Street, East Broadway, and then Pike, Eldridge, Forsyth, Chrystie, Grand, Allen, Canal, and Norfolk Streets, passing nearly every synagogue on the Lower East Side but pausing in front of only six for blessings and five-minute eulogies by the resident rabbis. Then it was back to Clinton Street, where children from the Hebrew Free School, on whose board the late rabbi had sat, joined the procession.

Estimates of the size of the crowds that lined the route ran as high as three hundred thousand, but most sources put the number closer to one hundred thousand. Jewish mourners came on foot to pay their last respects to their chief rabbi, and uncounted onlookers watched the procession from crowded windows, rooftops, stoops, and fire escapes. Thousands of these were curious gentiles.[19]

The *New York World* asserted that "not in the history of New York has there been so impressive a funeral as that which wound through the narrow streets of the Lower East Side today." That, however, was far from the truth; the chief rabbi's cortege was not even the grandest such procession in recent memory. Fully 1.5 million souls had lined up to pay their last respects to President Ulysses S. Grant in 1885 when his remains, accompanied by marching bands, were placed in a temporary tomb on Riverside Drive. And the parade of carriages that had conveyed mourners down Fifth Avenue to witness the interment of Catholic Archbishop Michael Corrigan's body in the St. Patrick's Cathedral crypt earlier that year had been a far larger spectacle. But this was surely the grandest convoy the Lower East Side had ever witnessed, with the most grief-stricken participants in attendance.[20]

Things were going smoothly as the procession turned from Clinton onto Grand Street. From there it was a straight shot eastward to the ferry house where the avenue met the East River. There the rabbi's remains were to be

Photograph of the Most Remarkable Funeral Procession Ever Seen in New York Streets.

9. A panoramic view of the vast crowd assembled to bid farewell to the chief rabbi. *New York World*, July 31, 1902.

placed aboard a Brooklyn ferry bound for Williamsburg and then finally to Cypress Hills for burial.

Four blocks down Grand Street, the street widened where it crossed Sheriff Street and East Broadway. The huge R. Hoe & Company printing press factory loomed over the intersection, opposite a triangular park. Passing Jews had often been harassed there by Hoe employees. But nobody thought anyone would dare to make trouble on a day like this, when a grieving community turned out in full force to bid farewell to a revered spiritual leader.[21]

8

"Get Out, You Sheenies! We'll Soak You!"

The imposing R. Hoe & Company plant took up the entire city block bounded by Grand, Sheriff, Broome, and Columbia Streets. Built of painted brick, it was actually made up of several buildings constructed at different times. Boasting two hundred thousand square feet, or more than four acres, of floor space, it featured a great clock tower that dominated the corner of Grand and Sheriff.[1]

The foremost manufacturer of printing presses in North America, R. Hoe & Company had gotten its start in 1805. The company had a proud history of innovations that had, several times in its past, revolutionized the printing trade. As the inventor of the rotary press, which had taken much of the cost out of printing newspapers, it was directly responsible for a boom in the newspaper industry in the late nineteenth century. In 1902, the company was under the stewardship of Robert Hoe III, a grandson of one of the founders, who had taken over after his father's death in 1884. The company employed some 1,800 people on Manhattan's Lower East Side.

Many of the young plant workers came up through the company's apprentice school, an institution in which Robert Hoe took special pride. There, neighborhood boys between the ages of sixteen and eighteen who had completed at least four years of schooling and passed an entrance examination were taught the mechanics of printing as well as English, mathematics, and mechanical drawing. Qualified applicants had to sign agreements that bound them to work for the company for five years in exchange for their training.

The boys were paid $2.50 a week and provided with sandwiches and milk for lunch. The consumption of alcohol and the use of tobacco were forbidden on the premises, and bad behavior was subject to punishment. Offenders, or simply those who could not keep up with their studies, were dismissed. Those who succeeded, however, were offered permanent positions as machinists or draftsmen.[2]

In mid-1902, fully three hundred such apprentices worked at the Grand Street factory. Despite the rigorousness of their program and the requirement that they be obedient and of "good moral character," however, they were often mischievous. It was difficult to control them, especially when they were off the premises. Even Robert Hoe admitted that they sometimes gave him trouble.[3]

On July 30, 1902, they would give him a great deal of it.

Many immigrants worked at R. Hoe & Company. The firm hired some Jews, but it was not an especially Jewish-friendly establishment, and there was a distinct undercurrent of antisemitism about the place. Gregory Weinstein, a Russian-born Jewish labor activist, had gotten his start as a printer there shortly after he emigrated to the United States in 1885. Years later, he recalled his treatment at the hands of some of his fellow workers:

> Every kind of annoyance and mental torture was heaped upon me: my frugal lunch package would disappear; a shower of fine nails would come down on my head from nowhere; my work would be spoiled. The climax was reached when I discovered, one afternoon, just before passing the time-keeper, that my coat pockets were filled with case nails. Exasperated by this mean attempt to expose me as a nail stealer, I took out the nails by the handfuls and showered them on the jeering youngsters, and I quit the shop in none too leisurely a manner.[4]

Hoe apprentices also had a history of tormenting Jewish passersby on their lunch breaks. Pulling the beards of elderly men, knocking their hats off, and hurling apple cores, banana skins, and melon rinds at them from above were common practice. "Jews had been attacked so often," the *American Hebrew* recalled later, that "that part of Grand Street is abandoned while the workmen have their lunches." Such incidents occurred especially frequently on Saturdays, when local Jews passed by on their way to Sabbath worship.[5]

According to the *New York Sun*, the anti-Jewish feeling at the factory was not exclusive to the apprentices. Jeering at Jews was something the boys had seen the men do time and again from the second- and third-story windows. The youngsters, the *Sun* insisted, were merely following an example set every day by the adults with whom they worked.[6]

Robert Hoe was well aware of these episodes. In fact, after several incidents the previous year in which the police had visited because his boys had assaulted passersby with snowballs, he had issued a notice to all employees:

> The police have been to see us in reference to the boys' throwing snowballs and other missiles at passersby on the street. Heretofore the officers have restrained from giving any trouble, but hereafter if the boys persist in assaulting or annoying people in the street, no matter who they are, they will be liable to arrest. We wish to protect our apprentices from any outrage enacted upon them, but if they offend in this manner in the future, we can do nothing for them.

This hardly amounted to disciplinary action, and Hoe admitted later that he had never been as strict with the young men as he should have been.[7]

This history was well known to Jews in the neighborhood, among whom the Hoe factory was sometimes referred to as the headquarters of the "whisker pullers." If any of the organizers of the chief rabbi's funeral cortege was wary of passing R. Hoe & Company at lunchtime on July 30, however, none apparently raised the issue. Not even the police were concerned. Although they, too, were fully cognizant of the pattern, there were very few officers in sight when the procession reached the intersection of Grand and Sheriff. Most members of the escort detail were already several blocks ahead, led to the pier by Captain Thompson to supervise the transfer of the casket to the ferry.[8]

The entourage reached the front of the factory shortly before 1:00 p.m., just as Hoe employees were returning to work after their lunch break. Even before the hearse was visible, several of the boys began jeering at the marchers and onlookers from the safety of windows on the factory's upper floors. That was the first break in the solemnity of the atmosphere.[9]

The hectoring continued when the hearse appeared, and as it proceeded past the factory, a few Hoe apprentices jettisoned scraps of dirty cotton waste onto the heads of four rabbis riding in a carriage behind the coffin

10. The R. Hoe & Co. factory at Grand and Sheriff Streets. Wikipedia.

and laughed as the men attempted to dodge them. These were followed by more dangerous projectiles. Wet overalls, scraps of steel, oil-soaked waste, blocks of wood, buckets of grease, iron nuts and bolts, flat irons, screws, tools, bricks, bottles, utensils, stones, and even a dead cat rained down on the pedestrians and those in the procession.[10]

The street was so crowded with people, it was impossible to move out of the way. Mourners "shouted and struggled and stampeded in vain to escape," the *Daily People* reported, but there *was* no escaping. Not even the hearse was immune. Its driver recalled later that it had been bombarded first with stale bread, and then a shower of small missiles, pieces of iron, and screws. They had been large enough, he was certain, to have broken the glass had they struck the side of the vehicle.[11]

Those below were initially bewildered and then outraged by this sudden turn of events. Some were resentful of what appeared an intentional affront to the memory of the departed rabbi. Others were concerned primarily with

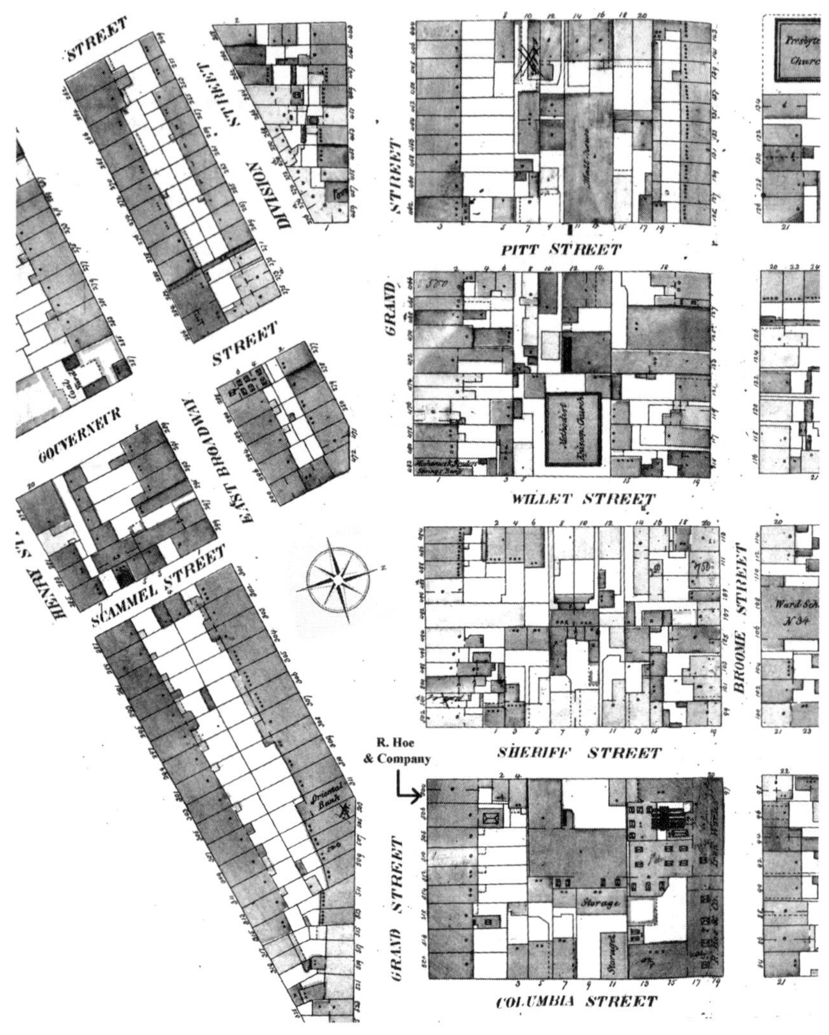

11. The Hoe factory occupied the entire city block bounded by Grand, Sheriff, Columbia, and Broome Streets. Its main entrance, shown on the map, was on the north side of Grand Street at the corner of Sheriff. New York Public Library.

the immediate imperative of protecting themselves from harm. "Is this *free America*?" a red-bearded, elderly man shouted in thickly Yiddish-accented English. "It is worse than Russia!"[12]

A half dozen men from among the mourners, including thirty-year-old, Russian-Jewish City Marshall Albert Levine, rushed into the factory office on the ground floor to demand that the assault be stopped. By one account, the men were received courteously and they secured a pledge from those in charge to investigate the complaint. By others, however, a clerk drew a pistol and a manager ordered them out of the building. As objects continued to rain down on the heads of the mourners, a second, larger group, very much agitated and crying out loudly in Yiddish, thrust its way into the building. The employees could not understand them and insisted later that they had believed themselves to be under siege.[13]

That is when a foreman took down a firehose from its mounting and, on orders from Robert Hoe himself, George W. Church, George Stillgenbauer, and Henry Stockhusen, three factory employees, grabbed it and began spraying a four-inch stream of water on the crowd. Its velocity succeeded in propelling them all out of the building This accomplished, the workers quickly cleared the steps at the building's entrance and shut the large iron gates to prevent any further intrusions.[14] Then Mr. Hoe called the police.

No one stopped the attack by the factory workers on the upper floors, who by now were directing as many as five high-velocity jets of water, some of it scalding hot, indiscriminately at those in the procession and at the bystanders below. Others emptied pails of water on them from the roof. Joseph Kaplan, riding in an open carriage, shouted up at Emil Adams, a Hoe machinist perched in a fourth-floor window who was directing a firehose at him.

"It's a shame if in a free country we can't hold a funeral without a disturbance," he recalled yelling.

"Get out, you sheenies! We'll soak you!" Adams shot back, using a thoroughly contemptuous and offensive slur for Jews, as he continued to rain water down on those below.[15]

Dora Schank and Sarah Rufusky were both burned by hot water. Mrs. Schank later recalled,

12. The chief rabbi's funeral cortege traversed Grand Street in front of the R. Hoe & Company factory just before the violence broke out. *Le Monde Illustré*, August 23, 1902.

> We were watching the funeral procession when, without any warning, we were drenched with scalding water from a hose playing down upon the crowd from a window on the fourth story of the Columbia Street side of the Hoe building.[16]

As more projectiles rained down on the Jews and injured many, some began to retrieve the missiles and hurl them back up at their attackers. Others shattered the factory's ground-floor windows with umbrellas they had brought along to shield themselves from the summer sun. "For once," the *New York Sun* wrote later, "the meek and futile protest of the pestered Jew was not forthcoming. In its place came a charge on the factory, the very suddenness of which took its defenders off their feet."[17]

The drivers of the hearse and the other carriages in the procession whipped their horses to escape the fray, but even this caused harm as the agitated beasts trampled people who were in their way. Groans were audible and blood was everywhere. But far more bloodshed was shortly to come from aggressors who were better armed and far more fearsome than the factory apprentices.

People for whom beating up Jews was all in a day's work.

9
"Club the Life Out of Them"

The hearse was long gone, as were many of the carriages, by the time Delancey Street Station Roundsman James M. Jackson and Officer William Maher, members of the escort detail, made their way to the front of the Hoe factory. They were the first of a handful of policemen to appear. As they approached, they drew their clubs. They arrested three men, even as some in the crowd attempted to pry the trio from their clutches. One of the men hit Jackson with a brick, injuring his head and causing him to fall.

The water hoses had been shut off and things had quieted down by 1:20 p.m., when reinforcements arrived to relieve the half dozen policemen already on the scene. Eight patrol wagons bearing two hundred officers hastily summoned from five nearby precincts and under the command of Inspector Adam Cross appeared at the factory. Hordes of Jews, many wounded, remained in the street, but despite the fact that the crowd was now calm, the police moved in with a vengeance. Inspector Cross made no effort to size up the situation or to distinguish aggressors from victims. He asked no questions. He issued no warnings to disperse.[1]

What he did do was to order his men to "club the life out of them" and "kill them." Whereupon his officers dutifully drew their billy clubs and started beating up Jews. And beat them they did, with the aid of a few Hoe employees who had brazenly joined them to finish what they had started. Here is how the *New York Post* described the melee:

> Men were flung down, women were dragged out by the arms and shoulders and pushed headlong down the street. But the crowd fell back slowly and stubbornly. One might have thought the police were

> putting down a riot from the way they handled many of the unfortunate men and women who chanced to be in front. . . . In several instances, those who were being battered back into the line by repeated pushings showed belligerent spirit, whereupon they were dragged out and sent stumbling off. It was somewhat difficult to reconcile this scene with the fact that these people had gathered there to attend a funeral, to show their veneration for a dead rabbi who was lying in the supremest [*sic*] peace and quiet less than a hundred yards away.[2]

The *New York Herald* noted that nightsticks were used "without discrimination as to age, creed or race" as police drove the mob from the factory. Old men, women, and boys were injured. As the beatings went on, a *New York World* reporter saw a policeman knock an aged Jew insensible. In fact, he reported, the police struck every man who *looked* like a Jew.[3]

Local Jews could be forgiven for distrusting the New York Police Department. Those from Russia and Eastern Europe had seldom had reason to appeal to the police for protection in their former countries; persecution was a more likely outcome. Sometimes the police in Russia or Poland had merely looked on passively and declined to intervene when peasants attacked their Jewish neighbors; at other times, they had actively participated.

But this was America, and although the immigrant Jews had every right to expect fair treatment from local law enforcement, they often didn't get it. Local Jews' experience with New York's finest had not been a happy one. Police had bashed many a Jewish head during the labor strikes of the past decade. And, of course, it was impossible not to compare this clash between Jews and police to that of the kosher meat boycott just two months earlier.[4]

During the meat strike, officers under the command of the very same Captain Thompson had dealt mercilessly with Jewish pickets. The police had been especially brutal with the mostly female crowds protesting rising prices of kosher meat that had made it unaffordable. Beating men who were out on strike from their jobs, which the New York bluecoats had done with abandon, was one thing; beating women was considered out of bounds, even though some of the women were wreaking havoc. The behavior of the police had not earned them any accolades then, and this time it was no better.[5]

For their part, some officers told the *New York Times* that neither the meat boycott nor the race troubles on the West Side two years earlier—when Devery had dispatched seven hundred police to beat Black men and women—could compare with the trouble outside the Hoe factory. That was probably an exaggeration, but the paper, no fan of the Irish or the police department, did detect a distinct atmosphere of antisemitism on the force. "It appears that the police, or a considerable proportion of them, regard the Jews of the Lower East Side not as claimants for protection, but as fit objects of persecution," it wrote.[6]

By the time the police gained possession of Grand Street, men with heads bleeding from the metal projectiles hurled from above and the police nightsticks that rained down on them pitilessly were lying prostrate in the street, as were women and children struck or trampled in the confusion. Hundreds had been injured; there were contusions and lacerations and sprained ankles, but there were also cracked skulls and internal bleeding. One man, a chair caner named Julius Weber, was knocked unconscious by a policeman, and no one thought he was likely to survive. Three ambulances arrived on the scene to minister to the injured. Doctors spent a full hour on-site treating flesh wounds, and took others, including Rudolph Gartenberg, who had suffered internal injuries, and another man whose leg was badly sprained, back to Gouverneur Hospital on Water Street.[7]

The newspapers recorded the names of some of the injured but missed the vast majority. Most of those who sustained blows from projectiles or batons simply returned home or went to their doctors to treat their wounds. As far as Hoe employees were concerned, only three had apparently sustained injuries, none serious.[8]

A few policemen were injured as well. Four Central Office detectives were struck with found objects, as was one officer. One of the detectives was knocked senseless and then carried into the Hoe factory, where an ambulance surgeon sewed up his wound with six stitches and then brought him to the hospital. Another, who had been detailed to look for pickpockets in the crowd, had sustained a severe cut to his head and been trampled. When he got back on his feet, he drew his pistol and fired into the crowd, although he did not hurt anyone. The others were not seriously injured.[9] The Hoe factory itself

13. Ambulances ferry wounded mourners to Gouverneur Hospital. *Black and White Budget*, August 30, 1902.

was badly damaged in the brawl. Every single one of the windows on the Grand and Sheriff Street facades of the building—there were more than one hundred of them—had been shattered.[10]

The fracas was still in progress when the hearse reached the Grand Street Ferry House. Some ten thousand mourners had gathered there, making it difficult for Captain Thompson and Sergeant John McSweeney to clear a path to the terminal. The ticket sellers were overwhelmed and could not accommodate all who sought passage to Brooklyn. Ten extra boats were commandeered to transport those in the funeral procession; spectators were compelled to reach the cemetery by an alternate route.

Anticipating the possibility of more trouble in Brooklyn, Captain Thompson telephoned his counterpart at the borough's Bedford Avenue police station and suggested he dispatch at least a hundred uniformed police to escort the procession to Cypress Hills, where the burial was to take place. Reserves were sent from eight stations.

Tens of thousands of mourners crossed to Brooklyn between noon and 2:00 p.m.; estimates ranged from 40,000 to 85,000. And these joined another 75,000 or so already waiting at the foot of Broadway in Williamsburg, which, like Manhattan's Lower East Side, boasted a sizable Jewish population. Business in Williamsburg was at a standstill, and many streets and sidewalks were impassible. Children were being crushed in the throng, which was larger than many had ever seen. Unable to forge a direct path down Broadway, the police decided to reroute the cortege onto Kent Avenue, to the profound disappointment of many who had been waiting along the original route for a glimpse of the hearse.[11]

When the procession, five hundred carriages strong even on the Brooklyn side of the river, reached the corner of Kent and South Sixth Streets, someone hurled a heavy block of wood from the top floor of an axle foundry. It struck one of the men in the procession, ruining his hat. He was not seriously injured, but several Jews, still smarting from the brawl at the Hoe factory, rushed into the foundry. They broke through a line of reserve police, burst through the building's door, and headed up a flight of stairs when the officers pursued them and a struggle ensued. Once a backup squad of police arrived with clubs drawn, the angry mourners were subdued and driven back into the street.[12]

There were no more major incidents, although some young boys hooted at the procession and pelted a few mourners with stones and mud as they made their way to Union Field Cemetery. It was about 4:00 p.m. when the hearse arrived. Thousands of people—estimates ranged from 15,000 to 60,000—had assembled for the chief rabbi's interment. They included five hundred children from Brooklyn's Hebrew Orphan Asylum.

There was disorder at the cemetery as people once again attempted to touch the casket. The location of the grave had not been announced, so when it was discovered to be in a far corner of the property, people rushed toward it, trampling other plots and jumping fences in the process. A dozen or so police had been detailed to the cemetery to keep the peace. There was plenty of disorder, but no real trouble.[13]

Eventually, individual groups coalesced around some sixty-five rabbis from New York, Boston, Philadelphia, New Haven, Rochester, Chicago, and other cities who spread out and delivered eulogies. Among the locals were Rabbi Philip Klein, a close associate of the chief rabbi in the supervision of slaughterhouses, who had led the service at the Joseph home that morning; Rabbi Israel Cooper, the longtime *chazzan* (cantor) of the Sons of Israel

Kalwarier Synagogue on Pike Street who was known as "the Jewish Caruso"; and A. S. Ratakowsky, president of Beis Hamidrash HaGadol.[14]

It was Rabbi Klein who officiated at the gravesite as the chief rabbi's family, including his widow, his son, two daughters, and a brother, stood by. The service was lengthy, and one of the daughters fainted under the hot July sun. The grave had not been dug prior to the event; this was done as everyone watched. Afterward, earth from Jerusalem was sprinkled into it and the coffin was lowered in. Finally, as evening approached, the pit was filled in and the eulogies ended, and New York's first and last chief rabbi was left to the ages.[15]

On the day before Rabbi Joseph's burial, some fifty-nine Orthodox rabbis from around the country had convened at the Machzikei Talmud Torah School on East Broadway, just two blocks from the rabbi's Henry Street residence. Their arrival in New York in time for his funeral had been serendipitous, as their meeting had been planned the previous May. Their goal was to establish a new union of Orthodox rabbis—to be dubbed the Agudas HaRabbonim—to preserve traditional Judaism by strengthening Jewish education, encouraging Sabbath observance, monitoring the kosher food industry, and regulating marriages and divorces. Ironically, these were the very same tasks Rabbi Joseph had been asked to shoulder in New York fourteen years earlier. There was now a shared understanding that such undertakings could not be entrusted to any one man but rather had to be part of a broad, shared responsibility.

There would never be another chief rabbi in New York.[16]

10

"Commissioner Partridge Is a Sleepy Old *Bubbie*"

The men who were arrested—all Jews, save three Hoe employees—were arraigned before Magistrate John B. Mayo at the Essex Market Police Court that afternoon. The Virginia-born Mayo, a Tammany Hall man, had been an assistant in the New York City Corporation Counsel's office before being appointed to the bench by Mayor Van Wyck in 1899. He was reputed to be well schooled in the law.[1]

Before the proceedings began, thousands of Jews gathered in front of the courthouse shouting excitedly in Yiddish. Inside, many victims had come to court bearing wounds and bandages for all to see. Hoe company representatives, police officers, and newsmen had also gathered, as had a team of lawyers hastily summoned to defend the accused men. The attorneys were something of a "who's who" of prominent Jewish figures in New York legal circles, and they represented a surprisingly broad spectrum of New York Jewry. They included the following:

Forty-six-year-old Democratic congressman Henry Mayer Goldfogle, of German Jewish extraction. Goldfogle had previously served as a judge of the municipal court of New York City and was active in the B'nai B'rith, a Jewish advocacy organization. He had been elected to the U.S. House of Representatives in 1900 and seated in early 1901.

Twenty-nine-year-old Otto Alfred Rosalsky, American born to Russian immigrants. The son of a butcher, he was raised on the Lower East Side, had graduated from New York University Law School, and had been a delegate to two Democratic national conventions. He had previously served as an assistant district attorney.

Russian-born Abraham D. Levy, thirty-eight, who had defended some high-profile criminals and whose name was mentioned frequently in the newspapers. He was a member of Rodeph Sholom, an uptown Reform congregation.

Morris H. Gottlieb, a former Tammany Hall operative who had resigned because he disapproved of the machine's poll packing. A British-born, uptown Jew of German descent, he appeared frequently in the police court.[2]

Isidor Cohn, a former New York State assemblyman; twenty-seven-year-old Alexander S. Rosenthal; forty-one-year-old Elias Rosenthal; and twenty-six-year-old Leonard A. Snitkin, all of Russian Jewish descent. Three of them were Tammany men.

What was notable about this group was that it encompassed nearly all of the disparate elements of the Jewish community: uptowner and downtowner, German and Russian, Tammany and anti-Tammany, Democrat and Republican. Only Sephardic Jews, a tiny minority, do not seem to have been represented. These factions had their differences and their members generally lived very separate lives, but when it came to a flagrant assault on Jews in New York, they came together in a heartbeat. An attack on one camp was an attack on all.

Although this alliance does not seem to have been planned, it was important because a couple of months earlier, during the kosher meat boycott, the "uptown" Jews, embarrassed by the disorder, had essentially kept quiet and stayed out of it. In a pointed column in the *American Israelite*, Bohemian-born, New Orleans–based Rabbi Max Heller, a pioneer in the Reform movement, warned how important it was for New York Jewry to unite this time. He wrote,

> These troubles will grow and spread unless they are stopped by emphatic and united protest. The wrong which the American Jew permits to be visited upon his Russian brother will find him out in due course of time. Let New York Judaism stand idly by these outrages, and the moral rottenness of such cowardice will draw upon itself the contempt it will merit.[3]

14. Essex Market Police Court. H. N. Tiemann & Co. Photograph Collection, 1880–1916, New York Historical Society.

Although in the coming months most of those who would lead the fight for justice would be downtowners, there would always be a few uptowners involved in the effort to secure justice for the victims, a sign of the seriousness with which they regarded the issue.

At the outset, the defense attorneys approached Magistrate Mayo in a body in an attempt to persuade him it had been the Hoe employees who were at fault and that the Jewish prisoners before him had acted only under provocation and should be released. Mayo, however, was not persuaded. He did not dispute the notion that the men might have been provoked, but he asserted that no one had the right to take the law into his own hands. "This spirit of lawlessness on the East Side should be discouraged," Mayo replied, "and I propose to go into each case carefully and try it on its merits."[4]

At least Mayo was not an unrepentant anti-Semite, as some Tammany-appointed judges were. Had the riot occurred several years earlier, the cases might have been heard by Police Justice John J. Ryan, a Tammany

Hall appointee who publicly denounced Jews as persecutors of Christians. Jewish defendants could never count on him for a fair shake. "I intend to see to it that the Hebrews of the East Side shall be taught that the Christians have rights as well as they," he had proclaimed in court one day while trying twenty-five-year-old peddler Morris Goodman for obstructing the sidewalk at Broome and Essex Streets. "The citizens of New York who live in other parts of the city have no idea of the outrageous methods of the Hebrews of the East Side in their relations with their Christian neighbors."[5]

After he was criticized for this brazen outburst, Ryan had paid a call on the mayor to explain himself, insisting he was actually a *friend* of the Jews. But he had only made things worse. He said,

> The Jews come to this country laboring under a delusion. They think they can do as they please. The police tell them they cannot . . . I am tired of hearing of persecution of the Jews in New York. . . . The trouble is emphatically among themselves, as any intelligent Hebrew in the other quarters of the city will tell you.[6]

The first to be arraigned in Judge Mayo's court was seventeen-year-old Harry Krinsky, charged by Patrolman Thomas F. Keenan of the Fifth Street Station with throwing a brick at the factory. He was fined $5. Next up were Harris Rosenblum, Samuel Rosenzweig, and Samuel Allenstein, the trio arrested by Roundsman James M. Jackson. The officer accused them all of having attacked him and fingered Rosenblum as the man who had hit him with a brick. Rosenblum was charged with felonious assault and the other two with inciting a riot.

"There is no possible thing to be said in favor of these men," Mayo opined from the bench, raising serious questions as to his own impartiality. He continued,

> The attack on the Roundsman occurred some distance away from the factory, and they could not possibly have been acting in retaliation for anything that the employees of the factory did. I will hold them on $1,000 bail for trial.[7]

It's unclear whether the judge had even bothered to hear from Rosenblum before he did so.[8]

15. Magistrate John B. Mayo. *New York Tribune*, January 25, 1907.

Then Mayo started handing out more fines. Jacob Feingold, accused by Hoe clerk George Williams of throwing stones at the factory, was assessed $5. Abraham Silverstein and Samuel Glicksburg each had to pay $5 for denouncing the police in front of the Delancey Street Station, and Louis Grambinsky and Abraham Postman were fined the same amount for overturning ash cans.[9]

Only Fred Levy escaped penalty. He had been driving a wagon and had been accused of striking an officer named McKean with a whip when the latter tried to stop him. Levy's attorney argued that McKean had been struck accidentally, and the defendant was released. And Morris Silverman, Henry Subhran, and Charles Reiff, all boys charged with throwing stones at McKean when he arrested Levy, were let off with a warning.[10]

16. Robert Hoe III. Wikipedia.

Among the three Hoe employees taken into custody was Harry Stockhusen, who had been arrested not because he sprayed water on the mourners but because he soaked a *policeman*—Patrolman William Maher. He argued he had done so under orders from his foreman and had merely "aimed the nozzle wrong," suggesting that it would have been less of an offense had he aimed it at a Jew. He and a colleague, George Stillgenbauer, were arraigned for disorderly conduct, as was a third, George W. Church, whom City Marshall Albert Levine accused of soaking him. All were held on $500 bail. Hoe factory managers paid the bond, and all three were released.[11]

Soon after the violence was over, Robert Hoe made a self-serving statement to Inspector Cross and also gave it to the newspapers. He placed all the blame for the trouble on the Jews:

> Just as the workmen and clerks of R. Hoe & Co.'s establishment were returning to their work at one o'clock, a number of men in the funeral procession of the rabbi, which was passing on the street, were seen fighting each other with their umbrellas, and a portion of the crowd,

> to get away from the fighters, rushed up the steps to the entrance of R. Hoe & Co.'s building, 504–520 Grand Street. Somebody threw a piece of cotton waste out of one of the windows. Thereupon the crowd rushed to get into the door of R. Hoe & Co.'s office, making a great noise and disturbance. They were forced out by the hands inside, and simultaneously the mob began throwing stones and other missiles at the windows and crowded against the entrance with the view of again forcing admission.
>
> In order to disperse them and save employees who were outside from being injured by the mob, some of the hands in the works turned on the fire hose, many of the employees not having succeeded in getting in, and some having been badly injured. The mob continued throwing stones, bricks and other missiles and breaking windows. The men upstairs, seeing their fellow workmen being mobbed in the street, threw missiles at the crowd. Stones and bricks and other missiles were thrown at the plate glass windows, breaking twenty-five in the old office and twenty-four in the new office, and of the small windows, fifty in one department and twenty-five in another.[12]

That was his public statement, which strained credulity. But he knew better, because it was not what he told Sergeant Henry Cohen privately. Cohen told the *Daily People* Hoe had admitted he thought the trouble had been caused by apprentices in his own factory who had dumped pails of water on the crowd while the procession was passing, prompting retaliation from those below.[13]

Nor was Hoe the only one to lay the blame on the Jews. Inspector Cross, too, told the newspapers he believed the attack on the factory had been premeditated. To bolster his case, he made the ludicrous assertion that there had been no stones on the street prior to the riot, ostensible proof that the Jews had carried them there with the intent to throw them:

> A strange thing connected with the riots, in my opinion, is that although the square in front of Hoe's factory is remarkably free from stones or other missiles, after the riot was over my men picked up a soap box full of rocks and other things. On one of the floors of Hoe's factory was found a glazier's hammer, which had been thrown from the street

> through a window, and which narrowly escaped hitting the head of a foreman. It seems to me to be the fact that the Jews went there with the idea of bombarding the factory.[14]

He continued by defending the behavior of the police with a couple of statements that were contradicted by virtually all other accounts:

> I don't know what happened before I reached the scene, but I do know that after I got there the behavior of the police was extremely mild. As soon as I arrived, I issued an order that clubs were not to be used, except in cases of extreme necessity, and they were not used.[15]

At closing time that afternoon, Cross went to great lengths to protect the factory workers from harm—something he had pointedly declined to do for the Jews. He kept patrolmen on duty near the Hoe building until closing time under the watchful eye of several captains and more than a dozen sergeants. He told the employees to leave by twos and threes and ordered them escorted up Grand Street toward the Bowery between a double line of police for several blocks until they were out of the neighborhood. Then he arranged for Robert Hoe to be driven home by a police detective.[16]

Asked by reporters whether he thought the police had acted with "unnecessary brutality," Commissioner Partridge was defensive. "What are they carrying clubs for?" he responded sarcastically. Then, as if realizing just how tone-deaf that remark sounded, he quickly added that he really could not answer the question:

> I am making an investigation for my own information based on what I have seen in the public press. I have my own opinion, of course. I would be an ass if I didn't form some opinion. I'll have to get more facts, however, and more information before I can express that opinion for publication.[17]

In other words, he had already decided the police were not at fault. He just lacked sufficient evidence to back up the ill-informed judgment.

Told by reporters that the police had "seemed to enjoy the discomfiture of the Hebrews who were being pelted from the factory window," that they had laughed at the Jews' plight, and that many on the street believed that if police had been present in sufficient numbers at the outset of the violence, they could have stopped it, Partridge claimed ignorance. "I have no official information on this point. You have just told me something that is news to me."

"Are you going to ask any of these East Side Hebrews, whose names are printed in the newspapers, to come to your office and substantiate their complaints against the police?"

"No," Partridge replied. "I am not sending out invitations to people to come here and tell their troubles. If anyone has a grievance, I expect them to call on me. I have never found people bashful under these circumstances."

"Then you do not intend to solicit such complaints?" a reporter asked.

"No. Why should I?"

"How, then, do you expect to get at the facts?"

"Never you mind," Partridge shot back, annoyed. "Leave that to me."[18]

The *Arbeiter Zeitung* (Workman's newspaper), the Yiddish-language organ of the Socialist Labor Party of America, took Partridge to task for his callous remarks. "Commissioner Partridge is a sleepy old *bubbie* [granny] who should be knitting socks, not be in charge of a police department," it wrote.[19]

Everyone, it seemed, wanted to blame the Jews for the attacks, even if that required lying. That made it all the more urgent, and all the more important, that the Jewish community ensure once and for all that the truth came out.

11

"There Never Was Such an Outrage on Our Race"

The Jews of the Lower East Side were indignant over the events of the day. They were angry at the Hoe employees, to be sure, but they were absolutely livid at the police. Officers of the law had brutally beaten Jews in the streets during the meat riots just two months earlier, and now it had happened again.

That evening, a dozen or so Jewish physicians, attorneys, and businessmen assembled in the office of Russian-born Dr. Julius Halpern on East Broadway to discuss how best to achieve a full and fair investigation. They wanted to ensure that those who had attacked innocent Jews were brought to justice and that the police not be permitted to blame the victims or sweep the matter under the rug to avoid consequences.

Among those assembled was Polish-born criminal lawyer Abraham H. Sarasohn, the son of newspaper editor Kasriel H. Sarasohn. A Republican, he would play the leading role in the effort. Also present was Russian-born Dr. Maurice Fishberg, a graduate of New York University Medical College who worked for the Bureau of Immigration.[1]

"Instead of protecting the Jews, the police attacked them," Dr. Halpern, forty-three, a pulmonologist who had emigrated to the United States in 1896, told the press. He continued,

> Talk of Russia, where the Jew is said to be oppressed. There never was such an outrage on our race as that which happened this afternoon. The action of the police in attacking and brutally beating with their sticks women and children in the performance of one of their most sacred religious rites—that of mourning for their greatest rabbi—is an outrage of which no barbaric country of the Middle Ages was ever guilty.[2]

The men knew full well that if any justice were to be obtained for the abused Jews, the city's politicians would have to drive the process. It was one thing for Jews themselves to launch an investigation, take testimony, and assign blame. They could certainly make some noise, and they fully intended to do so, but anything they did themselves would appear biased and lack credibility. It was quite another thing for any of those responsible for the attacks to be brought to justice. That would require the mobilization of the "system."

In this case, that really boiled down to three individuals. "We will thoroughly investigate the matter," Sarasohn vowed, "and our evidence will be placed before Police Commissioner Partridge. If he fails to act, we will call upon Mayor Low and District Attorney Jerome."[3]

Fortunately, by 1902 New York's Jewish community was ensconced in the political firmament as never before.

Jews had sometimes possessed, and occasionally wielded, a measure of political power in America in previous years. Editor, journalist, and playwright Mordecai Manuel Noah, of Portuguese Sephardic ancestry, for example, was a public figure important enough in the early nineteenth century for President James Madison to name him to consular positions in Riga and Tunis (although he was subsequently removed from the diplomatic service because of his religion by then secretary of state James Monroe). In 1862, prominent Jews had lobbied President Abraham Lincoln to rescind orders issued by General Ulysses S. Grant, ostensibly to combat war profiteering, that would have expelled *all* Jews from the district under his command, which was composed of parts of Kentucky, Mississippi, and Tennessee. Lobbied by at least one member of Congress and pressured by editorials in many of the newspapers of the day, Lincoln promptly complied.[4]

But this was something quite different. With the arrival of multitudes of Russian and Central European Jews at the turn of the twentieth century, Jewish people had acquired clout at the ballot box they had never before possessed. Jews now accounted for "every fourth man or woman you meet in Manhattan," according to *Di Yidishe Velt*, and they had been instrumental in electing both the mayor and the district attorney, something these newly minted officials understood quite well.[5]

Now it was time for those elected with their help to return the favor.

17. New York City mayor Seth Low. Library of Congress.

Seth Low, who had always been sympathetic to Jewish causes, had continued to be responsive to his Jewish constituents in his first months as mayor. For example, he had awarded patronage jobs to Jews like Philip Cowen, co-founder and publisher of the *American Hebrew*, appointing him supervisor of the *City Record*, a fairly important government office. And he had named jurist and Republican operative Julius B. Mayer to succeed newly elected District Attorney Jerome as justice in Manhattan's Court of Special Sessions.[6]

Both of those appointees were uptown Jews of German extraction. In February, Low had met with downtown Jewish delegates from the Lower East Side who had come to complain about recent oppression by the police. Jewish peddlers, they told him, were being harassed by local police officers. One might be arrested one day for peddling without a license and the next for peddling *at all*, even after a license had been secured. This law had been enforced only sporadically in the past, but now pushcart peddlers who had done nothing more than sell two cents' worth of peanuts or a hat feather were being hauled in. Furthermore, they were being fined by magistrates for doing business the city had *authorized* them to do. Several were even being driven out of the precincts in which they did business.

Jews had been the main targets of the crackdowns, and some interpreted the actions of the police, most of whom owed their livelihoods to Tammany Hall, as a malicious effort to "show the East Side what reform means"—that is, punish Jews collectively for supporting the fusion ticket. One member of the Citizens' Union who had previously run for alderman claimed that as long as Jews had remained politically subservient and supported Tammany candidates, they had not been singled out for brutal treatment, but that now that they had taken a more independent stance and supported the reformers, they had incurred the ire of the police.[7]

To others, however, the police were arguably more interested in embarrassing the new mayor and his administration than in punishing Jews per se. They were especially unhappy at the reorganization of the force ordered by his appointee Partridge, which included changes to their shifts, transfers, and even some demotions and salary reductions. By mid-April, Partridge had ordered the transfer of a dozen of the policemen involved in harassing the peddlers to distant parts of the city. The *Tribune* interpreted the action to mean that "the persecution of Hebrew tradesmen in the district east of the Bowery is not to be tolerated."[8]

It was a victory for the East Side Jews, if a limited one.

Also in mid-April, the mayor had intervened to solve a short-term problem many Jews were facing over the Sunday laws. In 1902, the first and last days of the eight-day Passover holiday fell on Mondays. Jewish butchers were forbidden by Jewish law to work on Saturdays, their Sabbath, and by state law to open on Sundays, the Christian Sabbath. This meant that observant Jews would be left with only a very brief window—a few hours after sundown on Saturday night, when Shabbos had officially ended—to purchase meat for the first night seder and the ritual meal on the last night of the holiday. This would pose a problem for many.

When this issue was brought to the mayor's attention, he had intervened with Commissioner Partridge, whose men frequently arrested Jewish merchants who operated illegally on Sundays. Asserting that "the spirit of the penal code, rather than its letter, should govern," he concluded that the situation called for leniency. He essentially ordered the police not to enforce the state law and to let the butchers do business, earning him the gratitude not only of the butchers themselves but also of the New York Board of Jewish Ministers, the *Hebrew Standard,* and no doubt, Orthodox families throughout the city.[9]

Jerome, for his part, had worked hard to secure the Jewish vote—so hard that during his campaign, he had pledged to move to the Lower East Side if he were elected. And he proved as good as his word. In early 1902 he moved his family into a rented, four-story home at 8 Rutgers Street. The Jewish community was delighted. The *Forverts* had declared him "not just a neighbor, but a protector." During the kosher meat boycott, his Jewish neighbors had sought his help, and he had walked the streets of the East Side trying to persuade the rioters to go home. Now his new neighbors sought his assistance on another issue: they wanted those who had so brutally attacked them to be brought to justice.[10]

Mayor Low proved not only willing but eager to assist. Upon his arrival at the office the morning after the Grand Street riot, he dispatched the following letter to Commissioner Partridge:

> New York, July 31, 1902
>
> John N. Partridge, Police Commissioner
>
> Sir—I desire you to make a careful report to me on the disturbance yesterday of the funeral procession of the Chief Rabbi Joseph. Such an incident is discreditable to our city, and I wish to be fully informed as to the origin of it, so as to be able, if possible, to see that those who are responsible for it are properly dealt with.
>
> Respectfully,
> SETH LOW, Mayor[11]

The city's board of aldermen also adopted a resolution calling for a "strenuous and thorough" investigation of the riot. Jerome, however, was hesitant to get his office too involved, at least at this early stage. He wanted to leave the investigating to the police. He did discern fault in the police response, however, and said so. "The police should have known from the crowds that commenced to gather in the morning that a big force of policemen would be needed," he asserted, "and it seems to me that if all precautions had been taken, there would have been no trouble." But then he added, "It is all a matter which concerns the police department and not the district attorney."[12]

More than a hundred Jewish societies passed resolutions demanding a thorough inquiry, and synagogues, lodges, and other Jewish organizations were urged to hold protest meetings. City Marshal Albert Levine chaired one of the larger ones on the evening of July 31 at Grand Street's Seminole Hall, just a few blocks from the Hoe factory. The police actually attempted to stop many from entering the premises, but it still attracted some ten thousand attendees. So many more people than could fit in the auditorium wanted to be there that a redundant session with the same speakers was convened in New Windsor Hall next door.[13]

Listeners heard from the attorneys who had represented those arrested. Democratic lawyer Benjamin F. Spellman, New York born but of Polish Jewish extraction, a critic of Jerome, told the audience to "watch Low, Jerome and Partridge, and slap them hard if they do not give you justice."[14]

Attorney Elias Rosenthal did not mince words:

> I was never so proud of my fellow countrymen, the Russian Jews, when I passed Hoe's factory on Wednesday and saw the whole front of the building smashed. I fully approve your course, and I would have counted you cowards had you done less. If I had my way the whole establishment should have been razed and wrecked utterly with dynamite. I am no anarchist, at that.
>
> And what shall we say about our beautiful, admirable Inspector Cross? You must demand the removal of Inspector Cross, and make the municipal government close up the factory of the Hoe firm if necessary.[15]

The most important gathering was an invitation-only meeting at the Educational Alliance, a settlement house on Jefferson Street established by German Jews in 1889 to help "Americanize" their Eastern European brethren. Dr. Halpern presided over an audience of about three hundred who voted to establish the East Side Vigilance League. To ensure credibility, the new organization was to include "only the most conservative and fair-minded" people—that is, it was to exclude radicals. It was tasked with collecting evidence and pressing for an impartial investigation into the causes and instigators of the riot.[16]

Establishing an ad hoc committee to deal with an emergent issue was common practice on the Lower East Side. A *kehillah*—a group that might speak on behalf of all of the Jews of the city—was still years from being formed, and there was no single, obvious organization to take up the mantle of pushing for justice and ensuring that such an event would not recur. Jews had used the same strategy during the kosher meat boycott, establishing first the Ladies Anti-Beef Trust and later the Allied Conference for Cheap Kosher Meat, and they would do the same in 1904 with the New York Rent Protective Association, formed during a tenants' strike. None of these organizations ever lasted beyond the crisis it was formed to address. For now, it would be the East Side Vigilance League that would fight for a fair investigation and for punishment of the instigators.

Halpern himself was appointed to chair the new league, and various subcommittees were established to raise funds, disseminate information, and present evidence to the mayor and Commissioner Partridge. The league's leaders immediately placed a call to Low's office and were able to get him on the phone. The mayor pledged his support for their approach and vowed to cooperate "as far as his official position would permit."[17]

Dr. Halpern then issued a public statement in the league's name:

> The Hebrews were entirely innocent in the affair, and it is too much to ask us to pass it over without a united demand for justice. The Vigilance Committee will insist on a rigid investigation. We are backed up by the mayor, and the Board of Aldermen is with us.[18]

This was an enviable position, and surely a first for New York's Jews. They had the political establishment firmly in their corner.

A second ad hoc committee, the Hebrew American League, was formed the following evening at an "indignation meeting" in Pacific Hall on East Broadway. Its goals were to unite the Jewish people and protect them from discrimination, and in service of the latter objective, it too would work to bring the assailants to justice. Charles Dushkind, a prominent corporate attorney, was chosen as its president; all of its officers were Russian born.[19]

Given the Jewish experience with the police department and Commissioner Partridge's revealing remark about clubbing, the members of the Vigilance League didn't trust that the department's investigation would be fair. They did not object, at this stage, to the inquiry being conducted within the police department, but they wanted their own lawyers present at all of the sessions to ensure that it was carried out impartially and that no whitewashing would occur. And they were adamant that Partridge *not* place the matter into the dirty hands of Inspector Adam Cross.

"We are determined to have the question of the conduct of the police inquired into by *other* than the Inspector," Halpern told the press, "for he has not proved himself a friend of the East Side Hebrews."

It was, to say the least, an understatement.[20]

12

"Action Is Called For! Examples Should Be Made!"

Despite the fact that Robert Hoe and Inspector Cross placed blame for the violence on the shoulders of the Jews and that Commissioner Partridge seemed headed in that direction, the newspapers weren't buying the story. Nor was the general public.

The *New York World*, a leading national voice for reform under publisher Joseph Pulitzer, had only opprobrium for the police and demanded an immediate investigation. "If there is any excuse for the department having made no preparations beforehand for handling the crowd at the funeral of Chief Rabbi Joseph, there is no excuse for the failure to act after the unprecedented crowd had gathered," it opined. And if it turned out to be true that the police had indiscriminately clubbed innocent men and women, then "everyone guilty of such an outrage should be speedily dismissed from the force."[1]

The *Brooklyn Standard Union* agreed. It believed the police guilty of just as much racial prejudice as the factory hands, and it accused the magistrates of bias as well. It also faulted Partridge for not immediately suspending Inspector Cross. "It is high time some of the Devery gang and at least a few incompetent Tammany police officers, of both high and low degree, were gotten rid of," it continued, "for 'the good of the force,' and the credit of the city."[2]

This latter comment was the opening salvo in a debate about who was responsible for police misconduct. Mayor Low and Commissioner Partridge had inherited the corrupt police force of which Tammany Hall and Devery had been the architects. But they had now been in office for more than half a year, and the riot had occurred on their watch. There would be a lot of finger-pointing over the next several months as the issue played out.

Several publications pointed out that resistance of the kind seen on Grand Street was out of character for Hebrews—in a *good* way. The *Sun* was glad that "for once, the meek and futile protest of the pestered Jew was not forthcoming." And the *Brooklyn Daily Eagle* was pleased that the Jews had struck out "in good American fashion" at their tormentors. It predicted that, having shown their willingness to fight, Jews would now be more likely to be left alone in the future.[3]

But then the *Eagle* segued into condescension, summoning the popular stereotype of the passive, frail, and defenseless Jew:

> Toward these poor Russian and Polish Jews, however, there ought to be a feeling of chivalry. They are small, bent, ill-fed, weak and ignorant. The man who picks them for the assaults of his fists or his wit is a man of whose presence in the community we are weary and ashamed; he is a scoundrel and bully and will beat women. But in the riots of yesterday the persecuted Jew proved that he could give an account of himself.[4]

In the same vein, the *Brooklyn Citizen* betrayed ethnic prejudice in its tongue-in-cheek comparison of the willingness of Jews to fight back against aggression and that of other ethnic groups in the city. Speaking of the Hoe employees, it declared, "Had they been indiscreet they would have attacked an Irish or an Italian funeral, in which event there would have been a great deal of work for the coroner, and maybe for the fire marshal."[5]

The *New York Times* received a torrent of letters to the editor about the riot, some of which had been written in language it described as "not wholly temperate." It ran a few of the printable ones, including one that compared the melee to the funeral of Catholic Archbishop Michael Corrigan, for whose interment in the crypt of St. Patrick's Cathedral on Fifth Avenue the previous May, several *hundred* police officers had been assigned to keep order. Another suggested that Robert Hoe would have been better off making no statement at all, since the one he issued strained credulity.[6] Even the *Catholic Mirror* condemned the attack on the Jews. In an editorial reprinted in the *Irish World*, the paper called it an example of religious intolerance that reflected poorly on the city and the police.[7]

It's doubtful the papers received many letters accepting the Hoe or Cross versions of the stories, but if they did, they did not print them. The public seemed nearly of one mind on three basic facts: that Jews hadn't started the riot, that the Hoe employees had, and that both the factory workers and the police had behaved abominably.

To the *Forverts*, and likely to many of its Russian Jewish readers, the whole sordid event was nothing more or less than a pogrom—a bloody attack on Jews not unlike those many remembered bitterly from the old country. Some surely found the analogy especially appropriate in light of the participation of the police. But exactly how apt was it? The Russian word means "to wreak havoc; to demolish violently." The first such incident was an anti-Jewish riot in Odessa in 1821, and the expression was later employed to describe the spate of antisemitic violence in the Russian Empire that followed the 1881 assassination of Czar Alexander II.[8]

Most such attacks in Europe were far more violent than the 1902 Grand Street riot, however. They were often planned in advance; they often included rape, murder, and substantial destruction of property; and they were sometimes followed by the exile of the survivors. Not infrequently, police were known to stand by and decline to intervene, and the Jews had no recourse with higher authorities. When the East Side Jews became victims of gentile citizens whose attacks were abetted by law enforcement, it was entirely understandable that some would draw the comparison, even though this had been no massacre.

Nonetheless, the *Forverts* decried the "bloody pogrom" in the banner headline of its July 30 edition and in subsequent articles. The paper might have employed some other, less loaded term but instead made a conscious choice to use the highly charged Russian analogy.

The socialist paper, which saw capitalist conspiracies wherever it looked, took a "plague-o'-both-your-houses" approach to the two dominant political parties. In an editorial likely penned by Abraham Cahan, its editor, it actually blamed Jews, if only indirectly, for the attack. The *Forverts* held Jewish voters responsible for having unwisely supported the reformers in the previous election. As far as the paper was concerned, the Democrats and Republicans were two sides of the same coin. Only the socialists truly had the Jews' interests at heart:

Forward Vorwarts

פאָרווערטס

Vol. VI No. 1661 New York & Philadelphia, Wednesday July 30 1902 Price One Cent

א בלוטיגער פאגראם ביים רב הכולל'ס לויה.

ליפערס בעפאלען טרויענדער אידען שפאל... טען קעפ מיט שטיינער און בריהען מיט זודיגע וואססער.

דיא פאל'ציי מאכט יד אחת מיט דיא ליפערס און מ'טען און פערוואונדען צעהנדליגע אידען.

3 גרויסע מאנופעקטשורערס פון אסאסיאיישען גיבען נאך.

18. The front-page headline of the *Forverts* on July 30, 1902, which translates, "A Bloody Pogrom at the Chief Rabbi's Funeral."

> Who *are* these police? It was Tammany who nurtured them. Now you're beholding the aristocratic "reform" government. The mass of Jewish citizens whose heads were split open yesterday and who got trampled, they *themselves* have put the clubs into the hands of those who are antisemitic and anti-worker.[9]

Cahan had as little use for Judge Mayo as he did for the police:

> Instead of damning the men who wear blue coats with bronze buttons and get fat from bribery for the savagery they showed yesterday, those who were supposed to defend the Jews, this justice did the same thing that the police did. He treated the victims as perpetrators. He punished the Jews who came with bloodied heads with five- or ten-dollar fines.[10]

Di Yidishe Velt, noting that the riot on Grand Street was the only incident in the history of New York City it could recall in which Jews had been brutally and badly treated by ruffians *and* police, put the total number of Jews who had been injured at no fewer than two hundred.[11] And it printed a strident, open letter to "the highest officials of New York" with an admonition and an implied threat that read, in part,

19. *Forverts* editor Abraham Cahan. Wikipedia.

Di Yidishe Velt, speaking for three hundred and fifty thousand outraged citizens of the East Side, by whose grace you are in office, demands of you, Mayor Low; of you, Commissioner Partridge; and of you, District Attorney Jerome:

that the police officers who have been engaged in this brutal course of conduct shall be removed from the offices they have shown themselves unfit to fill;

that their commanding officer, who gloats at the wickedness that has been perpetrated, shall no longer wear the uniform of a body which cannot but be demoralized under such leadership;

> that the wretched Jew-baiters who vented their venom upon this defenseless multitude be punished by criminal law, which is administered by you, Mr. District Attorney; and
>
> that their employers, who were in a position to command them and who did not hesitate to aid in the assault upon this funeral procession . . . should not be permitted to skulk behind the pitiable pretense that they could not control their own apprentices.

"*Di Yidishe Velt* and those whom it represents will hold you responsible!" it went on to declare. "Fine words, promises, assurances as to the future will not suffice! Action is called for! Examples should be made!"[12]

13

"Cross Is Cross with the Jews"

On August 1—just two days after the riot, and one day after his boss had requested it—Commissioner Partridge sent his report to Mayor Low. It had been prepared by none other than Inspector Adam A. Cross, despite the fact that the Jews had made it clear they had no faith in the inspector's objectivity.

They were, of course, right to be concerned. Cross's report contained the preposterous assertions he had already made verbally: that the violence had been entirely the fault of the Jews and that it had been premeditated.

Partridge refused to comment publicly on the document in any detail, but he did tell the *New York Press* that he thought the police had performed well under the circumstances, citing the fact that there had not been too many serious injuries.[1]

In five typewritten pages, Cross had doubled down on his dubious assertion that the street had been free of stones and bricks when the procession began, and he detailed the detritus found inside the Hoe factory after the melee: eighteen pieces of broken brick, twenty-nine pieces of broken stone, eight iron bands, four iron bolts, one twelve-pound keg, one hammer, and three bolts. He then made a huge leap of logic and deemed it all conclusive evidence that "those who broke the windows and destroyed the property of Hoe & Co. came there prepared to do what they did do." He also repeated that he had witnessed no clubbing or any other violent action by the police.[2] Anything to deflect blame from himself and his department. Even barefaced lies.

Partridge, however, had gotten the message that Cross was not the man to investigate his own actions, and although he did not take the advice of the *Brooklyn Standard Union* to suspend the inspector, he did the next best thing: he summarily transferred him. The official word was that Cross's transfer to

20. Cartoon from *New York World*, August 2, 1902, referencing Inspector Adam Cross's summary transfer to the Bronx, "among the goats and pumas."

the Bronx had been in the works *before* the Grand Street riot, but few believed Partridge would otherwise have exiled his right-hand man to work "among the goats and the pumas," as the *New York World* put it. It was a jocular reference to the recent escape from the New York Zoological Park—today's Bronx Zoo—of a young puma that had roamed the borough freely for two days until it was captured.[3]

"It is taken as an indication that Commissioner Partridge has thrown Devery's friend overboard," the *World* noted. The paper even printed a cartoon mocking the transfer with the caption "Cross gets the double-cross."[4]

Several members of the East Side Vigilance League called at police headquarters on Mulberry Street to present the evidence of police brutality they had collected so far. While they were waiting for Colonel Partridge, they told reporters they were there to lodge complaints against Roundsman James M. Jackson and Sergeant John McSweeney as well as several patrolmen.

They brought along twenty-two-year-old Harris Rosenblum, the tailor Jackson had accused of attacking him with a brick. Hauled before Judge Mayo the day before on a charge of feloniously assaulting Jackson, Rosenblum had turned out today to return the favor. Appearing with a bandaged head, he accused Jackson of clubbing him unmercifully, knocking him down, throwing him into a patrol wagon, and continuing to throttle him all the way to the station house. And he had a witness who was prepared to testify that Jackson had singled Rosenblum out and chased him into the park across the street from the factory. Rosenblum had then grabbed hold of a railing, but the roundsman had pried his hands off of it and clubbed him, opening a wound on his head.[5]

The other witness they brought was Herman Serels, known as Harry, whom the newspapers described as the only Jew in the employ of R. Hoe & Co. He was there to confirm that it had been his fellow factory workers, and *not* the mourners, who had initiated the trouble. A machinist in charge of manufacturing screws who had been working on the fourth floor of the building, he was quite nervous about testifying because he was sure that doing so would put his job in jeopardy.[6]

When the delegates were admitted to Partridge's private office and began to state their grievances, however, they were cut short.

"Gentlemen, nobody wants to go more thoroughly into this matter than I do, and I will have an honest and thorough investigation of the charges made," the commissioner promised them. "I am a very busy man, and I hope you will pardon my seeming indifference if I refer the matter to Inspector Brooks. He is in charge of the district where the riots occurred, and he will make a better investigation than I could, knowing the ground more thoroughly."[7]

Partridge certainly had reasons apart from the press of other business for wanting the investigation off of his desk. The whole matter placed him in a quandary. If he came down too hard on the police, he would be perceived internally as an enemy, and it would undermine his ability to command the department. If he were seen as too lenient, it would confirm for many that he had failed to reign in bad police behavior, one of Mayor Low's most important campaign promises.

Two days earlier, the *New York Tribune* had speculated that despite the fact that Partridge had been in his position only seven months, he might be a short-timer. Two powerful civic organizations, it wrote, were preparing reports about conditions within the police department that did not reflect well on his management. The Hoe investigation promised to be contentious, and the last thing he needed was more controversy.[8]

Having made his statement, Partridge touched a button, and Inspector Nicholas Brooks entered the room. Brooks, who commanded the district east of the Bowery, had just returned to New York from vacation. Had he been in town, it would have been he and not Cross who commanded the police reserves called to Grand Street. Putting him in charge took the onus off Partridge himself, and it also satisfied the Jewish community's demand that Cross not be given charge of investigating his own conduct.[9]

When Cross was questioned about the inquiry by reporters, he was strident and showed no remorse. He declared defiantly,

> I court the fullest kind of an investigation into these charges. I have absolutely nothing to fear, for I can prove that everything that was done was on the level. No clubbing was done after I got there. And I made inquiries of the officers in charge when I arrived, and *they* know nothing of any clubbing.[10]

He ginned up a good conspiracy theory to deflect the allegations:

> The people who are making these charges are after the police in general. I suppose they want to make a complaint against me because I was in command in the absence of Inspector Brooks and made a report about the riot. They want to make the trouble go up as high as they can. . . . A

> thorough investigation of this trouble will go to show that the police did their duty.[11]

"It is absolutely untrue that there was any disturbance among the marchers themselves," Serels told Inspector Brooks. "The employees on the floor on which I was working . . . threw screws and bolts, such as were being manufactured there. The crowd below hurled back these missiles, thus inflicting heavy damage and breaking many of the windows of the factory." He then averred, "I come here to make this statement, although I know that this will cost me my place, but I am a Jew and I saw my brethren attacked."[12] Moreover, he added, the harassment of Jews had been going on for some time:

> It has been the practice of the employees of the Hoe Company to throw pieces of cotton waste, banana skins and other refuse down upon the Jewish people as they were on their way to worship in the various synagogues. . . . This annoyance is not confined to Saturday afternoon, but to any day there is a crowd upon the streets.[13]

That evening, a mass meeting of about five thousand was held at Cooper Union. Uniformed police and Central Office detectives were scattered through the aisles to keep order. Those officers who spoke German or Yiddish could understand the many denunciations of the police force that were made, but they took no obvious umbrage, and everything remained peaceful. The meeting was organized and dominated by socialists: Louis Miller, editor of the *Arbeiter Zeitung*, chaired it; and speakers included Abraham Cahan of the *Forverts* and union organizer Joseph Barondess.

"The Bronx has got used to beasts at large of late, so, perhaps the people up there will stand the rule of Cross better than we could," Miller joked. He went on to lament the fact that the recent funeral had been for the chief rabbi and not for Cross himself. "I never admired Partridge, but I have changed my opinion today," he said, referring to the commissioner's decision to exile the inspector.[14] He would soon have good reason to return to his earlier judgment.

Quipping that if Cross had lived in Russia, he would surely have been sent to Siberia, Cahan suggested the inspector harbored anti-Jewish sentiments. "Cross is cross with the Jews," he declared, because

> Cross and men of his stamp clogged Allen Street with immorality and then fattened on it.[15] Devery made his pile and skipped. Cross was making his pile fast when the Jews broke up his graft. He has never forgiven them.

This was a reference to the complaint against Cross and Captain Herlihy lodged two years earlier by Episcopal Bishop Potter and Jewish reformers Felix Adler and Jacob Schiff, in which they suggested the police refusal to close down the brothels was because they were being paid off.[16]

The Ukrainian-born Barondess, a prominent labor organizer who had masterminded the 1891 cloak makers' strike and more recently helped negotiate an end to the kosher meat boycott, recounted his own experience with police aggression against the heavily Jewish Cloak Makers' Union. "When the cloak makers paraded, they set on them and clubbed them as they did you on Wednesday," he recalled. He condemned the mayor, District Attorney Jerome, and Commissioner Partridge, the latter of whom was still resented by some for having denied Jewish protesters a demonstration permit during the meat boycott. Barondess appealed to all to support socialist candidates over Democrats and Republicans. And he added, "Let us not rest until we have got Cross and Thompson out of the department."[17]

For the latter, he didn't have to wait long. The very next day came the unexpected news that Captain William Thompson, the Devery man in charge of the funeral procession's police escorts, had retired "at his own request" at the age of sixty-two after thirty-six years on the force. Colonel Partridge insisted Thompson's decision had nothing to do with the funeral riot.

"There were no charges against Captain Thompson," Partridge told reporters defensively. "At least there was nothing tangible. It was a case of bad judgment at the worst. He looked all worn out, and I agreed with him that it was time for him to quit." It's doubtful anyone believed the colonel, however. The riot had occurred in Thompson's precinct and on his watch. Had he and his men been on the scene instead of riding ahead with the hearse, it is entirely possible the violence would quickly have been suppressed. There was every reason to believe Thompson would have to face a hearing if he remained on the force.[18]

21. Joseph Barondess. College of Charleston Library.

The fact that the captain was now safe from discipline angered some Jews, many of whom remembered that police under his command had dealt harshly with their women during the meat boycott. But taken together with the transfer of Inspector Adam Cross, his sudden retirement was, in a way, a second victory for the Jewish community.

It was clear they were no longer powerless. And they had not even really begun to fight.

14

"Driving Them like a Lot of Hogs"

Although the press was silent on the ethnic makeup of the Hoe labor force, later chroniclers of the riot have generally taken it as an article of faith that the Hoe employees were predominantly Irish and that they had acted out of hatred for Jews. There are no extant rosters from that period that give insight into the makeup of the Hoe workforce, but recent scholarship suggests that not a few were probably of German extraction, because those arrested, those who testified, and those whose names appeared in the newspapers in connection with the riot had German-sounding surnames or because census and vital records confirm their German ancestry. Even though many were immigrants themselves or the children of immigrants, this did not preclude them from being hostile to the "foreigners" who came after them. And many had no doubt brought with them age-old prejudices from Europe, including antisemitism.[1]

Most local Jews believed the factory workers' attack had been motivated by Jew hatred, though at least one editorial writer in the Socialist Labor Party's *Arbeiter Zeitung* disagreed. "Some hot Jewish 'patriots' are trying to construe from this tragic opera an antisemitic danger in this land," he wrote. "Several stupid workers in the Hoe factory who perpetrated this riot would have done the same to Chinese, Italians or other foreigners who, like the Jews, would have marched in large numbers without police protection."[2]

Indeed, the same might well have happened at a Chinese funeral; the Chinese in New York were probably even less liked and respected than the Jews. But that does not absolve the Hoe hands of antisemitism. Harry Serels certainly felt it at the factory. To him, not much had changed since Gregory Weinstein's hazing in the late 1880s. And Robert Hoe himself conceded there was anti-Jewish feeling in the company when he told the *New York Times* right after the riot that among the three hundred apprentices who worked for him, "some of them have a dislike for the Jews."[3]

This was not, however, the antisemitism of the Patrician Protestants who, beginning in the late 1870s, declined to socialize with even well-established Jews in their hotels, clubs, and resorts in places like Saratoga Springs and Coney Island because they found them uncouth or distasteful. Neither was it the later antisemitism of people who believed Jews controlled the media or the banking system, nor the Jew hatred engendered by the Russian forgery *The Protocols of the Elders of Zion*, which claimed a Hebrew plot to take over the world but which had not yet been published in 1902. Nobody could mistake the poor Lower East Side Jews for captains of industry who had grandiose plans for global domination.

It was, rather, the Jew hatred of the urban working class, the blue-collar laborers, many of whom were recent arrivals themselves or the children of immigrants. It was the condescension of earlier arrivals toward an impoverished, unkempt group of latecomers who more or less kept to themselves, spoke their own language, dressed peculiarly, and in many cases, seemed either uninterested in assimilation or unable to blend in. Jews were also convenient scapegoats in times of economic uncertainty, and some were seen as too radical: socialists and anarchists like Emma Goldman and Alexander Berkman, for example, were alive and well in the Jewish ghetto and deeply unpopular in many circles.

The attitudes of these workers sometimes came with a side order of dislike for the Jewish merchants of the ghetto, whom some perceived as greedy and moneygrubbing, or jealousy of the upward mobility of Jewish immigrants, many of whom did not stay poor for long. And there were deep roots of antisemitism in most forms of Christianity, especially Catholicism. Many Christians also subscribed to the blood libel, the European canard that falsely accused Jews of murdering Christian children for their rituals.

To be fair, for some participants in the riot, there probably *was* no serious antisemitism involved. There surely was an element of teasing and harassment motivated by nothing more odious than youthful indiscretion. Jewish passersby were convenient victims for the immature apprentices at the Hoe factory who enjoyed harassing the odd-looking bearded men who passed the factory on their way to worship. That sort of mischief was probably not motivated by any well-considered ethnic animus on their part.

But well considered or not, there definitely *was* animus, as Harry Serels demonstrated on August 2, when he failed to show up in court. Although it was the Jewish Sabbath, it was not a day of rest for attorneys Abraham H. Sarasohn and Alexander Rosenthal of the East Side Vigilance League, who went to the Essex Market Police Court to file more charges. The attorneys had expected to find Serels there to testify in support of several of the complaints.

When he did not show up, they sent out a party to search for him. And although they wished the court to issue a summons for him, they hoped, for his own protection, to keep his identity a secret. So they asked the judge for a subpoena for "John Doe," who was described as an employee of R. Hoe & Company and an important material witness in the prosecutions of both Hoe employees and the police.[4]

It didn't take long for Serels's identity to be revealed, however, and when Robert Hoe learned of the summons, he criticized the Vigilance League. He complained that there was no call for secrecy and asserted that his firm would cooperate fully with an investigation. He also used the occasion to take issue with newspaper reports that Serels was the only Jew employed at the factory. "We have fully fifty Jews," he insisted. "Some of them have been with us many years." He added, "We have no prejudice against the Jews."[5]

Hoe's assertion notwithstanding, the league's attorneys had been right to be cautious about revealing Serles's identity. Finally located at the home of a friend, Serles explained that he had failed to appear not because he was observing the Sabbath but because his life had been threatened. He not only dreaded showing up in court; he was also deathly afraid of returning to the factory. He was served with a subpoena to appear the following Tuesday, but there was still the matter of protecting him in the interim.

Members of the Vigilance League arranged lodging for him, and he asked Delancey Street Station Captain Charles L. Albertson for police protection. Albertson initially declined, telling Serels that he seemed to him a big, husky fellow able to take care of himself. But when he also refused to issue Serels a

22. New York police captain Charles L. Albertson. *Waverly Free Press*, January 19, 1906.

permit to carry a weapon for protection, representatives of the league went public with the captain's lack of cooperation.

Sarasohn told the press,

> Serels promised to tell all he knows, but he had been warned that if he does the police will not protect him. We know it is a fact that a guard has been denied him, and it is also true that he has been refused to carry a revolver to protect himself from the rowdies, who, encouraged by the attitude of the police, are ready to set upon him. . . . Captain Albertson has promised protection, but his promises have not been kept.[6]

The bad press was apparently enough to make Albertson relent and provide the requested protection. The league also arranged to pay Serels his salary and promised to help him find a new job.[7]

As protest meetings continued among all sorts of organizations in the Jewish quarter—fifteen synagogues held them, as did various clubs and mutual aid societies—and as those who had caused the violence were condemned even in some New York churches on Sunday, August 3, the East Side Vigilance League issued a new statement intended to turn up the heat on the police:

> It has been conceded by the police that there were four policemen in front of the Hoe factory at the time of the outbreak of the trouble. This means that the police admit that a mob of hoodlums was permitted to abuse and assault a peaceable and lawful assemblage in the presence of at least four guardians of the peace. The police did nothing to suppress the onslaught of the ruffians in the factory.

The league went on to assert that the Jews had retaliated only after efforts to get Hoe management to stop the violence had failed and those officers had declined to protect them. And it promised to make a formal complaint against Inspector Cross and to demand that Commissioner Partridge fire him.[8]

Both the Vigilance League and the Hebrew American League went on collecting testimony. They had already recorded thirty additional, well-substantiated complaints against Hoe employees and police, and on Monday they handed them all over to Inspector Brooks, who continued his inquiry. Some one hundred Jews converged on Mulberry Street to testify or to listen. At least twenty of them still had bandaged heads.

Also present were District Attorney Jerome and Florence J. "Big Florrie" Sullivan, the Tammany leader of the Eighth District. He had come, he said, "to make sure justice was done." The investigation had the potential to benefit Tammany Hall if police misbehavior could be demonstrated and laid at the feet of the Low administration.[9]

Much of the hearing that morning was devoted to the case of Julius Weber, the man clubbed by police whom several mourners had taken for dead.

"I was marching in the funeral procession when they began to throw things at us from the Hoe factory," Weber told Inspector Brooks. He continued,

> With several others I went into the factory to protest. We threw no missiles at that time, and our sole objective was to have the boss make his men stop pelting us with iron and other things.
>
> The door of the office was slammed in our faces and we were hustled to the street. Just as we got outside, they turned the hose on us and I started to run for a safe place. I ran up against a policeman. He and another policeman with a red mustache were the only ones I saw up to that time. The policeman grabbed me by the neck and slugged me over the head with his club. I fell unconscious, and when I came to, I was lying on the floor of a drug store in Grand Street.[10]

Weber's testimony was confirmed by Jacob Rubel, who had witnessed the incident. "This man Weber was running away when the policeman grabbed him and slugged him over the head," Rubel recalled. He went on,

> He had slugged others before. I went up to him and asked him for his number. He told me to "get the hell out of here" and made a grab for me with his club upraised. I managed to escape, but I saw his number and as soon as I got to a safe place I wrote it down—number 4404.[11]

Di Yidishe Velt reported separately that the policeman whose badge number was 4404 had also beaten a boy on the stoop of the Young Men's Benevolent Association just across the street from the Hoe factory. The boy's head had been split open and he appeared to be dead, but he had been dragged away by police before anyone could find out what his name was. The paper wrote to Commissioner Partridge asking that the officer be punished and sent out reporters to see if they could locate him.[12] Badge number 4404, it turned out, belonged to Irish-born Officer Henry Doupe of the Eldridge Street Station.

Sam Shrednesky recalled that another officer had pushed his way into the crowd but had *not* used his club. The attorneys for the Jews pointed out the significance of the observation: it demonstrated that there had been no necessity for clubbing and that doing so had constituted an excessive use of force.

WITNESSES AT RIOT INQUIRY TELL OF CLUBBING DONE BY POLICEMEN.

MEMBERS OF THE EAST SIDE VIGILANCE COMMITTEE AND SOME OF THEIR WITNESSES.
(Photographed to-day by an Evening World photographer.)

23. Members of the East Side Vigilance League and some of their witnesses. City Marshal Albert Levine is at top center. *New York World,* August 4, 1902.

Moses Cohen testified through an interpreter that while he was standing on the north side of Grand Street, he had overheard Roundsman Jackson order Policeman Charles Merrill to use his club and witnessed the pair of them rush into the crowd together, swinging. David Dorman testified through an interpreter that he had heard Jackson cry "Club the Jews!"

"I thought this man didn't understand English," Inspector Brooks interjected. The interpreter conferred with the witness for a moment and then reported that Dorman knew *enough* English to know what "Club the Jews" meant.

Dorman also recounted that Merrill had used his club savagely against women as well as men, "driving them like a lot of hogs." Merrill categorically denied this; he claimed he had not arrived until the riot was over and that, even then, he had left the station house in such a hurry that he had forgotten his club.[13]

When, after hearing some forty witnesses, Brooks announced that he would reconvene the hearing the following Friday, attorneys Benjamin F. Spellman and Abraham H. Sarasohn asked if he really thought further testimony was necessary. Although they were prepared with about sixteen additional witnesses, they believed they had already more than made their case.

"Before I take any action in this matter," Brooks responded, "I'm going to hear the testimony of *all* the witnesses on *both* sides."

The attorneys objected in a chorus. "You're not a trial judge," one reminded him. "The testimony of forty witnesses has established a *prima facie* case against the officers and warrants your making charges against them," one of them added.

"I was directed by Commissioner Partridge to make a thorough investigation of this affair and unless I receive orders to the contrary," Brooks retorted, "I shall hear the statements of everybody concerned in the case who chooses to testify."

Jerome, who backed Brooks in this, then made a patronizing remark that suggested he had not been impressed by the accusations he had heard that day. "In that great crowd," he said, "there must have been many persons prominent by reason of their profession or calling who would have made strong witnesses, and it seems strange that none of them has come forward to testify." In other words, the elitist Jerome would have found professionals more convincing than those the *Sun* referred to as members of "the extremely poor and ignorant class," the very people for whose votes he had pleaded just a few months earlier.[14]

That morning, Jerome had promised representatives of the United Hebrew Community that he would see to it that the guilty were punished and told them he had designated Assistant District Attorney Isidor J. Kresel, a Yiddish-speaking Jewish immigrant from Ukraine, to investigate their complaints. But the truth is he was still hesitant about bringing charges. He had already signaled this a few days earlier when he stated that he thought the matter concerned the police department and not the district attorney. Now he told the press,

> Always in matters like this, self-seekers, men who want to see their names in print and to pose as benefactors and public-spirited citizens before their fellows, harangue public meetings and start committees. Our difficulty is to sift the wheat from the chaff. Mr. Kresel is well-balanced and able. He speaks the East Side languages and can get at the truth for us. If his report shows that there is just cause for complaint, the facts will be laid before the Grand Jury and to the fullest extent of our ability we will see that the guilty are punished.[15]

That day also brought the first civil suit against R. Hoe & Co. Thirty-five-year-old Rudolph Gartenberg, a locksmith and one of Rabbi Joseph's pallbearers, who had only just been discharged from Gouverneur Hospital, sued the company in the Supreme Court (as trial courts in New York State are still confusingly designated). He had been assaulted by Hoe employees when he tried to get inside the factory to remonstrate with its managers and was struck by a brick hurled at him from an upper-floor window. He was seeking $25,000 in damages.[16]

The same delegation from the United Hebrew Community that had called on Jerome that morning had paid a visit to the mayor's office. It included Rabbi Bernard Drachman, Congressman Henry Goldfogle, and eleven others. Low's private secretary, James B. Reynolds, received the men. They asked that the mayor, either through his own office or by request to the board of aldermen, launch an "open, public, impartial and searching investigation" so that blame could be fixed and the guilty could be punished.[17]

Rabbi Drachman, who read a statement that tarred the managers and employees of R. Hoe & Co. as "despicable and deserving of the condemnation of all good and true people" and excoriated the police for their brutality, announced that $100 would be offered for evidence leading to the arrest and conviction of any Hoe employee connected with the attack. For information leading to the arrest, conviction, and dismissal of any member of the New York Police Department who had assaulted any of the mourners or refused to render assistance when asked, $200 would be paid.[18]

The East Side Civic Club, a nonpartisan group dedicated to the improvement of the Lower East Side, also petitioned the mayor, but in a letter. Although the club members appreciated his order to the police commissioner to undertake a careful investigation, they pointed out that the July 30 riot was only the latest in a series of hate-inspired police attacks on peaceful people. To wit, they asked that he broaden the scope of the investigation to include an examination of the "longstanding antagonistic attitude of the police toward the law-abiding people of the East Side."[19]

All of this essentially amounted to a resounding vote of no confidence in the inquiry then going on at police headquarters. Nobody in the Jewish community trusted the force to police itself. Although the Jews would cooperate with the Brooks investigation, they had little faith in it.

They wanted something bigger and meant to get it.

15

"The Well-Considered Opinion of a Committee of Citizens"

On Tuesday morning at Essex Market Police Court, Magistrate Peter T. Barlow considered the cases of the three Hoe employees who had been arraigned before Magistrate Mayo and also presided over the arraignment of Emil Adams, a Hoe machinist arrested on the complaint of Chrystie Street livery stable owner Joseph Kaplan. All were accused of hosing people from above. The *New York Post* couldn't help but remark on the "formidable array of legal talent" that had assembled in the courtroom both to prosecute and defend the accused.[1]

The first case called was that of Adams, the man who had been overheard threatening "sheenies" with soaking. Kaplan had been part of the funeral cortege, riding in an open carriage with three friends. He testified that when they got within twenty-five feet of the Hoe factory, he saw missiles thrown from the upper stories and Adams holding the nozzle of a hose. Shortly afterward, water came raining down on him and his fellow passengers. When he shouted to Adams to stop, he said, he received only a raft of insults in return. Kaplan's testimony was corroborated by his friend Bernard Freedman. Adams offered no defense. He was arraigned that morning and held for trial on $500 bail.

As for the others, George W. Church, a factory superintendent accused by City Marshal Albert Levine of soaking him who bore marks on his body he said had been inflicted by Jews, continued to be held on $500 bail. But Barlow dismissed the cases against George Stillgenbauer and Henry Stockhusen; he did not appear to attach much weight to the accusation that they had sprayed a police officer.[2]

That same day, Marshal Levine dropped another bombshell. He produced an affidavit from Samuel Feinberg, who claimed a representative of the police had offered him a bribe to decline to testify before Inspector Brooks. Feinberg had given this statement:

> The policeman told me, or suggested to me, that it would be a fine thing for me if I could go back to Warsaw and spend the rest of my life in luxury. He said that there was a certain way I could get sufficient money to do this, and insinuated that if I failed to show up to give my evidence in the riot hearing I would be furnished with cash enough to get me out of the country and keep me out. He also suggested that I had lots of friends among the other witnesses and that it wouldn't hurt me to go around and ask them what they thought it would be worth to them to keep still.[3]

The allegation got some play in the newspapers, but there does not appear to have been any meaningful follow-up, since it was not backed by corroborating evidence, and the name of the officer was not revealed, if indeed Feinberg even knew it. Still, the *American Israelite* spoke out about it. "It is painfully evident that the police officers are lying to shield themselves," it wrote in an editorial. "Other witnesses testify hesitatingly, or hide themselves and fail to appear because their lives have been threatened if they give evidence."[4]

It had begun to appear as if there was no depth to which the police would not stoop to avoid blame. But Mayor Low was listening. He understood that the conclusions of the police department's internal investigation were unlikely to mollify any of the victims. Just as he had not hesitated even a day when he ordered Commissioner Partridge to investigate the riot, he responded promptly to the message the Jewish community had sent. They had demanded a broader, more objective inquiry apart from the sham investigation going on at police headquarters, and he announced that he was going to give it to them.

The mayor selected five prominent citizens to serve on a committee to look into exactly how the disturbance originated and whether any of those involved in it should be charged. Of the five, all of whom were professional men-about-town, two were Jewish. All had demonstrated a serious interest in civil affairs.

The independent, blue-ribbon committee was to consist of the following:

Edward Baldwin Whitney, a Yale-educated attorney who had served as assistant attorney general under President Grover Cleveland. He had been working to improve conditions on the Lower East Side. The mayor asked Whitney to chair the committee.

Louis Marshall, an American-born attorney of German Jewish extraction. Educated in the Syracuse, New York, public schools, he had gone on to study law at Columbia. He was heavily involved in Jewish affairs and in 1902 began publishing *Di Yidishe Velt*, a progressive Yiddish daily aimed at helping Americanize the Russian and Central European newcomers. He was also extremely well connected among the "uptown" Jews, including Schiffs, Warburgs, Guggenheims, Bloomingdales, Strausses, Loebs, and Lehmans.[5]

Thomas Maurice Mulry, New York born to Irish immigrants, had been educated in Catholic parochial schools and was president of the Society of St. Vincent de Paul, an organization devoted to helping the poor. He had experience working with immigrants and was connected to several Catholic charities.

Boston-born William Henry Baldwin Jr., president of the Long Island Rail Road. A Harvard graduate, he was a reformer and a philanthropist who had served as president of the Committee of Fifteen, a body that had investigated vice in the city the previous year. He was a strong supporter of African American industrial education and served on the board of Tuskegee University.

Nathan Bijur, a forty-year-old, American-born attorney whose parents were Prussian Jewish immigrants. A graduate of Columbia College and Columbia Law School, he had also earned a PhD in political science. Admitted to the bar in 1884, he was an accomplished corporate lawyer and a Republican. Active in local Jewish affairs, he sat on the board of the United Hebrew Charities. Not coincidentally, he had been a strong supporter of Mayor Low's campaign.[6]

In his formal invitation to the men, the mayor asserted that the two inquiries would proceed simultaneously and, he hoped, be complementary. He expected the "official" account from Partridge, but he said he would also value the opinion of men known to be "in sympathetic relations with the East Side," which, of course, strongly implied that he believed the police were not.

The new committee would actually be the fifth body to look into the causes of the riot, the others being the East Side Vigilance League, the Hebrew American League, the police department, and the office of the district attorney. But when the members called on the mayor to accept his invitation formally, Low also made it clear that they were under no obligation to limit their inquiry to the Grand Street riot. They would be free to give it as broad a scope as they felt necessary. In other words, they were welcome to investigate and opine on police misconduct on the East Side generally.

The committee was not empowered to summon witnesses; it would have to seek voluntary cooperation. And it would not be authorized to employ counsel. But Whitney was undaunted by those restrictions. "There are many ways of learning what we want to find out," he promised the press.[7]

The appointment of a blue-ribbon citizens' committee was an important achievement for the Jewish community. There had never been an opportunity for anti-Jewish violence in New York to be examined and discussed publicly at such a high level. As a matter of fact, the mayor was actually making history: he had appointed the first citizens' committee in the nation ever to investigate an ethnic riot.[8]

On Friday, August 8, Inspector Brooks reconvened his inquiry. Assistant District Attorney Kresel was present, as were attorneys Sarasohn and Spellman. Three more Jews testified with a Yiddish-speaking Central Office policeman acting as interpreter. Two related their experiences but were unable to identify their assailants. A third, however, could. Harry Krinsky, who had been fined $5 in police court because Patrolman Thomas F. Keenan had accused him of throwing a brick at the factory, had come to accuse Keenan of handling him roughly.

After this, Sarasohn rested the case and asked Brooks to place six men before the police commissioners on charges of felonious assault and conduct unbecoming to officers. Roundsman James M. Jackson and Patrolmen Henry Doupe and Joseph H. McKeever, all of the Delancey Street Station; Patrolman Thomas F. Keenan of the Fifth Street Station; and Patrolman Charles Merrill of the Elizabeth Street Station were all named. The sixth was identified only as the police officer whose badge number was 1271; he had been accused of using profanity.

But Brooks refused. He still had the names of twenty-five additional witnesses he had received from Charles Dushkind of the Hebrew American League, and before he was finished, he meant to hear from all of them—as well as from anyone prepared to testify in favor of the police.[9]

Spellman rose to his feet and once again pointed out that Brooks's role was not to try the men but merely to decide whether there was enough evidence to convene disciplinary hearings. The proceedings were more analogous to a grand jury investigation than a jury trial, and Brooks had already heard plenty of evidence. But the inspector was adamant, insisting he was going by police department rules.[10]

The beatings by the police of innocent Jews during the riot on Grand Street had convinced some Jews they could never be safe in America as long as they relied on the authorities for protection. It gave new energy to the argument that Jews in New York needed to become more assertive in defending themselves, and in particular to an idea that had been floated two years earlier. A man named Moses Gottlieb, formerly a bandmaster in the Third Cavalry Regiment of the Russian Imperial Army, had suggested in May 1900 that New York Jews organize their own regiment. At the time he told the press he already knew of six hundred Jewish boys ready to sign up, and by the end of that year, he claimed that twice that number had expressed interest. Gottlieb was never very clear about the actual mandate of the regiment, but his idea was that a Hebrew militia, once formed—with financial support from the local Jewish community—might be admitted to the National Guard of the State of New York as a constituent force.[11]

There had been little support for the concept among establishment Jews or the larger community. The *Jewish Messenger* had warned that "the general public does not need any special object lesson in Jewish patriotism or militarism." It derided the idea as distasteful and unnecessary. The *Reform Advocate* thought the organizers would make a laughingstock of themselves. And the *New York Tribune* had pointed out that earlier attempts to form ethnic regiments had failed and that, in any event, such organizations tended to emphasize racial differences.[12]

24. New York police inspector Nicholas Brooks. Author's collection.

The militia idea had more or less been put to rest by the end of 1901, but the Jewish experience on Grand Street suddenly breathed new life into it. A certificate of incorporation was secured and a drillmaster and a venue for training recruits identified. One of the organizers—it was now a new cast of characters—made the link to the Hoe riot clear:

> If there had been no riot, the regiment would not have been formed. . . . After the riot the recruits came so fast and made such persistent demands for official recognition that we decided upon the present move. . . . It is not our intention to oppose the police, but what we are aiming at is to perfect a body that will protect East Siders from persons like those who assaulted the marchers in the funeral procession.[13]

On August 13, the *Tribune* pointed out the fallacious thinking behind the idea:

> Does the brave East Side Mars think that if another riot took place like the one of a few days ago, and it was believed that the police failed to do its duty, he could call out his regiment and settle matters? If he had the right to go to the rescue of his people with his rifle, why could not another regiment, with headquarters next door, march against the Jewish soldiers?[14]

It didn't take long for the New York Guard itself to disabuse the organizers of the notion that their effort would in any way be welcome. Once a prominent officer pointed out that the guard's numbers were limited by law, that it already had all the men it needed, and that the idea of a Hebrew regiment was "sheer nonsense," it was no longer discussed seriously.[15]

16

"The Trouble Was All Over When We Got There"

Inspector Brooks reconvened his inquiry on the morning of Monday, August 11, to hear witnesses for the police. By now, the accused policemen had retained an attorney. He was Foster L. Backus, who earlier that year had become famous for securing the acquittal of a well-known socialite accused of murdering her paramour. That case had made headlines across the country.[1]

Backus put up Sergeant Henry Cohen, thirty-eight years old, New York born to German Jewish parents. He was the member of Inspector Brooks's staff who had received the first report of the riot by telephone and had summoned reinforcements. Cohen had arrived on the scene in the patrol wagon with Inspector Cross.

"The trouble was all over when we got there," Cohen testified. Cross had conferred with Robert Hoe and his son, he said. That, however, had been the sum total of his investigation at the scene; he never spoke to a single victim. On cross-examination, Cohen was asked if he had heard Cross tell a reporter at the time that "the Jews had it in for the Hoe people and had brought missiles with them and made the funeral procession an occasion to get even." But after Backus objected, Brooks, for some unknown reason that strongly suggests bias on his part, did not permit Cohen to answer the question.[2]

Next up was ex-captain William Thompson, who had headed the funeral's escort detail and had retired shortly after the riot. He had not personally witnessed the violence at the Hoe factory because he was already at the pier when it broke out. He recalled that at that time, one of his men had reported, "Captain, they have thrown water out of the windows of the Hoe building on the passing crowd."

Thompson had then sent a sergeant back to the Hoe plant to investigate. The officer returned about ten minutes later and reported that Cross had already arrived with reinforcements and that there was a lot of trouble going on there. This directly contradicted Cohen's testimony, and Cross's public assertion, that all had been calm when Cross arrived.[3]

The hearing ended at 3:30 in the afternoon, at which time the mayor's committee went into session. A huge number of people showed up to testify. The first witness to appear was attorney Sarasohn himself. He spoke generally of outrages committed by police against East Side Jews, blaming the police department's inadequate punishments for abuses of power and dereliction of duty. He was followed by Julius Bloomberg, a lifelong East Side resident, who asserted that the police bullied local Jews because they knew they were unlikely to fight back.

The commissioners heard from Mrs. Mary Greenfield, whose nine-year-old son Nathan had been among the psalm-singing boys who had marched with the chief rabbi's hearse. She had watched the procession from a nearby stoop and confirmed that both debris and water from the Hoe building had injured mourners. She herself had been almost blinded by a torrent of dirty water, after which she had been struck by a police officer.

Before Mrs. Greenfield ran for home, she saw a little boy get hit in the head with a large iron bolt without realizing it was her son. A painter named Max Singer, who testified next, had carried Nathan out of harm's way. The boy, whose head was still bandaged, also appeared at the hearing.[4]

Alexander Lemar, a non-Jewish immigrant from Transcaucasia (a region that corresponds roughly to modern Armenia, Georgia, and Azerbaijan) who worked on the East Side, also testified. Lemar said that if he told all he knew of police cruelty, he would have to speak for three days. He asserted that the New York police were "worse than the Bashi-Bazouks," a reference to Ottoman army irregulars known for their brutality and lack of discipline.[5]

Most of the other witnesses told similar stories. Several rehashed what they had already reported to Inspector Brooks. There were accounts of clubbing, scalding, and even one of a civilian who, wielding a heavy stick, had merrily joined in on the beating of Jews. One witness recalled that the police pursued even fleeing mourners, raining blows on their heads and backs as they sought only to run away.[6]

Mayer Schoenfeld, a well-to-do saloon keeper and former labor leader who had been a fusion candidate for alderman the previous November, ascribed the violence on Grand Street to revenge, but not on the part of the Jews. He asserted that the police, unhappy with the results of the recent election, had wished to punish East Side Jews for the role they had played in it:

> Do you remember the Negro riots on the West Side?[7] That was because the police had to get square with the Negroes for their independence in politics. The same cause led to the clubbing at the funeral of the Chief Rabbi.... Before the Jew became independent in politics ... there was none of this trouble. But since he has voted against the wishes of the police, he must be punished. *That* is the reason for the actions at the riot.[8]

The most compelling testimony that evening, however, didn't relate to the chief rabbi's funeral at all. The committee had made it clear it would consider reports of abuses that predated the riot, and much of what the members heard that first day had little or nothing to do with the events on Grand Street. Rather, it involved the laying bare of earlier instances of police brutality, police persecution, and police blackmail aimed at Jewish people and the appalling lack of punishment of the offending officers. It was as if the Lower East Side Jewish community, suddenly able to air grievances against the police in relative safety, dredged up a huge backlog of complaints it had been storing up. The pent-up frustrations of years of abuse had finally found a safe outlet for expression.

Dr. Maurice Fishberg of the Bureau of Immigration provided details about exactly how police officers blackmailed Jewish peddlers. The police had a regular schedule of prices, he told the committee. Men who sold their wares from baskets were assessed twenty-five cents per week; women only ten cents. Men who sold from pushcarts had to pay fifty cents a week. The money, ostensibly a "contribution" to the peddlers' association, was paid to a civilian middleman who made weekly rounds.

"But there *is* no East Side peddlers' association," Fishberg insisted to the committeemen. "If the peddlers do not pay the blood money," he continued,

25. Members of the mayor's committee to investigate the Grand Street riot. *From left:* Edward Baldwin Whitney, Louis Marshall, Thomas Maurice Mulry, William Henry Baldwin Jr., and Nathan Bijur. *Sources:* Ancestry.com (Whitney), Public Domain (Marshall, Mulry, Baldwin), and the Historical Society of the NY Courts (Bijur).

"they are shoved from pillar to post by the police who seem by some underground method to know when this or that man or woman has not contributed to the common blackmail fund."[9]

Dr. Joseph Barsky said he knew of a boy who had been clubbed into unconsciousness by a policeman simply because he had told the officer to mind his own business. The boy had then been fined $10 in police court for this transgression. Barsky said he had witnessed many such abuses but had not complained because his experience had taught him that to do so would do no good.

Jacob Phillips, a schoolteacher, recalled a trip to the Madison Street Station during which he asked that a policeman be detailed to guard the door of his synagogue during a special service. The sergeant there had insulted him. He added that he had learned to submit to almost anything a policeman dished out because talking back might get him killed.

Perhaps most discrediting to the police was a story known locally as "the Dooley case," told by Mrs. Sarah Goldstein and corroborated by her husband, Abraham. One hot night early in the summer, she recalled, their family was sitting out on the stoop of their tenement house for relief from the heat. Their eighteen-year-old daughter was seated on a chair on the sidewalk when a patrolman from the Eldridge Street Station named Dooley walked by.

The officer objected to the girl sitting where she was and ordered her into the house. When she remonstrated with him—after all, she wasn't breaking any laws—he had hurled her bodily into the vestibule. After the girl asked her brother to take down the policeman's badge number, Dooley arrested her. As her parents followed them to the station house, Mrs. Goldstein pleaded with the officer to let her go. In response, he struck the mother violently on the chest and head, knocking her unconscious. He sent her to the hospital and arrested all of the other family members—father, daughter, son—on charges of disorderly conduct.[10]

Mrs. Goldstein suffered hemorrhaging after the incident and reported that she had been spitting up blood since then. The family had filed a complaint with police headquarters, and Dooley was brought before Deputy Commissioner Nathaniel B. Thurston. The patrolman brought two false witnesses to the hearing, however, and nothing was done. This story, which had circulated widely, was one reason "Peggy" Thurston, as he was known from his National Guard days, was so reviled in the Jewish community.[11]

Thurston had played no role in the Hoe riot, but because of the mayor's committee investigation, several other serious complaints about him came out in the newspapers and at the hearings. One involved a patrolman named John F. Lope. He had arrested a Jewish man he felt had not been sufficiently respectful and charged him, falsely, with having run over a child with a pushcart. In court the following day, the officer's story had changed: the pushcart had become an express wagon, and the child had allegedly been seriously injured.

Despite the fact that several witnesses testified against Lope, that there was no record of an ambulance call, that the officer could not produce the child, and that the man owned neither a pushcart nor an express wagon, Thurston took no action against the patrolman. Nor did he punish Patrick Hogan of the Eldridge Street Station, who had declined to arrest a man he saw assault a Jewish man. What Thurston did do was to remark to a fellow policeman about the Jewish witnesses waiting to testify: "Now wait until you hear how all these persons will testify to exactly the same thing. They are always well-rehearsed."[12]

Thurston did little to salvage his reputation when he was approached by the *New York Herald* to explain himself. Although he claimed to be unbiased, his words belied this:

26. Col. Nathaniel Blunt "Peggy" Thurston, New York deputy commissioner of police, 1898. New York Historical Society.

> In my judgment, the Hebrews are excitable; they may interfere in some way when a man is arrested or they may consider one of their number has not been arrested justly. They come here, complain of the matter, and they have witnesses enough to fill this room. I believe all they want is to get a decision here against the policeman, so they may have justification for bringing a civil suit against him and recover judgment. I do not think we should be used in furtherance of any such plan.[13]

This was the man Colonel Partridge, the mayor's choice to reform the police department, had chosen to be his first deputy.

17

"The Attack Was Deliberately Planned"

The *American Hebrew* was jubilant about how well the mayor's committee hearings were going. "The wisdom of the appointment of an unofficial committee," it gushed, "becomes more apparent at every session." It added that the testimony given before it would never have come out before, because witnesses would have felt they were taking their lives into their hands by testifying.[1]

It also would likely never have come out if the Jews in the city had not amassed the necessary political clout to force an investigation. The *New York Herald* agreed that the Jews were getting results. "Their representatives are gathering evidence daily to prove their assertions that they are oppressed and cannot get just treatment at police headquarters," it noted. "They are proceeding quietly, but nonetheless effectively."[2]

Tuesday, August 19 brought even more evidence of their success when District Attorney Travers Jerome's office finally sought grand jury indictments. In keeping with his elitist class prejudice, Jerome had called only those he deemed "the more intelligent" participants in the funeral procession and residents from the neighborhood, as the *Herald* put it, to give testimony. Not for him were the unwashed or the unlettered. Some fifty witnesses had been subpoenaed; more than a dozen were called that day. The grand jury was expected to deliberate for about three days.[3]

In the meantime, the mayor's committee heard from R. Hoe & Company employees. The witnesses were presented by Ira B. Wheeler, the company attorney, and all hewed closely to the party line first articulated by their boss, Robert Hoe, who had insisted that the violence had begun among the Jews. Hoe himself, who had been on the premises during the riot and who had promised complete cooperation, declined to appear.

After a brief opening statement by Wheeler in which he promised to show that there had been no aggression on the part of the factory workers until "action became necessary to save property and life," Edward A. Collins, the general foreman of the plant, was called. He said he had been out to lunch as the procession passed and claimed to have heard someone in the crowd cry, "Look out for the fight!" He also testified that he had heard someone say that the trouble was due to an altercation between cigar makers and cloak makers.[4]

Collins allowed that the factory's apprentices had jeered at the procession from the safety of the building and acknowledged that someone had dropped a piece of cotton waste—Robert Hoe had admitted this previously—but insisted it had fallen on the crowd rather than on the procession, as if that made a difference.[5]

Collins also acknowledged that in the past, the company had received many complaints from Jewish people victimized by its employees, but he used this fact to serve his own ends. Because of this, he told the committee, his impression was that the crowd had arrived intent on attacking the factory in retaliation. "In my opinion," he suggested, "the attack was deliberately planned by the roughs on the sidewalk, not for loot, but in revenge for some fancied wrong." He was suggesting that the Jews had come to a funeral bent on payback but offered no evidence to substantiate his statements. And he rejected the notion that hoses had been used to spray water on the crowd because, he claimed, no hose in the building was long enough to have reached the windows.[6]

Another foreman produced two bushels of debris—broken bricks, stones, pieces of iron, nuts, bolts, and screws—that he claimed had been collected from the factory floor after the fracas. He and the next witness testified that the screws, nuts, and bolts retrieved were not of the kind used in the factory and suggested they might have come from the construction site of the new Williamsburg Bridge a block and a half away. This was another attempt to suggest that the Jews had come prepared to cause trouble.[7]

The only problem with this theory was that it wasn't true.

Sixty-four-year-old William Spalckhaver, the company's chief draftsman, insisted that more than sixty Jews were employed at the factory and that the place was entirely free of prejudice. And Richard Fichte, like Spalckhaver of German descent, claimed he had seen women in the crowd hand the men stones they had collected in their aprons to hurl at the building. He characterized the police response as "very gentle." Fichte also stated that after the riot was over, all employees had signed statements affirming that they had done nothing to start the trouble.[8]

And finally, the committee heard from Irving B. Dwyer, a clerk in the office on the ground floor who had seen Jews enter the building. He said some thirty or forty had surged in, that they had smashed the office doors, and that a half dozen clerks had ejected them. He did not mention who had ordered that they be hosed—only that after about five minutes, it had been Mr. Hoe who had ordered the water shut off.[9]

The committee took a recess and reconvened for an evening session in which members heard from a dozen more Jews. Benjamin Asht, a Grand Street merchant, testified that Hoe employees began throwing melon rinds at the crowd as soon as the hearse passed and that the spraying had started well before anyone threw anything back at the building. Celia Aberman, who lived nearby, confirmed that some of the water was scorching hot; she had seen steam as it fell. And Sigmund Schwartz, a Forsythe Street undertaker, insisted he had warned Captain Thompson ahead of time that there would be trouble when the procession passed the factory. He had never taken a Jewish funeral procession past R. Hoe & Co. without problems, he asserted; just three weeks earlier one of his drivers had been pelted with an apple.[10]

That same day, the grand jury surprised everyone. In session for only one day, it had heard from twenty witnesses and found their testimony persuasive enough to return three indictments against two members of the police force. All were for assault in the second degree, a charge that assumed intent to cause serious physical injury.

Two of the indictments were against Roundsman James M. Jackson, one of the first officers to arrive on the scene of the riot. Jackson, who had been heard to shout, "Club the Jews!" had been accused of indiscriminate beatings. The third was against an officer not named publicly because he was on vacation. It took another day before the papers learned that he was Patrolman

Henry Doupe, officer number 4404. He had been accused of brutality by Julius Weber and allegedly told Jacob Rubel to "get the hell out of here" when the latter asked for his badge number.[11]

The following morning, escorted by Inspector Brooks and their counsel, Foster Backus, Roundsman Jackson and Patrolman Doupe appeared at the Court of General Sessions, where both pled not guilty to charges of assault in the second degree. Jackson was held on $1,000 bail; for Doupe, only $500 was demanded. Bondsmen posted the money, and the officers were freed the same day.[12]

Charges had also been filed against a third officer, policeman Charles Merrill, who had been accused of striking people savagely. But Merrill argued persuasively that he had forgotten his club that day and that, in any case, he had not been on the scene at the time. His case was dismissed.[13]

Partridge was asked by reporters if the indicted men would be suspended. He said he had not yet made up his mind:

> If I discipline a policeman who has used his club in a legitimate manner, I could soon get the police so that they would be afraid to use their clubs for the purpose for which they were intended. On the other hand, if I do *not* discipline them, a patrolman who uses his club without justification will have the police department doing nothing *but* clubbing. That is the reason why I want to go to slow in a case of this kind.[14]

Even as he dithered about suspending the men, he knew it would not be prudent to leave them on the Lower East Side. So the next day, it was announced that Doupe was being transferred to the East Sixty-Seventh Street Station and Jackson to the Brooklyn Bridge squad.[15]

In the meantime, the mayor's committee of five continued to hear testimony. On close questioning, committee member Louis Marshall was able to get one of the witnesses to confirm that the screws, nuts, and bolts that had been brought in as evidence earlier *were*, indeed, of a type used at the factory. This had been denied earlier. The revelation corroborated the story of the Jewish witnesses who testified that the projectiles they threw at the building had first been hurled at them by factory hands.[16]

The next day, Inspector Brooks figured out a way to wriggle out of any further investigation of his colleagues. Now that Jackson and Doupe had been indicted, he said, he didn't believe it would be fair to them to continue his hearings. He sought, and received, permission from Partridge to suspend his inquiry indefinitely.[17]

Indefinitely, of course, meant forever.

18

"Because We Are Hebrews and the Police Are Irishmen"

A full complement of police officers, including Captain Albertson, Sergeant McSweeney, and Roundsman Jackson, appeared at the mayor's committee's final public session. The star witness, however, was Inspector Cross.

The initial questioning centered on the issue of preparedness. Cross testified that the police had had no idea the funeral would be as large as it was until 10:30 that morning, when Captain Thompson first called for reinforcements and 52 more officers were sent. It was a lie; Sergeant Brady had received warning ten hours earlier that the crowd would be huge and that more police officers would be needed. Cross asserted that funerals with twenty thousand attendees were not unusual on the East Side and said that if he had known that as many as one hundred thousand would turn up, he would have sent 750 or so more officers.

"You know, they are a very peaceful lot down there. We never had any trouble before," he said, conveniently omitting mention of the meat riots that had occurred just two months earlier. "Had there been no interference at Hoe's factory I think the policemen there would have been sufficient."

Commissioner Louis Marshall challenged that remark in view of the numerous reports the police had received over and over again from Jews who complained of being assaulted there. Cross admitted there had been many such incidents but insisted that a number of arrests had been made and that Robert Hoe had terminated some of the young troublemakers.

"Do you think the clubbing justifiable?" Marshall asked.

"I can't say as to that," Cross responded disingenuously, reiterating his lie that he knew nothing of the clubbing that he himself had ordered. "I arrived on the scene about 1:30," he said. "I heard no complaints of clubbing then, but I heard that several policemen had been badly hurt." In other words, in this preposterous, made-up scenario, Jews or Hoe employees had attacked and injured the police, but the police had not responded with their clubs.

Asked if clubbing would have been justified if the trouble had already subsided, Cross was forced to agree that it would not. "I don't think it justifiable for policemen to club a crowd if they are peaceable and have not refused instructions to move on. If they are riotous, heroic action must be taken."[1]

But no one had testified that any instructions had been given to the crowd before the beatings began. And many witnesses had confirmed that the crowd had been calm when the police reinforcements arrived and began their attacks. Furthermore, there had been accounts of police clubbing people who were trying to do nothing other than flee the scene.

Commissioner William Baldwin asked if it was possible the mourners had armed themselves with bricks and stones in anticipation of an attack from the Hoe factory. "I sometimes think that those who had known of previous interference from the factory employees had decided to be prepared," Cross responded.

"Then your opinion is that the Jews were not the aggressors?"

"I can't say that," Cross replied. "In the report I have indicated some aggression came from the Hoe building, but sometimes I think one thing and sometimes I think the other."[2]

He had been far more certain when he wrote, in his report to Partridge, that "those who broke the windows and destroyed the property of R. Hoe & Co. came there prepared to do what they did do." But in fact, neither this assertion nor that of attorney Sarasohn that he possessed evidence of premeditation on the part of the factory employees was either credible or persuasive. The idea put forth by Inspector Cross, that the Jews had come laden with projectiles, was as absurd as his claim that the police had not used their nightsticks and was especially improbable given the nature of the event, a funeral. Neither he nor Sarasohn ever produced any evidence to support either contention.[3]

In the meantime, because the grand jury's indictment of the two police officers had given Inspector Brooks a convenient excuse to suspend his internal inquiry, there was no longer any effort being made within the police department to hold anyone accountable. This incensed the East Side Vigilance League, and attorney Sarasohn wrote Partridge in protest. He did not mince words:

> Over five weeks have passed since the mourners at the funeral were beaten and clubbed by the police officers and although their victims and their counsel have been untiring in their efforts and their labor to obtain the punishment of the police officers, in the police department they have not even been able to . . . have charges formulated against the officers charged with such brutality. . . .
>
> As counsel for the assaulted citizens, I demand that these five officers be placed upon trial, under charges of assault and clubbing, and that the two men indicted be suspended from duty until the determination of the charges or the result of the trial upon the indictment.[4]

When Partridge failed to act, the committee took it as prima facie evidence that the commissioner was not the man to deliver on Mayor Low's campaign promise of meaningful reform of the New York Police Department. So they decided to call the mayor himself to account.

At noon on September 8, a delegation of three paid a call on Low. Sarasohn did the talking. He complained to the mayor that Partridge and Thurston had treated the dossiers they had provided "with scant attention" and had let off with nothing more than a reprimand several police officers who deserved more serious punishment.

"Because we are Hebrews and the police are Irishmen is not a sufficient reason that we should be murdered and assaulted without redress," Sarasohn declared. He explained that the indifference of the high officials in the department had made those in the lower ranks believe they could treat Jews any way they pleased without fear of retribution. As an example, he cited an incident that had occurred in Jackson Square just the previous night in which a band of toughs had beaten up a party of Jews. The police had declined to interfere.[5]

The memorial the men left with the mayor laid out a litany of complaints: about the fact that Commissioner Partridge had conducted his investigation through a subordinate and that it had been adjourned indefinitely; about the

27. Attorney Abraham H. Sarasohn. Columbia University Library.

lack of power granted the mayor's committee to compel testimony; about the initial reluctance of District Attorney Jerome to bring charges to the grand jury; and about Partridge's refusal to suspend the officers under indictment.

The document also made it clear that as much as the Vigilance League wanted individual offending police officers punished, the broader problem would remain. It ended, however, with two rather fuzzy demands: that the police commissioner "administer his position with the realization that a large number of men under him are brutal" and that "a policy be inaugurated that will result in the dismissal from the police force of all men found guilty of unwarranted clubbing."[6]

The *Jewish Messenger*, ever nervous about how their downtown Russian counterparts might tarnish the reputation of the uptowners, worried out loud that the Vigilance League had gone too far in criticizing the mayor, who had been supportive of the Jewish community:

> We can understand that the patience of our East Side brethren has been sorely tried, but there is no advantage in losing self-control. Mayor

> Low needs no reminder in the style of a sharp political harangue. The community can depend on his sense of justice without distinction of party or creed. He realizes the weakness in the police problem, but it takes time to cure long-rooted evils.[7]

Presenting the mayor with a memorial hardly amounted to a loss of self-control, however, nor is there any indication that Low took umbrage at the Vigilance League's appeal. It was lobbying, plain and simple. But the mayor did feel obliged to await the findings of his own citizens' committee before taking any additional steps. As it happened, he did not need to wait long. That report reached his desk just two days later.[8]

In the five-thousand-word document drafted by Commissioner Louis Marshall, the mayor's committee did not pull punches. It fixed "primary responsibility" for the violence on employees of the Hoe factory. It stated flatly that "those who actually took part in the funeral procession are entirely without fault" and that Inspector Cross's attempt to blame bystanders for initiating the disturbance was "entirely unsupported by the evidence."[9] It disparaged the management of R. Hoe & Company for failing to take action against those who attacked the Jews, for insufficient cooperation with the committee itself, and for orchestrating "a concerted effort to hush up the affair" in order to fend off blame.

But it reserved its sharpest criticism for the New York Police Department. It found the headquarters staff negligent for "accepting the judgment of an unskilled civilian" about the number of police officers required for the funeral and for failing to heed the message subsequently received by telephone—that many more officers would be needed. It faulted Captain Thompson for failing to give sufficient notice to headquarters about the size of the crowd and Commissioner Partridge for halting the internal investigation. It asserted that the trouble had been over and the crowd quiet before the arrival of Inspector Cross and his reinforcements, who had nonetheless attacked the mourners "without a word of warning or any request to disperse." And it claimed that the commissioners had heard very strong evidence that some policemen clubbed a number of people "without the least excuse."[10]

As far as antisemitism within the force was concerned, the committee found that instances of rough treatment of local Jews were "inexcusably common" and that punishment of individual officers, when it occurred at all, was too lenient and virtually never involved dismissal. It called for more care in selecting the officers assigned to duty in the Jewish quarter.

The committee also took aim at the judges: "It is charged by residents of this district that magistrates are very arbitrary in their action, often deciding cases against the weight of evidence and frequently even refusing to hear the witnesses produced." And it added that "certain magistrates appear to have developed such prejudice against Jewish witnesses that they refuse them a fair hearing, even when of the highest character and fully corroborated." It believed the matter worthy of investigation but acknowledged that conducting one was not within the purview of the mayor.[11]

Mayor Low's office released the report the following day, and reporters scrambled for comments. The mayor himself told them he intended to take further action and promised to announce specifics soon. Colonel Partridge reverted to his usual woe-is-me whine: "Can't you see that I have too much to think of to read anything or talk of anything else?" He tried to leave the impression that he had more pressing matters on his hands.[12]

Robert Hoe was out of town, but the most senior officer of his firm available, Charles W. Carpenter, decried the report as "full of inaccuracies and statements made for political effect." He insisted that "the shop was stormed by a mob of men intent on killing us" and that the use of hoses was therefore justified—even though his colleague, Foreman Collins, had testified that no hoses had been used. He said he had no personal knowledge of anyone dropping anything out of the factory windows and—incredibly—insisted he did not believe anything *had* been thrown. "There may have been some jeering," he conceded, "but I do not believe it went beyond that."[13]

District Attorney Jerome said the conclusions of the committee concurred with those he and Assistant District Attorney Kresel had reached. He predicted that the two officers whose indictments his office had secured would be tried soon.

Inspector Cross was in Europe and unavailable for comment. Captain Albertson refused to say anything. But Inspector Brooks spoke out, though he did so—astonishingly—as a defender of the department, sounding like anything but an impartial investigator in charge of a supposedly incomplete inquiry:

> It never occurred to us that an unusual number of men would be needed for a funeral. A riot was the last thing on earth that could have been expected at such an event. Therefore, after we had received the application for a permit it never seemed necessary to make any further inquiry.
>
> It is stated that information was received at police headquarters at midnight to the effect that there would be an unusual crowd at the funeral. This information came from a man of whom we knew nothing. . . . If the police department paid attention to all such telephonic communication, we would be sending out reserves at all hours of the day.
>
> It should also be said that under the penal code a policeman is compelled to use force to stop a riot whenever such an event occurs. . . . It was the duty of the police to take every necessary means to stop the lawlessness at once.

In that one biased defense of the department, Inspector Brooks essentially rendered a verdict on the investigation he never completed. It should have been ample evidence to all who were watching that there was nothing remotely impartial about Brooks and that the police department could in no way be trusted to police itself.

The reaction of the press to the mayor's committee report was uniformly positive. The *Sun* lauded the body for exposing "a faulty condition of things that demand a prompt and efficient remedy." And the *Brooklyn Standard Union* hoped the report would be followed by concrete action—that is, actual punishment of miscreants.[14]

Although the *New York Times* was surprisingly forgiving of the "blackguard boys in Messrs. Hoe's establishment," writing simply that "they acted after their kind," it had nothing but opprobrium for the police. "It appears that the police, or a considerable proportion of them, regard the Jews of the Lower East Side not as claimants for protection but as fit objects of persecution," it wrote. "These unhappy Jews are not only not protected by the police; they are in need of protection against the police."[15]

Nor did the *Times* have anything good to say about the magistrates, whose actions, it insisted, ensure that "the policeman is in effect instructed from the bench that outrages upon the Jews of the East Side, when they stop short of murder or grievous bodily harm, come under the application of the legal maxim, *de minimis non curat lex*" (i.e., the law is not concerned with insignificant or minor matters).[16]

"The report reads remarkably like what any body of disinterested citizens would have said about the conduct of the police in the Negro riots on the West Side when Tammany was in power," the *Tribune* observed. It continued,

> The rowdies who think it smart to pummel "Niggers," stone poor Russian Jews, kick over Syrians' fruit stands, annoy industrious "Dagos," pull the pigtails of the "Chinks" and trample under foot plain citizens of American blood are generally friends of the policemen.[17]

The *Post* gave voice to what everyone was thinking when it wrote that "in every essential the police force of Col. Partridge is the police force of Devery." Not much had changed. And it warned that there was every reason to believe the police would continue to act as persecutors in the future.[18]

The Jewish newspapers were delighted with the report. The *Forverts* was especially pleased that the committee had confirmed what the paper had known all along: that the police treated Jews far worse than other citizens and that magistrates were predisposed to believe the police over the Jews. Philadelphia's *Jewish Exponent* predicted, rather too optimistically, that "the result cannot but be far-reaching and wholesome."[19]

Although he did not personally come in for criticism in the committee report, Mayor Low surely felt the heat generated by its wholesale indictment of the police department. He had campaigned on a platform that promised reform of the force, but the man he had chosen to clean house was falling down on the job and making the mayor himself look bad.

It was time to take matters into his own hands.

19

"A Direct Snub to the Commissioner"

Mayor Low's immediate response to the outrages cataloged in his committee's report was not to summon his police commissioner and call him on the carpet. His first call, rather, was to George L. Rives, the city's corporation counsel. He asked Rives to prepare charges against Inspector Cross and Sergeant Brady—and possibly against Captains Herlihy and Albertson as well.

Cross was to be charged with neglect of duty: for not taking proper precautions to prevent trouble, for failing to make a prompt investigation, and for submitting an incorrect and misleading report about the riot. Brady was also to be so charged: in his case, for accepting the opinion of a layman in deciding how many officers to send and for disregarding the warning to deploy more policemen and failing to report it to his superiors. The mayor left to Rives's discretion whether or not to charge Herlihy.

He also made it clear he would have ordered Captain Thompson charged as well had the latter not already resigned. And he suggested that Captain Albertson might also be a target, even though the committee had not criticized him, as it appeared that he had gone out to lunch just before the trouble began.[1]

Only then did Low write Partridge to inform him of the pending charges against his men, which, of course, Partridge himself, as head of the department, would have to adjudicate. He also directed him to supply the names of any other officers guilty of clubbing people on Grand Street without first warning them to disperse and arrange for them to be charged as well. Nor did the mayor stop there. Recognizing that the problem went far beyond bad police behavior at the funeral riot, he asked for a copy of the department's regulations on clubbing, a list of all officers accused of assaulting citizens improperly since 1895, and another of all officers then under indictment for any reason.[2]

It was not a discourteous letter, but neither was it warm. The mayor communicated his extreme dissatisfaction with the status quo, and it was clear he was giving an order and not simply making a request. Low also wrote Travers Jerome, sending him a copy of the committee report and asking him to "do what is called for" to bring the guilty Hoe employees to justice.[3]

And finally, he sent a copy of the report to Joseph M. Deuel, chairman of the Board of City Magistrates. The magistrates were part of the judicial system and not under Low's jurisdiction, but he wanted them to know what the committee had concluded about their "uneven action" that had ostensibly led to the abuse of citizens at the hands of the police.[4]

In most circles, the mayor earned kudos for his decisiveness. His action seemed to the *New York World* a direct snub to Partridge, and there was much speculation that the latter might resign or be fired. There was even a rumor that some members of the mayor's committee had privately urged a change at the top of the department.

Partridge himself, who had said in the past that he would step down if there ever came a time that he ceased to be the "real" head of his department, refused to comment on the letter, but he did visit the mayor's office the following day. Low wasn't in, so he spoke to James B. Reynolds, the mayor's secretary. Reynolds would not comment publicly on the nature of the visit, but he did feel obliged to stifle rumors of a shake-up. He insisted that Partridge was not angry about the letter and that "not the slightest mention was made of resignation."[5]

The immediate upshot at the police department was Sergeant Brady's announcement that he would follow Captain Thompson's lead and put in for retirement. Citing his age and the fact that he had never had a charge preferred against him, he said he wanted to go out with a clean record. The truth, of course, was that by retiring, he conveniently placed himself out of harm's way. Partridge approved his application, and Brady left the same day.

Neither Mayor Low's letter nor the committee report went over well with the magistrates. Predictably, Deuel rejected the criticisms as unfounded. He also complained that he and his colleagues had been disparaged based on

"THOU SHALT NOT CLUB!"

Mayor Low Has Ordered Charges to Be Preferred Against Policemen Who Attacked Peaceable Citizens at the Funeral of Rabbi Joseph.

28. Cartoon from the *New York World*, September 18, 1902.

statements made in secret sessions and had not been given an opportunity to be heard. He had a point, but his suggested solution—to break the seal and publish the proceedings of the committee—was rejected by committee chair Edward B. Whitney, who insisted it would be improper to reveal confidential sources.[6]

The magistrates may not have been happy with the mayor, but the Jewish newspapers certainly were. The *Yidishe Velt* heralded the arrival of the "judgment day" for the police and celebrated the fact that "this time, the protests of the Jews were not for nothing." And although it must have stuck in the craw of Abraham Cahan of the *Forverts* to praise Low, he did just that in an editorial. He wrote,

> The *Forverts* is a socialist newspaper, and Mayor Low is a representative of the capitalist classes. . . . Mr. Low is not one of us. But he is a

> *responsible* "not one of us." In this story of the pogrom, he behaved in a way that should call forth the respect of all our brothers, socialist or not socialist.[7]

Before the end of September, charges against Cross, Herlihy, and Albertson were filed. Only the latter two were served, because Cross wasn't due back from Europe until October 8. As soon as the charges were announced, Partridge transferred Herlihy—who, as it happened, was also awaiting trial in the criminal courts for failing to suppress vice dens while he commanded the Eldridge Street Station—from police headquarters to Grand Central Station, a traditional place of exile for captains being disciplined.[8]

Although Deputy Commissioner "Peggy" Thurston had not been mentioned at all in connection with the funeral riot and was not under indictment, he knew he had been vilified in testimony before the mayor's committee, and he saw the handwriting on the wall. He, too, submitted his resignation. "I had been informed that a lot of people were knocking me with Mayor Low," Thurston told the *New York Times*. "The mayor, I think, has decided that I am the cause of the dissatisfaction expressed in various quarters about the department." According to the *Times*, one of those arrayed against him was District Attorney Jerome, who had made no secret of his dislike for the man.[9]

"I guess I am the goat," Thurston told the paper, adding that he had been sick and tired of his job for a long time, something that certainly could also have been said about the Jewish community's view of his performance. In fact, many placed the responsibility for his resignation on the community. It was said that the Jews had complained to Mayor Low that every time they tried to get satisfaction at police headquarters they were blocked by Col. Thurston.[10]

Another of Colonel Partridge's closest advisers who had run afoul of the Jewish community was now gone. And this one had not been a man, like Cross, whom he had inherited from Devery but rather one of Partridge's own choosing.

Many now believed Partridge himself would be next.[11]

20

"These People Are Ignorant"

On the morning of October 20, hearings on the charges against the accused officers began at police headquarters on Mulberry Street with Commissioner Partridge presiding. Although these were internal disciplinary hearings and not proceedings in a court of law, the press referred to them as "trials" and to Assistant Corporation Counsel Chase Mellen as the "prosecutor."

Because the cases against Herlihy and Cross were so closely linked, they were heard together. Both men, good friends of "Big Bill" Devery, would be defended by Devery's own lawyer, Abram I. Elkus, an Orthodox Jew who was an expert on police law. Albertson had a different attorney. Herlihy's case would be heard first, and it was agreed that any relevant testimony would also be considered in the other cases.

Herlihy, who pled not guilty, had been in charge the night before Rabbi Joseph's funeral, when the permit for a funeral procession was issued. Ex-sergeant James Brady, first in the witness chair, identified the application he had received from funeral committee member Israel Levy that night. Then counsel Mellen began the questioning.

"Was Captain Herlihy present when you received this application?"

"No, sir," Brady replied.

"Was he in the building?"

"I suppose so, somewhere."

"Will the blotter show?"

"It should."

The police blotter was produced. It revealed that Herlihy had reported for work at 6:00 that evening.

"The captain was on reserve duty, then?"

29. New York police headquarters at 300 Mulberry Street, 1903. F. V. Greene, *The Police Department of the City of New York: A Statement of Facts; Address by Police Commissioner Greene* (New York: City Club of New York, 1903), frontispiece.

"Yes, sir."

"What does 'reserve duty' mean?"

"It means he goes to bed."

"Did you notify Captain Herlihy of the application for the funeral procession?"

"I did not."

"I find in the blotter this entry: 'Seventh precinct, one roundsman and seven men.' Did you make that entry?"

"I made the entry, but it was an error," Brady said. This was a crucial piece of evidence, because it made it clear that when Herlihy affixed his signature to the blotter, he had signed off on what would prove to be a wholly inadequate escort detail for such a large funeral procession. "It must have been a mistake," Cross called out from his seat at the counsel's table, presumably out of order.

Brady admitted he had received a later call from an unidentified citizen suggesting that the crowds would be very large and questioning the adequacy of the detail. "You did not tell Captain Herlihy anything of this, did you?" Elkus asked.

"No, sir."

Then, in a surprise move, the prosecution called Herlihy himself to the stand. "Is he called to testify against *himself*?" Inspector Cross asked Elkus in a stage whisper. The latter rose to object vehemently, but Partridge overruled him, insisting that he didn't see the harm in Herlihy answering a few questions. Eventually, Elkus relented on the condition that the questioning not stray from the matter at hand.

Herlihy used the opportunity to shift the blame to Brady, who, having retired, was out of danger. "What steps did you take that night to inform yourself as to what was going on in the districts under your supervision?" Mellen asked.

"I said to the Sergeant when I came on duty, 'Is there any news, Sergeant?' And he said no."

Mellen then asked if Herlihy had given instructions to Brady to notify him if anything important came up. "It wasn't necessary," the captain answered. "He knew the rules."

30. Principal figures in the police trial. *New York Tribune*, October 21, 1902.

"Did you not consider a parade of 20,000 persons in the streets of the city important?"

"He evidently didn't think so," Herlihy replied.

Mellen then moved for dismissal. The case for neglect of duty had not been made, he insisted, because Herlihy had not been made aware of Levy's visit.

"The record shows that Captain Herlihy was present and did not know what was going on. He was put in charge and it was his duty to see that the men under him did their duty," Partridge responded. "It has not been brought out by the evidence that Captain Herlihy looked at the blotter further than to see if there was any place where his name should be signed. The motion is denied."[1]

Next up was the case of Adam Cross. He, too, pled not guilty. The first witness called in his trial was Sergeant Henry Cohen, who produced the police blotter proving that Cross had been in charge of the district where the riot took place. It also included a record of the phone call from the Hoe factory, which Cohen himself had fielded, after which he had ordered reserves to the scene. After an additional call came in at 10:50 a.m. asking for even more men, he testified, fifty more patrolmen were dispatched.

He had not personally seen Cross that day, he said, until he was ordered to accompany the inspector to Grand Street. Cross himself drove the patrol wagon. When they reached the intersection of Grand and Sheriff, he saw no evidence of rioting, nor had any occurred afterward, he said. "Everything was quiet."

"Did you see any injured people?" Partridge asked.

"Only a detective-sergeant who had a cut on his head," Cohen said.

"Did you see any ambulances?"

"I saw one going away as we came up." The *World* observed that Cohen searched Cross's face before he answered each question.[2]

After a break for lunch, several Jewish witnesses were called. They described attacks on the Jews by both Hoe employees and the police reinforcements who had arrived with Cross. Then the following afternoon, Partridge heard from William F. Wilbour, a tenement house inspector who happened to have been near the Hoe building on the day of the riot. He had probably been chosen among many potential witnesses because he was *not* Jewish, a fact that may have added to his perceived credibility. He testified that he had seen police reserves charge the crowd and wield their clubs freely.

Then it was former captain Thompson's turn. He testified that he had arranged the night before the funeral for ten men from other precincts to augment fifteen from his own and that he thought that would be enough. He had not communicated with Inspector Cross about it because he had felt competent to make the decision himself. He added,

> The escort was certainly enough for the purpose. It was as large an escort as was ever furnished a funeral. They sent me fifty men from Headquarters later without my request. I think I would have got along without them, but as I had them I used them to good purpose around the house of the late Chief Rabbi.[3]

The following morning, October 23, the prosecution put up Patrolman Michael Scrieber of the Delancey Street Station. He testified that those in the crowd had been orderly and well behaved until they had been attacked and that afterward, he had seen missiles thrown by both sides. Roundsman Lonergan of the Madison Street Station—who "appeared fearful, lest he should give testimony adverse to the accused men," the *Times* observed—agreed. He added that he had heard cries of "Kill the police!" but did not know where they had come from.[4]

At this point, attorney Mellen rested the case. Partridge did not reconvene the proceedings until October 31, when it was the turn of other bluecoats to speak in support of their comrades. Captain James K. Price, who had formerly commanded the Eldridge Street Station, was up first. "Do you think that sufficient protection was furnished by the police on this occasion?" Assistant Corporation Counsel Chase Mellen asked him.

"I believe there ought to have been more," Price answered, "because I never saw such a large crowd of people gathered at any funeral in my life before. But I sent all the men I was ordered to send."

"You weren't present when the riot occurred?" Mellen asked.

"No. It's lucky I *wasn't* there, for if I had been I would have been a policeman and done something *myself* to those who started the trouble." He made it clear, however, that he didn't mean the Hoe employees when he added, "I think Jackson should get a gold medal for what he did."[5]

Next up was ex-inspector Alexander "Clubber" Williams, known for his brutality. He was the man who, in 1894, had been quoted as saying he would never believe a Jew under oath.

"Did you ever, in your experience, find it necessary to line the streets with policemen at a funeral, Mr. Williams?" attorney Elkus asked.

"I never did."

"How many men did you ever find necessary as a detail at a funeral as big as Rabbi Joseph's?"

"Oh, about twenty-five. Fifteen in front and ten in the rear."

"Do you think there was enough police protection at Rabbi Joseph's funeral?"

"There was a large enough escort." When pressed under cross-examination, however, he was forced to admit that at President Grant's funeral in 1885, the entire police force had been called out.[6]

31. Scene at the 1902 trial of New York police inspector Adam A. Cross. *New York World*, October 20, 1902.

When the trial reconvened on November 10, Cross himself finally took the stand. Asked by Mellen about the events leading up to the funeral, he stated, "I knew nothing of the funeral of Rabbi Joseph when I reported for duty on the morning of the riot. I had never heard of Rabbi Joseph and did not know that such a man existed."

"But don't you read the newspapers?"

"Yes. I read the papers every morning."

The funeral, of course, had been announced in at least three local papers. Cross then recounted,

> I went in a patrol wagon. Sergeant Cohen went with me, and I drove as hard as I could. When I reached Hoe & Co.'s, the riot was over. People I saw were covered with blood and were standing around the building. The funeral had passed, and comparative quiet had been restored. I

32. New York police inspector Adam A. Cross. *New York Tribune*, May 10, 1907.

then started an investigation, talking first to Mr. Hoe and then to as many as knew anything about the trouble.

Under cross-examination, Mellen asked about the report Cross had prepared for Commissioner Partridge in the immediate aftermath of the riot, forcing him to admit it had contained many inaccuracies. Cross attributed his mistakes to his haste in producing the document. He insisted he had done his best under the circumstances.[7]

"Could any steps have been taken to prevent this occurrence?" Mellen asked.

"I don't know of any," Cross answered.

"You didn't take all the precautions in the case of the funeral, did you?"

"Not knowing about it, I didn't."

"Was a sufficient number of men furnished to prevent trouble?"

"I say yes," he answered defiantly.

"If there was a sufficient number of men to prevent trouble, why did it occur?" Partridge asked.

"It was something unforeseen."

"I think that answer needs qualification," Partridge said.

"It was like the explosion of a bomb in front of Hoe & Co.'s place."

"The men didn't happen to be in the right place at the right time. Does that explain it?" Partridge continued.

"That is it," Cross agreed. "I presume if we had been notified in advance and had had five men on a block, we could have prevented the trouble."

"Why?" Mellen asked.

"Because these people are ignorant. A great many of them."

"Now you are speculating," Partridge admonished.

"Perhaps I am," Cross shot back. "But I say this: that they were so excited at that time in consequence of some wrong that had been done them . . ."

"I don't believe we can gain anything by all this speculation," Partridge interjected. And that ended Cross's testimony and, shortly afterward, the defense's case. What *had* been gained, of course, was insight into Cross's complete disdain for people he had sworn to protect.[8]

21

"I Don't Need This Job"

While the Herlihy and Cross trials were going on at police headquarters, the grand jury, after hearing from twelve witnesses, declined to indict George W. Church, the Hoe employee City Marshal Albert Levine had accused of spraying him. But the cases of Roundsman James M. Jackson and Patrolman Henry Doupe, who had both been indicted in August, were referred to the Court of General Sessions for trial.[1]

The two men were tried separately. Three days into the Jackson trial, the jury decided to acquit him of the charge of clubbing Harris Rosenblum. Since that was the stronger of the two cases against him, District Attorney Jerome concluded that it was unlikely he would be convicted in the Israel Schaefer case. He also believed that Patrolman Doupe, against whom there was even less evidence, would not be found guilty of assaulting Julius Weber. The remaining charge against Jackson and the charge against Doupe were therefore dropped.[2]

The Jewish press was indignant. The *Forverts* lamented the fact that now "nothing will come of the riots at the funeral of the *rav ha'kolel*," and *Di Yidishe Velt* wrote sarcastically that "Roundsman Jackson will now be able to continue to show off his talent for splitting heads with his club." It went on to decry the fact that the jury had preferred the *bubbemeise*—literally, a "grandmother's fable"—of this "club-wielding hero" over the sober testimony of the Jewish witnesses against him.[3]

December 1902 brought small victories, however. Robert Hoe got a comeuppance of sorts. He had applied to the city's office of the comptroller for compensation for his factory's broken windows. Claiming the building had sustained $870 in damages, he had the temerity to blame the city for it. The claim was flagged by the city's auditor and disallowed by Comptroller Edward M. Grout after he questioned several Hoe employees under oath and reviewed the testimony Inspector Brooks had received during his investigation.

In rejecting the claim, the comptroller asserted that the complainants were practically unanimous in their view that it had been Hoe employees who incited the riot. This, Grout concluded, released the city from any liability. The newspapers speculated that Hoe might sue the city, but there is no indication that he ever did.[4]

The *American Hebrew* saw it as a victory. Yet another investigation had exonerated the Jews. But that news was quickly overshadowed by Colonel Partridge's surprise announcement that he would resign effective January 1, 1903, the first anniversary of his assumption of office.[5]

In his letter of resignation, Partridge boasted of his many achievements during his eleven months in office. Internally, he had racked up 115 retirements and 76 dismissals, 764 reprimands and 1,463 fines, all totals substantially higher than those of the previous year. Externally, he counted 1,434 arrests for gambling, 155 for keeping betting parlors, 565 for keeping disorderly houses, and 13 for blackmail, also up from 1901. He cited ill health as the reason for his departure, and though he did not specify what ailed him, he assured the mayor that it was not serious but that it required that he get some rest.[6]

The *New York Times* was only too happy to set straight anyone who actually believed Partridge was resigning for health reasons. It suggested he was trying to get out ahead of the two prominent "good government" organizations that were expected shortly to be calling for his head. One was the City Club, a decade-old group that included many of New York's most prominent men who had supported Mayor Low's candidacy. The group believed the police force had become demoralized under Partridge, who enjoyed little respect among the rank and file; that "haunts of vice of the worst character still existed" on the force; and that the only serious effort to break up blackmailing and gambling was coming from District Attorney Jerome's office. It also asserted that promotions within the department were still being bought and sold.

The second organization clamoring for Partridge's removal was the Citizens' Union. It had been founded five years earlier and, as a partner in the fusion ticket, had also helped elect Seth Low. In an open letter released on the eve of Partridge's resignation, it deplored the fact that "the prevalence of vice and crime, the glaring offenses against decency and order and the connection of the members of the police force with illicit business that characterized the last administration have not been adequately diminished."[7]

No one doubted Partridge's personal rectitude; he was, rather, seen as unequal to the task of running the department and guilty of exercising poor judgment. Under his stewardship, the police department had simply not changed enough. It still looked much as it had under "Big Bill" Devery.

Partridge was slightly more candid about his decision when cornered by reporters. "Is overwork the only reason for your resignation?" one asked. "Not the only one, but the impelling one. There are a great many people who I think are Mayor Low's supporters who think there are better men for commissioner than I," he answered. "So far as I am concerned, I am going to give Mr. Low a chance to put one of them in."

The *New York World* couldn't resist giving Devery himself a shot at Partridge, and the ex-chief was only too happy to provide an assessment. "I won't say anything about Partridge," he said, before doing just that:

> He was a nice old man, and now that he has put away his knitting needles and gone home, I hope he'll have the quiet his nerves deserve. He's had his fling and I guess he's sick of the whole reform bunch.[8]

Mayor Low was gracious in his acceptance of Partridge's resignation, praising the latter's "fidelity and complete integrity" in his acknowledgment letter. There was no percentage in any other public response; after all, Partridge had been his own choice. Behind the scenes, however, the parting of the ways was far less cordial. Quoting one of Mayor Low's friends it declined to name, the *Tribune* recounted a conversation between the commissioner and the mayor a few days before the resignation letter was submitted. Partridge had allegedly said,

> From what I can learn, you have been listening to some men who think they know a lot about running the police department, and who think I don't. I don't need this job, and I'm not holding onto it for the love of

> work or the fun I'm having in doing it. Now you just keep on listening to these folks and maybe you'll hear them tell you of someone who will take this job off my hands. I'll turn it over to you for a New Year's present.[9]

Neither of the groups that had sought Partridge's ouster explicitly mentioned the police brutality of the Grand Street riot or the investigations that had followed it. But these were certainly precipitating factors—in Partridge's resignation and in Mayor Low's readiness to accept it. When, without consulting Partridge, Low initiated action against those officers accused by the citizens' committee, it was the ultimate vote of no confidence, and Partridge could not have misconstrued it. The department's unwillingness, or inability, to discipline its officers was deeply embarrassing to a mayor who had promised to clean it up. Partridge read the tea leaves: if he did not go of his own volition, it was only a matter of time, and probably not very much of it, before he would be forced out.

Mayor Low didn't waste time dithering about a replacement. To succeed Partridge, he named General Francis Vinton Greene, a Republican and a U.S. Army veteran who had fought in the Spanish-American War.[10]

Partridge, however, had one more errand to discharge before he exited the Mulberry Street building: the delivery of a Christmas present to Inspector Cross and Captains Herlihy and Albertson. On the day before the holiday, he ruled them innocent of the charges arrayed against them.

"Having maturely considered evidence adduced I find that it does not sustain the charges and that the defendants are not guilty. The complaint is dismissed," he said. With one stroke, Partridge thus brought an end to the possibility of any punishment for members of the force who had abused the Jewish mourners at the rabbi's funeral.[11]

One can only speculate as to his motives for clearing the men, but doing so had certainly not been the result of having "maturely considered" the evidence. He would not have pursued charges against any of them had he been left to his own devices; the hearings had been forced on him by the mayor. He had been close to Cross from the time he took office, had been a reliable champion of the inspector, and had always interceded on his behalf when he could. Given how his relationship with Mayor Low had deteriorated by the end of his tenure, it is also possible, even likely, that he saw exonerating the men as a final poke in the eye to the soon-to-be ex-boss he felt had humiliated him.

Partridge had consistently exhibited devotion to Cross, but had the loyalty been reciprocal? A writer for the *Arbeiter Zeitung* didn't think so. He believed Cross had all along been "helping to discredit the reformers," deliberately undermining Partridge and his boss, Mayor Low, in order to help Tammany Hall in the next election. Cross, after all, was a Devery man who owed his livelihood to Tammany Hall, and the police force as a whole, with its large complement of Tammany appointees, was annoyed at Partridge for the changes he was trying to make. Many, and especially Cross, had a strong vested interest in avoiding a crackdown on corruption. Cross certainly also blamed Partridge for his role in Devery's ouster from the force.

In the public mind, the Hoe riot posed a big test for the reformers, who had promised to clean up the police department. No matter how many Tammany men remained on the force, it was now the reformers' watch, and it was up to Low and company to reign in the police.[12]

If undermining the reformers was truly Cross's motive, then Partridge had been duped. He had chosen to depend on Adam Cross from the time he took over, and if he was being double-dealt, he couldn't see it. He supported the inspector to the bitter end.

Thanks to his close relationship with Partridge, the wily Cross had beaten the system once again, though within months, without Partridge to protect him, he would be dismissed again for dereliction of duty in a matter unrelated to the Hoe riot.

Partridge's departure was another victory for Jews who had been appalled at his unquestioning support for the hated inspector, not to mention his appointment of equally reviled, now ex-deputy commissioner Thurston. In a speech the following year, Commissioner Greene delivered a remarkably frank verdict on his predecessor:

> Commissioner Partridge took no adequate measures either to break up the alliance between the police and crime or to get a proper

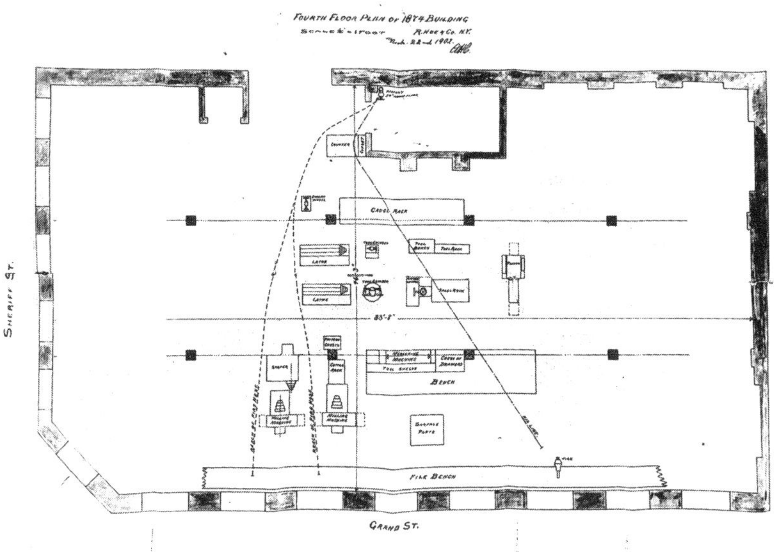

33. Diagram of the tool room on the fourth floor of the R. Hoe & Co. factory purporting to show that the firehose was too short to have reached the building's Grand Street windows. Produced as evidence in the case of *People of the State of New York v. Emil Adams*, Municipal Archives, City of New York.

> understanding of the underlying conditions in the department. On the contrary; he showed his continued ignorance of the problem with which he had to deal by making his principal uniformed adviser Inspector Cross, who has since been dismissed from the force, and whose reputation among policemen and others familiar with the affairs of the force was of the worst.[13]

The case against Emil Adams, charged with soaking Joseph Kaplan with a hose, was not heard by the Court of General Sessions until 1903. Adams put up a strong defense. He insisted that on the day of the riot, after briefly viewing the funeral procession, which at the time was entirely peaceful, he had returned to his workstation in the tool room on the fourth floor of the Hoe factory. He had not, he claimed, so much as touched a hose that day. He also maintained that no water had been turned on and that, in any event, the fifty-foot hose, kept on a shelf on the back wall of the tool room, was three feet too short for its nozzle to have reached the windows. Adams's attorneys even presented a diagram of the tool room that purported to illustrate this.

The lawyers produced affidavits from Adams's co-workers to support his testimony, and a few of them—chosen, no doubt, because they were Jewish—testified to essentially the same set of facts, adding that no jeering or shouting had been heard, nor had any projectiles been thrown from the windows.[14]

It was, apparently, enough to get the case dismissed, which meant that no one from the Hoe factory was ever punished for a role in the riot.

22

"I Withdraw the Statements Challenged"

At the end of December 1902, immediately after Partridge's exoneration of the officers, the *Yidishe Gazeten* asked Louis Marshall, one of the members of the mayor's committee, what he thought about the termination of proceedings against the men.

Marshall owned up to his personal disappointment that there had been no convictions or dismissals, but he was nonetheless generally satisfied:

> I . . . believe that the effect of the agitation and investigation which followed the occurrences at Rabbi Joseph's funeral has been most wholesome and that there is no occasion to fear a repetition of the offenses which so greatly moved the entire community last summer.

Even though there were no convictions, he told the paper,

> it does not follow that the Jewish community should be discouraged or even feel that its rights have been disregarded. On the contrary . . . the public authorities recognized it to be their duty to thoroughly investigate the affair and to place the blame where it belonged. Such investigation took place and the responsibility was fixed after a thorough and impartial hearing.

He also cited the extremely favorable news coverage that had been garnered: "Press of the entire country with remarkable unanimity and without regard to political or other affiliations condemned those who were responsible for the wanton attack upon the funeral procession, and the police." He went on to predict that the police would "recognize their obligations and the necessity of treating the residents of the East Side with humanity and the consideration which they deserve."[1] He surely overstated the case, but he was no less optimistic two years later in a letter in which he laid out exactly what had been accomplished:

> There was a very full report rendered, a number of policemen were disciplined, the blame was placed where it belonged, the captain who was guilty of dereliction of duty resigned, an inspector was put on trial, and the effect has been most salutary, the Jewish people being now protected by the police against similar outrages, where before, their complaints were unnoticed. Moreover, they now receive better treatment in the police courts, whereas, prior to this episode, they were treated with brutality by everybody.[2]

The Jewish community had forced five investigations: one within the police department, one by the district attorney, one by a citizens' committee appointed by the mayor, and two by committees of its own. The mayor's committee they had caused to be established was the first in American history to review an ethnic riot. And all of the inquiries—not one of which might have taken place but for pressure from Jews—had absolved them of responsibility.[3]

They had also made a dent in the police department. The investigations resulted in, or contributed to, three disciplinary hearings, half a dozen accelerated retirements, several transfers out of the Lower East Side, the resignation of the commissioner and first deputy commissioner, and two trials of officers charged with assault. In addition, a handful of Hoe employees had been arraigned, though neither they nor the police officers was ultimately punished.

The city magistrates, many of whom were typically unsympathetic, condescending, and patently unfair to the Jews hauled before them, had at least been put on notice that they were being watched. They had been chastised by the mayor himself, who warned them publicly that their prejudice had permitted the police to take far too much license in carrying out their responsibilities. And, if Marshall is to be believed, their treatment of Jews did improve somewhat as a result.

One other success was internal to the Jewish community. The common revulsion to the antisemitic violence managed to unite the fractious community in a common effort. The fact that those who pushed for justice and the slate of attorneys who defended the accused Jews consisted of uptowners and downtowners, Germans and Russians, Republicans and Democrats, and Reform Jews and Orthodox Jews was an achievement in and of itself.

Nothing of the scale of the Grand Street riot ever happened to New York's Jews again. One factor may have been the muscular Jewish response to the riot, but other things were changing too, including the police department itself. Beginning with Theodore Roosevelt's stewardship, the department underwent a lengthy process of modernization and professionalization. Among the innovations in the first decade of the twentieth century were the establishment of a Criminal Identification Bureau to maintain criminal records, a new fingerprint identification system, and the establishment of a Police Athletic League on the Lower East Side.[4]

Of course, antisemitic violence did not suddenly cease. There was, for example, a brawl in Brooklyn in June 1904, when twenty young toughs known as the Rainmakers Gang savagely attacked a group of Jews with bricks, rocks, and sticks without provocation. The gang, many members of which lived under the docks along the waterfront and slept in tenement basements, had been accused previously of theft, assault, and arson, among other crimes, not all of this criminal activity directed at Jews.

Jews, however, were its unmistakable targets in the riot, which occurred in Williamsburg and was premeditated. Pushcarts in the heavily Jewish area were overturned and store windows were smashed; beards were pulled, women and children were struck, and one man's skull was fractured. More than a dozen people were hurt in the half-hour fracas.

The Jews fought back, just as they had on Grand Street, and although most of the rowdies fled when they saw the police coming, a group of Jewish men managed to restrain two of them long enough for the bluecoats to arrest them. Some five hundred Jews followed them to the station house, not trusting that justice would actually be done. But it was. The police did their jobs, and the two were quickly arraigned and held on $1,000 bail each. It turned out to be the gang's last hurrah; by the following month, the police succeeded in breaking it up for good.[5]

Subsequent events that bore similarities to the chief rabbi's funeral were all tame affairs. When Kasriel H. Sarasohn, the editor of the *Yidishes Tageblatt* and the father of Abraham, died in early 1905, an estimated seventy-five thousand people turned out to watch the procession, which was similar to the chief rabbi's funeral, though not so large. But the police had learned much from the Jacob Joseph funeral debacle. Ordered not to use their clubs, they nevertheless managed to keep the crowds in check, and there was no real trouble. In fact, two Jewish newspapers actually wrote to the police commissioner after the funeral complimenting him on the manner in which the force had handled the event. And the *New York Post* drew an explicit comparison to the chief rabbi's funeral, pointing out that the three hundred policemen "preserved excellent order, which was in sharp contrast to the riots of two years ago." Sarasohn, it is worth noting, was interred in a plot adjacent to Rabbi Joseph's grave.[6]

Similarly, when the popular playwright Jacob Gordin, known in some circles as the "Yiddish Shakespeare," died in 1909, an estimated twenty-five thousand of his fans thronged the Bowery to watch a procession of some ten thousand souls from five hundred Jewish societies and labor unions make their way through the Lower East Side and across the Williamsburg Bridge to Brooklyn. There were no incidents. The same was true of the 1916 funeral of writer Sholem Aleichem, whom the English newspapers referred to as the "Jewish Mark Twain" and whose funeral also attracted tens of thousands.[7]

Measured narrowly by the fact that there was never a repetition of the R. Hoe & Co. riot, that no attacks on Jews of its kind and scale by police or anyone else ever again occurred in America, Louis Marshall's optimism has been borne out. Antisemitic violence of any significant scale was rare in the early part of the twentieth century and gathered momentum only in its closing decades. And even those incidents were generally quite different from the 1902 attack, as they were largely premeditated and perpetrated by individuals who associated Jews with political causes like civil rights or Zionism rather than those motivated strictly by racial or ethnic animus.

The paucity of violent incidents, however, cannot be taken as an indication that American gentiles, the police among them, ceased to hold antisemitic

34. U.S. Army brigadier general Theodore A. Bingham, later chief of the New York Police Department. U.S. Army Corps of Engineers.

prejudice. As soon after the Grand Street riot as 1907, Theodore A. Bingham, the third man to hold the position of police commissioner after Partridge, unfairly castigated New York's Jewish community. Appointed by Mayor George B. McClellan Jr., the Tammany candidate (and son and namesake of the Civil War general) who unseated Seth Low at the end of 1903, Bingham was a West Point graduate and a former brigadier general in the U.S. Army.

In a signed article in *Harper's Magazine* published late in 1907, Bingham asserted that "of the two thousand pictures added to the rogues' gallery during the last year, more than sixty per cent were those of Russian Jews." The gallery was a collection of mug shots of criminal suspects maintained by the New York police, and although being included in it was thought to be disgraceful, it was in fact not a compendium of those convicted of crimes—merely of those under police suspicion.[8]

The following year, however, Bingham doubled down on his invective in a polemic called "Foreign Criminals in New York" that appeared under his byline in the *North American Review*, a leading intellectual journal of the era. He made the shocking statement that Jews were responsible for fully *half* of the crime in the city. He went on to declare that Jews were leaders among pickpockets, burglars, arsonists, and highway robbers, the first being "the one to which they seem to take naturally."[9]

Now most Jewish leaders felt that they had to do something. Those figures simply couldn't be true, nor could the allegation be allowed to stand. Several "indignation meetings" were held and research was undertaken in the Court of General Sessions. It concluded that only 14.5 percent of the 4,573 indictments handed down in all of 1907 were of Jews and that of those indicted, only 69 percent were convicted.

Many spoke out against Bingham and his bogus statistics. Magistrate James J. Walsh, a non-Jewish former member of the House of Representatives, insisted that the statement was not based on fact. "The Jews have some criminals—so have we gentiles," he asserted. "But fifty percent, or even twenty percent, is out of the question." Adolph Radin, the Jewish chaplain to those incarcerated in New York's jails, supplied figures that showed that Jews made up only a tiny percentage of the prison population. And Rabbi Martin A. Meyer of Brooklyn's German Jewish Temple Israel told the *Brooklyn Daily Eagle* that "no words of ours can be too strong condemning such wholesale indictments of our people, nor too pointed in refuting them." The list went on and on.[10]

The *New York Times* didn't believe antisemitism had been Bingham's motive; it suggested the commissioner was merely attempting to "set forth the needs of his department." As the paper explained it,

> His plea is not that the foreigners in New York are peculiarly of a criminal disposition, but that the police, because of their ignorance of foreign languages, habits and customs, are peculiarly unfitted to cope with the criminal conditions which beset every race.

Bingham had, indeed, made such a case at the very end of the piece, but the *Times* was being far too charitable. The vast bulk of his article was a lengthy xenophobic rant, excoriating not only Jews but Italians and other "foreigners" as well.[11]

Whatever Bingham's intent, this time the Jewish community was not out for blood. Perhaps because they felt they had less influence with the current mayor than they had had with Seth Low, because they knew police reform was not high on Tammany Hall's to-do list, because they didn't want to undertake a new battle against a police commissioner they might not win so soon after the debacle with Partridge, or because they calculated that calling for Bingham's resignation might invite retaliation, they chose not to demand his badge. All they wanted from him was a public retraction and an apology.

They got the retraction. The very first thing the commissioner did when he returned from vacation on September 16, 1908, was to admit publicly that the *North American Review* statement in his article had been based on inaccurate information that he had not gathered himself. He declined to reveal his source, which suggests that he may have been lying, but he did issue a satisfactory public statement disavowing the erroneous statistic. His purpose, he insisted, had been essentially what the *Times* had suggested: to make a plea for more money for "additional weapons to cope with crime."

Whether he actually apologized, however, is questionable. "In view of . . . the fact that many estimable citizens feel hurt by what I wrote without the slightest malice, prejudice or unfriendliness, for I have none," he wrote, "I withdraw the statements challenged, frankly and without reserve." It wasn't exactly a full-throated act of contrition, but it was enough to put the matter to rest.

However he may have felt privately, Louis Marshall offered a gracious response:

> I am convinced that in writing his article he was not actuated by the slightest feeling of hostility toward the Jews, but that he was merely seeking to support his thesis by what he considered to be the proper arguments, but which, unfortunately, were in part based on incorrect premises. His frank recognition that he had unwittingly wronged the Jewish people will be accepted by them in the same frank and manly spirit. The incident should be considered closed.[12]

Bingham's retraction ended the matter, but it was a good example of the growing sophistication of the Jewish community in how and when to deploy its newfound political clout. And it did not stop the momentum his article had generated in the Jewish community to organize a permanent institution that might fight such battles in the future.

During the kosher meat boycott, the Hoe riot, and subsequently, the Lower East Side rent strikes of 1904 and 1907, ad hoc organizations had to be established on the fly to speak out and act for those affected. Without exception, these ceased to exist once the crises that had brought about their formation had passed. After the Bingham affair, the Jewish community finally acted on the need for a permanent organization to shoulder these tasks.

In 1909, just a few months after Bingham's retraction, representatives of some 218 New York Jewish societies, prominent Jewish merchants, and rabbis from sixty congregations met in the United Hebrew Charities building to adopt a constitution—in English and Yiddish—for a new group that was to encompass the uptown German Jewish elite as well as the downtown Orthodox leaders. Led by prominent Reform rabbi Judah Leon Magnes, it was to be a nonpartisan, nonpolitical entity whose purpose was to "further the cause of Judaism in New York City, and to represent the Jews of this city with respect to all local matters of Jewish interest."[13]

This was not the first time something like this had been tried. In the mid-nineteenth century, efforts had been made to promote cooperation among the various Jewish factions in America, and in 1859, a few years before the Civil War, a national-level organization was created in New York. The Board of Delegates of American Israelites, modeled on a similar British group, had among its objectives "to keep a watchful eye on occurrences at home and abroad." It would also "see that the civil and religious rights of Israelites are not encroached on, and call attention of the proper authorities to the fact, should any such violation occur."

Among its activities, it had fought efforts to limit army chaplain positions to Christians, opposed General Ulysses S. Grant's infamous 1862 order to expel all Jews from his military district, and helped defeat efforts by the North Carolina legislature to bar Jews from holding public office. It had opposed efforts to establish Christianity as America's national religion and lobbied against Sunday laws that discriminated against Jewish businesses. The board had also mounted the first systematic effort to obtain statistical information about America's Jews. But it didn't last very long, at least as a stand-alone entity. In 1878, it merged with the Union of American Hebrew Congregations (now the Union for Reform Judaism) and became one of the latter's standing committees.[14]

The 1908 effort, which, by contrast, was entirely local, came to be called the New York Kehillah. A term for an organization that deals with Jewish life issues in a given community, *kehillah* is from the same Hebrew root as *kahal,* a local Jewish governing body responsible for administering religious, legal, and communal affairs. Now, whatever their internal differences, the local Jewish community would have an inclusive vehicle that would speak with a single voice on issues like opposing the Sunday laws. If attacks on peaceful Jews happened again, they might presumably find protection and support from a ready-made defender and advocate.

Ironically, the Kehillah was organized more or less according to the *kahal* model Chief Rabbi Joseph had tried to import from the old world when he arrived in 1888. It had worked successfully in Europe but had proven wholly unequal to the task of organizing the huge and highly balkanized New York Jewish community, especially since it got no official backing from the government. Its efforts in 1909 to assert authority over kosher supervision in New York were no more successful than those of the chief rabbi years earlier.[15]

Rabbi Joseph had failed to unify even New York's Orthodox Jews, still less to fulfill the vain hopes of some to bring those Reform Jews who had "strayed" back to the Orthodox fold. But although he had not been much of an ambassador to the gentile community, he had, during his short tenure, tried to speak for the entire Jewish community on matters of common concern, such as the outrageous seizure of a little Jewish girl by Elbridge Gerry's cohorts in 1889 and their refusal to restore her to her father. The New York Kehillah was to play a similar role as an advocate for *all* the Jews of New York, in addition to addressing issues internal to the Jewish community such as promoting Jewish education—another of Rabbi Joseph's unfulfilled tasks.

As a practical matter, however, no attacks like the Rabbi Joseph funeral riot happened during the short life of the Kehillah, which lasted only until 1922, when it collapsed from internal conflicts. And so it was never called on to intervene. But the mantle of fighting discrimination and promoting religious and civil rights was borne by three national-level organizations, the American Jewish Committee (AJC), the Anti-Defamation League (ADL), and the American Jewish Congress (AJCongress), which had all been established in the years immediately following the Grand Street riot.[16]

Perennial organizations like the AJC, the ADL, and the AJCongress have remained essential through the modern era. They defended American Jews when violence against them surged in the 1950s and 1960s, largely because of widespread Jewish support for civil rights. And they continue to do so today. As tax-exempt organizations under the Internal Revenue Code, they are prohibited from participating in political campaigns or supporting particular candidates for public office. But they are still able to build relationships with politicians and speak up and demand justice, especially at a time like the present during which America is once again witnessing an alarming rise in attacks on Jews.[17]

In 2021, the AJC published the results of a survey of American Jews—the largest ever taken, it asserted—that contained the shocking statistic that that some 3 percent of America's 5.8 million Jewish adults reported having been victims of *physical* antisemitic attacks during the previous twelve months, fully one-third of them asserting they had been targeted more than once.[18] That figure has undoubtedly risen since the 2023 Israel-Hamas war.

If there is a lesson to be drawn from the Grand Street riot, it is that resistance to these outrages is both necessary and possible. The key lies in unifying, in organizing, in building alliances, and in amassing political power and influence. And in using that influence wisely to hold the government accountable for prosecuting and punishing civilians who commit violent acts and police who condone, perpetuate, inflict, or fail to prevent them.

The Jews of New York learned that even if they had to accept a certain amount of antisemitism in the *goldene medine* that was America, their growing numbers had delivered to their grasp the means to extract a cost from those who perpetrated violence against them. Beginning in 1902, they served notice on all who would attack them that what they could expect in return was to be doggedly pursued and brought to justice.

ACKNOWLEDGMENTS

First and foremost, I am most grateful to Dr. Steven I. Levine, University of Montana Emeritus Professor of History, who, fortunately for me, takes great pleasure in editing history manuscripts. He gave generously of his time to review several drafts of this book. His wry humor made him a pleasure to work with, and his insightful suggestions made this book a far better work than it otherwise might have been.

In addition, I received invaluable help from four luminaries in the field of Jewish American history:

Dr. Jonathan Sarna, Joseph H. and Belle R. Braun Professor of American Jewish History at Brandeis University

Dr. Pamela Nadell, Patrick Clendenen Chair in Women's and Gender History and director of the Jewish Studies Program at American University

Dr. Kimmy Caplan, chair of the Department of Jewish History and Contemporary Jewry at Israel's Bar-Ilan University

Dr. Jeffrey Gurock, Libby M. Klaperman Professor of Jewish History at the Bernard Revel Graduate School of Jewish Studies of Yeshiva University

I am also deeply indebted to Dr. Edward T. O'Donnell, associate professor of history at the College of the Holy Cross, a recognized authority on American history and Irish American history in particular, who has written about the Jacob Joseph funeral riot.

All of those mentioned above reviewed the manuscript, offered wise counsel, and helped me avoid pitfalls, ruts, and potholes along the way.

My need to understand how the Yiddish-language press viewed the events chronicled in the book gave me a second opportunity since the publication of *The Great Kosher Meat War of 1902: Immigrant Housewives and the Riots That Shook New York City* (2020) to work with Rivka Schiller of Rivka's Yiddish, who tracked down newspaper coverage of the riot and its aftermath. It also reunited me with the delightful Dr. Miriam Isaacs, former visiting associate professor of Yiddish language and culture at the University of Maryland, who sat beside me for many enjoyable hours translating and helping me understand the nuances in the material.

Heartfelt thanks to my dear friends Marsha Cohan, Glenn Sugameli, Suzanne Zunzer, and Stephen Mink, who have always given generously of their time to read and critique my manuscripts, as well as Sharon Graham, for whom this is the first time.

Attorneys Paul M. Sandler, Peter Robertson, and Steven Herman fielded my innumerable legal questions, and author Allan Levine, who has also written about the chief rabbi's funeral riot, gave the manuscript a once-over to my distinct benefit. I am also grateful to Grace Wagner of the New York Historical Society, Ken Cobb and Cristina Stubbe of the New York City Municipal Archives, and Victoria Bijur for help in obtaining source materials and images.

Finally, my thanks to my indefatigable literary agent, Peter W. Bernstein, who advised me on shaping the book proposal, Brianna Blackburn and her colleagues at Scribe Inc. for a meticulous job of copyediting, and Tom Swanson, Taylor Gilreath, Ann Baker, Kayla Moslander, Nathan Putens, Sarah Kee, Tish Fobben, Rebecca Jefferson, Tayler Lord, Leif Milliken, and my many friends at Potomac Books for their continued confidence in me.

CHRONOLOGY

1888

Rabbi Jacob Joseph, hired by several Orthodox congregations for a six-year term as chief rabbi of New York, arrives in America from Vilnius to a tumultuous welcome.

Rabbi Joseph preaches his inaugural sermon at the Beis Hamidrash HaGadol synagogue on Norfolk Street, pleasing the elderly congregants but failing to inspire younger, American-born Jews.

The rabbi introduces the *plombe,* a lead seal, to signal consumers that they are buying meat slaughtered according to Orthodox requirements. The well-meaning policy meets a firestorm of resistance from producers, butchers, consumers, and other rabbis.

1892

Rabbi Joseph engages in a public spat with Reform rabbi Isaac Mayer Wise over the issue of circumcision.

Charles H. Parkhurst, pastor of Manhattan's Madison Square Presbyterian Church, launches an attack on corrupt Tammany Hall politicians.

1894

New York State senator Clarence Lexow initiates a probe and reveals widespread police corruption in New York City. Captains "Big Bill" Devery and Adam A. Cross are caught in the crosshairs, tried before the police commissioners, and dismissed from the force.

Voters agree to merge all of New York's boroughs into a single entity, effective January 1, 1898.

1895

Devery and Cross appeal their dismissal from the police department and are reinstated by the courts.

Joseph's term as chief rabbi is concluded, and he is no longer being paid by the United Orthodox Congregations. Some wholesale butchers continue to employ him.

1897

Reformer Seth Low, running on a fusion ticket, a coalition of the progressive Citizen's Union and Republicans, fails to oust Tammany Hall in his quest to become mayor of the new, expanded City of New York.

1898

Chief Rabbi Joseph suffers a stroke that partially incapacitates him, but he continues his work.

"Big Bill" Devery becomes acting chief of police.

1901

Rabbi Joseph becomes bedridden and unable to discharge his duties.

Adam Cross is named acting deputy chief of police.

Seth Low makes another run for the mayoralty and is elected, as is William Travers Jerome, the fusion candidate for district attorney.

1902

JAN. 1

Mayor Low assumes office, as does his choice for police commissioner, John Nelson Partridge.

Devery is ousted from the department. Partridge vows to reform the corrupt department but unwisely chooses Cross as an adviser.

JULY 28

Chief Rabbi Jacob Joseph dies at the age of sixty-two.

JULY 29

A committee meets with the chief rabbi's family to discuss his funeral arrangements. It is decided he will be buried the following day in Union Field Cemetery at Cypress Hills in East New York.

Israel Levy, a funeral committee member, applies to police Sergeant James Brady for a permit for the funeral procession, which will traverse the Lower East Side and then depart for Brooklyn from the Grand Street ferry terminal. The police promise twenty-five officers to escort the procession. Some twenty thousand people are expected.

At midnight, a Jewish newspaperman telephones Brady to suggest that the crowd will be much larger and that far more police will be needed. The warning is ignored and never reported to Inspector Adam Cross, who is in charge the following day.

JULY 30

The funeral procession, escorted by Captain William Thompson and a squad of patrolmen, makes brief stops at several synagogues as it traverses the Lower East Side.

On the final approach to the ferry terminal, young workers in the R. Hoe printing press factory at Grand and Sheriff Streets harass the mourners and throw debris at the cortege and those amassed on the street. A delegation of mourners that enters the factory to demand that the harassment cease is repelled. Hoses are turned on, and water, hot and cold, is sprayed on pedestrians who hurl the missiles back at the factory and break its windows.

A call is placed to the police, and reinforcements arrive under the command of Inspector Cross. Although the violence has already subsided, the police issue no warning. Goaded by their commander to "club the life out of them," they set on the Jewish mourners and beat them unmercifully. Many are seriously injured and several are arrested.

A missile is also thrown when the cortege arrives in Brooklyn, but the police keep order. The interment takes place without incident in Cypress Hills.

Those arrested are brought to Essex Market Police Court. Many bear bruises. Several prominent Jewish attorneys appear for them. Some are fined; others are held over for trial.

Robert Hoe III, owner of the Hoe factory, issues a self-serving and inaccurate statement that places all blame for the trouble on the Jews. So does Inspector Cross.

That night, a dozen Jewish doctors, lawyers, and businessmen decide to bring all the Jewish lodges and societies together in a protest to Commissioner Partridge and, if he refuses to act, to District Attorney Jerome. A committee is formed to investigate and formulate charges.

JULY 31

Mayor Seth Low asks Police Commissioner John Nelson Partridge for a report on the riot. The board of aldermen unanimously demands a "strenuous and thorough investigation."

Jewish organizations throughout the city hold meetings to condemn the Hoe employees and the police. At one, the East Side Vigilance League is formed to secure a fair investigation and punishment of the offenders.

AUG. 1

Commissioner Partridge sends a report to the mayor that was prepared, over the objections of the Jewish community, by Inspector Cross. In it, Jews are accused of premeditation and blamed for starting the melee. Cross is summarily transferred to the Bronx.

A delegation from the East Side Vigilance League pays a call on Partridge to lodge complaints against several police officers. Rather than accept personal responsibility to carry out an investigation, he fobs it off on Inspector Nicholas Brooks.

Brooks hears testimony from several Jews who refute Cross's statement that Jews were responsible.

AUG. 2

Captain William Thompson, who had been in charge of the police escorts detailed to the funeral procession, suddenly announces his retirement, thus avoiding the possibility of a disciplinary hearing.

AUG. 4

Inspector Brooks hears more testimony from witnesses provided by the East Side Vigilance League. Over the objections of the league's attorneys, he also insists on hearing from "defense witnesses" even though he is only supposed to prefer charges where deserved and not conduct a trial.

District Attorney Travers Jerome, initially hesitant to get involved, designates Assistant District Attorney Isidor Kresel to investigate complaints and bring charges where indicated.

AUG. 5

Two Hoe employees are arraigned at Essex Market Police Court on charges of assault; two others have their cases dismissed.

Attorney Abraham H. Sarasohn submits a dossier to Assistant District Attorney Kresel containing affidavits from sixty witnesses.

Mayor Low, lobbied by Jewish groups dissatisfied with the police department investigation, names a blue-ribbon committee of five citizens to conduct an independent review.

AUG. 8

Inspector Brooks reconvenes his inquiry and hears from more Jewish witnesses.

AUG. 11

Inspector Brooks hears the testimony of witnesses for the police. There is disagreement as to whether Grand Street was calm when the police reinforcements arrived.

That afternoon, the mayor's committee conducts its first hearing and hears many stories of police brutality, persecution, and blackmail that preceded the Hoe riot. Commissioner Partridge and his first deputy, Col. Nathaniel B. Thurston, are criticized. Several witnesses testify about the assault by the police and the Hoe employees in front of the factory.

AUG. 18

District Attorney Travers Jerome submits evidence to the grand jury and seeks indictments of several individuals.

The mayor's committee reconvenes and hears testimony from Hoe employees. All appear to be reading from the same script: that Jews had come prepared for the fight and had started it as "payback" for recent harassment by factory employees.

AUG. 19

The grand jury returns two indictments against Roundsman James M. Jackson and one against Patrolman Henry Doupe. They are arraigned the next day, and Partridge transfers, but does not suspend, both men.

AUG. 20

The mayor's committee continues to hear testimony, but Inspector Brooks uses the indictment of Jackson and Doupe as a pretext to suspend his inquiry indefinitely.

AUG. 25

The mayor's committee holds its final public session. Inspector Cross is the star witness. He sticks to the script that the Jews had arrived intending to attack but presents no evidence to support this contention.

SEPT. 8

A delegation from the East Side Vigilance League calls on the mayor and complains about the investigation at the police department and about Commissioner Partridge.

SEPT. 10

Mayor Low receives the report of his citizens' committee, which exonerates the Jews. It disparages the management of R. Hoe & Co. and finds police headquarters staff negligent. It also asserts that the crowd was quiet before the arrival of Inspector Cross and his reinforcements, who nonetheless began to club people indiscriminately for no good reason.

The committee also finds that instances of "uncivil and even rough treatment" of local Jews were "inexcusably common" in the police department and that punishment has been too lenient. And it criticizes the city magistrates for prejudice against Jewish witnesses.

SEPT. 15

In what the *New York World* calls "a direct snub to the commissioner," Mayor Low informs Partridge after the fact that he has instructed the city's corporation counsel to prepare charges against Inspector Cross, Sergeant James Brady, and possibly Captains John D. Herlihy and Charles L. Albertson.

To avoid discipline, Brady immediately files for retirement, as, soon after, does Deputy Commissioner Thurston, who is not accused of anything but feels pressure from the mayor's office. Before the end of the month, charges against Cross, Herlihy, and Albertson are filed.

OCT. 20

Hearings on the accusations against Captains Herlihy and Albertson and Inspector Cross begin, with Commissioner Partridge presiding. The three men are tried together.

At the same time, the cases of Roundsman Jackson and Patrolman Doupe are heard at the Court of General Sessions.

DEC. 12

Commissioner Partridge announces his resignation, effective January 1, 1903, the first anniversary of his assumption of the job.

DEC. 24

Partridge finds Inspector Cross and Captains Herlihy and Albertson not guilty of the charges arrayed against them.

1908

SEPT.

In an article in the *North American Review,* commissioner of police Theodore Bingham cites bogus statistics charging Jews with responsibility for half of the crime in New York City. Jewish community leaders meet and, armed with statistics of their own that put the rate at 14.5 percent, speak out.

Led by Reform rabbi Judah Leon Magnes, they establish a federation of Jewish organizations to unite the various local Jewish societies into a single, nonpolitical entity. It will be known as the New York Kehillah and will last until 1922 before collapsing due to internal conflicts. Among its purposes will be to counter bogus accusations such as those in the Bingham article.

SEPT. 16

Under pressure, Bingham admits publicly that the statement in his article had been based on inaccurate information that he had not gathered himself, though he does not reveal his source. He doesn't actually apologize, but he does withdraw his statement. It is enough for the Jewish community, which has not sought his ouster and is eager to turn the page.

GLOSSARY

Agudas Hakehilos B'Amerika. Formally the "Association of the American Hebrew Congregations," but colloquially the "United Orthodox Congregations."

Agudas HaRabbonim. The Union of Orthodox Rabbis, established in 1902 in the wake of the death of Rabbi Jacob Joseph.

bar mitzvah. Literally, "son of the commandment." A ceremony marking the progression into adulthood of a thirteen-year-old Jewish boy.

beis din. Jewish rabbinical court.

Beis Hamidrash HaGadol. New York's leading downtown Orthodox Jewish synagogue during the mass immigration era.

bubbemeise. A wives' tale; literally, a "grandmother's fable."

bubbie. A grandmother.

charif. Literally, "sharp." "Yankele Charif," i.e., "Jake the Sharp," was the nickname given to Rabbi Jacob Joseph for the acuity of his intellect.

chazzan. Cantor in a synagogue who helps lead the congregation in prayer.

cheder. Elementary school in which Hebrew and religious knowledge are taught.

chevra kadisha. Literally, "holy society." An organization of Jewish men and women tasked with accompanying a corpse after death and before burial and ensuring that it is ritually cleansed, properly dressed, and interred according to Jewish tradition. Often referred to as a "burial society."

Galicianer. A Jew from Galicia, modern-day southeastern Poland and Ukraine.

goldene medine. "Golden land," a Yiddish term for an idealized version of America.

hechsher. Rabbinical certificate that certifies that food sold in an establishment is kosher.

kahal. The local governing body of a Jewish community responsible for administering religious, legal, and communal affairs.

kashrus. The body of dietary laws prescribed for Jews.

karobke. Tax levied on kosher meat in Russia.

kehillah. A Hebrew word that literally means "congregation." In New York, it referred to a federation of Jewish organizations established by Reform rabbi Judah Leon Magnes that united the various local Jewish societies into a single, nonpolitical, voluntary entity.

kosher. Food that conforms to Jewish ritual dietary regulations and is thus considered fit to eat.

Litvak. A term denoting a Jew from Lithuania or one of its neighboring regions.

maggid meisharim. "Preacher of righteousness." A rabbi contracted by a Jewish community to deliver sermons on Sabbaths and Jewish holidays.

mashgiach. A Jew who supervises the kosher status of an establishment to ensure adherence to orthodox Jewish practices. Plural: *mashgichim*.

matzoh. Unleavened bread, especially consumed during the Passover holiday.

mechitza. Partition used to separate men and women in a synagogue or elsewhere.

plombe. A small leaden seal attached to a piece of meat or poultry to certify that it was properly slaughtered on a certain date and can be made kosher for consumption.

pogrom. An anti-Jewish riot in czarist Russia or other Eastern European country. From a Russian word meaning "to demolish violently."

rav ha'kolel. Term sometimes translated as "chief rabbi" of a Jewish community.

Shabbos. The Sabbath; the Jewish day of rest. It is celebrated from sundown on Friday to sundown on Saturday.

sheeny. An offensive slang term for a Jew. Plural: *sheenies*.

shoychet. A slaughterer officially certified as competent to kill cattle and poultry in the manner prescribed by Jewish law. Plural: *shoychtim*.

shul. A synagogue.

talis. A prayer shawl.

Talmud. The central text of rabbinic Judaism and the primary source of Jewish religious law.

Talmud Torah. A school for young children that offers after-school classes in Hebrew and the Jewish religion.

Torah. The Five Books of Moses; the first five books of the Hebrew Bible.

treyf. Nonkosher; forbidden according to Jewish dietary laws.

yeshiva. An Orthodox Jewish elementary or secondary school.

yeshiva *bocher*. A young, unmarried, male yeshiva student.

NOTES

Preface

1. Anti-Defamation League, *Audit of Antisemitic Incidents 2023*, ADL.org, accessed March 28, 2023, https://www.adl.org/resources/report/audit-antisemitic-incidents-2023.
2. "Protest Meeting Tomorrow at Cooper Union," *Forverts*, July 31, 1902.
3. Samuel Oppenheim, "Disgraceful Acts of a Mob at a Jewish Funeral in New York, 1743," *Publications of the American Jewish Holocaust Society* 31 (1928): 240–41; Jacob Rader Marcus, *The Colonial American Jew*, vol. 3, *1492–1776* (Detroit MI: Wayne State University Press, 1970), 1127.
4. Isabel Fattal, "A Brief History of Antisemitic Violence in America," *Atlantic*, October 28, 2018.
5. Christopher Wray, Address at the Anti-Defamation League Never is Now Summit, November 10, 2022, Federal Bureau of Investigation, accessed November 29, 2022, https://www.fbi.gov/news/speeches/director-wray-addresses-adl-never-is-now-summit-111022.
6. An outlier was the Crown Heights riot, in which a gang of Black men fatally stabbed a Jewish student to avenge the lives of two Black children hit by a car in the motorcade of the Lubavitcher Rebbe, Menachem Mendel Schneerson.
7. "News Roundup for November 11, 2022," J Street, accessed November 22, 2022, https://jstreet.org/news-roundups/news-roundup-for-november-11-2022/#.Y3zTW3bML98.

Prologue

1. "Harris Rosenblum in the 1900 United States Federal Census," Ancestry.com, accessed May 8, 2024, https://www.ancestry.com/discoveryui-content/view/18926394:7602?tid=&pid=&queryId=77c4102f-8acf-4f1f-b743-ea5c8abd23eb&_phsrc=gHP69&_phstart=successSource; "Hundreds Hurt in Riot of East Side Hebrews and Many Arrests Made," *New York World*, July 30, 1902; "Hebrews Accuse Cross of Ordering Use of Clubs," *New York World*, August 1, 1902; "Riots at Rabbi's Funeral," *New York Tribune*, July 31, 1902; "Hebrews Given Hearing by Police Officials," *Brooklyn Citizen*, August 1, 1902; "Hebrews Accuse Policemen," *Brooklyn Times Union*, August 1, 1902; "Hebrews Make Formal Charges," *Brooklyn Standard Union*, August 1, 1902.

2. "Adam Augustus Cross in the U.S., College Student Lists, 1763–1924," Ancestry.com, accessed May 8, 2024, https://www.ancestry.com/discoveryui-content/view/387475:2207?tid=&pid=&queryId=c07143d1-fbd8-4dc5-92b7-9542db96c5aa&_phsrc=gHP75&_phstart=successSource; "Police Mont Pelee Explodes," *New York Tribune*, June 10, 1902; "Adam A. Cross in the 1880 United States Federal Census," Ancestry.com, accessed May 8, 2024, https://www.ancestry.com/discoveryui-content/view/38898881:6742?tid=&pid=&queryId=f44a9476-2d67-4a15-9a7e-1d4a17f3932e&_phsrc=gHP78&_phstart=successSource; "Adam A. Cross in the U.S. Passport Applications, 1795–1925," Ancestry.com, accessed May 8, 2024, https://www.ancestry.com/discoveryui-content/view/1212562:1174?tid=&pid=&queryId=ba5ac416-6efc-42c6-91f7-371cdfccccec&_phsrc=gHP80&_phstart=successSource; "Police Inspector Cross Married," *New York Times*, December 21, 1901.
3. "Robert Hoe, 3D, Dies in London," *New York Times*, September 23, 1901; "Robert Hoe in the 1900 United States Federal Census," Ancestry.com, accessed May 8, 2024, https://www.ancestry.com/discoveryui-content/view/49241765:7602?tid=&pid=&queryId=f4e445d8-64f3-4ee7-becd-b7c0c5f9f158&_phsrc=gHP84&_phstart=successSource; "Robert Hoe: Catalogue of the Library, 1912," Christies, accessed May 30, 2022, https://www.christies.com/en/lot/lot-6297004.
4. "Mary Greenfield in the 1900 United States Federal Census," Ancestry.com, accessed May 8, 2024, https://www.ancestry.com/discoveryui-content/view/18951845:7602?tid=&pid=&queryId=b57df8ca-c66c-4477-88ba-d0b77527734e&_phsrc=gHP87&_phstart=successSource; "Stories of Clubbing at Riot Hearing," *New York Times*, August 14, 1902; "Accused of Blackmail," *Daily People*, August 15, 1902.
5. "Candidates to Be Voted For. Men Who Have Asked for New York City's Suffrage," *New York Herald*, November 8, 1892; "Legislative Acts–Legal Proceedings," *New York Herald*, November 9, 1892; "A. H. Sarasohn Dies; Lawyer 51 Years," *New York Times*, June 21, 1940; "Abraham H. Sarasohn in the 1900 United States Federal Census," Ancestry.com, accessed May 8, 2024, https://www.ancestry.com/discoveryui-content/view/18934720:7602?tid=&pid=&queryId=950954b1-877d-4be7-a1ce-1ba0f47525b6&_phsrc=gHP91&_phstart=successSource; Cyrus Adler and Frederic T. Haneman, "Sarasohn, Kasriel H.," Jewish Encyclopedia, accessed May 31, 2022, https://www.jewishencyclopedia.com/articles/13197-sarasohn-kasriel-h.
6. "Emil Adams in the 1900 United States Federal Census," Ancestry.com, accessed May 8, 2024, https://www.ancestry.com/discoveryui-content/view/55710511:7602?tid=&pid=&queryId=2b264777-a218-4e73-904a-0c25b7f5920d&_phsrc=gHP93&_phstart=successSource.
7. *The Police Department of the City of New York: A Statement of Facts; Address by Police Commissioner Greene* (New York: City Club of New York, 1903), 401.
8. "Partridge Rumors Again," *New York Tribune*, July 29, 1902; "Col. J. N. Partridge Dies at 82 Years," *New York Times*, April 9, 1920; "Col. John N. Partridge Dies," *New York Tribune*, April 9, 1920; "Col. J. N. Partridge Dies at Age of 83," *New York Herald*, April 9, 1920.

1. "Unite the Hearts of Our Brethren"

1. "Number of Jews in Greater New York," *New York Times*, August 17, 1902.
2. "The City," *American Hebrew*, March 30, 1888.
3. Jonathan D. Sarna, "The 'Mythical Jew' and the 'Jew Next Door' in Nineteenth Century America," in *Anti-Semitism in American History*, ed. David A. Gerber (Urbana: University of Illinois Press, 1986), 63.
4. Abraham Cahan, *Yekl and the Imported Bridegroom and Other Stories of Yiddish New York* (Mineola NY: Dover, 1970), 13–14.
5. "A Voice from the Ghetto," *American Hebrew*, December 26, 1902.
6. "Number of Jews"; Paul Ritterband, "Counting the Jews in New York, 1900–1991: An Essay in Substance and Method," in *Papers in Jewish Demography, 1997*, ed. Sergio Della Pergola and Judith Even, Jewish Population Studies 29 (Jerusalem: Avraham Harman Institute of Contemporary Jewry, 1997), 202.
7. "Reform Judaism: The Pittsburgh Platform," Jewish Virtual Library, accessed March 26, 2022, https://www.jewishvirtuallibrary.org/the-pittsburgh-platform.
8. Moses Rischin, *The Promised City: New York's Jews, 1870–1914* (Cambridge MA: Harvard University Press, 1962), 76–78; Cahan, *Yekl*, 13–14.
9. Eugene Markovitz, "Henry Pereira Mendes: Architect of the Union of Orthodox Jewish Congregations of America," *American Jewish Historical Quarterly* 55, no. 3 (March 1966): 364, quoting Morris Weinberger, *Ha-Yehudim veha-Yahadut be-New York* (New York, 1887).
10. Timothy D. Lytton, *Kosher: Private Regulation in the Age of Industrial Food* (Cambridge MA: Harvard University Press, 2013), 14–15.
11. Harold Philip Gastwirt, "Fraud Corruption and Holiness: Kashrut Supervision in New York City, 1881–1940" (PhD diss., Columbia University, 1971), 10–11.
12. "A Chief Rabbi Needed," *New York Herald*, August 4, 1879; Dovi Safier and Yehuda Gerberer, "The Malbim of Manhattan," Mishpacha.com, November 4, 2020, https://mishpacha.com/the-malbim-of-manhattan/; Abraham J. Karp, "New York Chooses a Chief Rabbi," *Publications of the American Jewish Historical Society* 44, no. 3 (March 1955): 131; Markovitz, "Henry Pereira Mendes," 372.
13. "The Orthodox Congregations," *Hebrew Leader*, September 8, 1882.
14. "Orthodox Congregations."
15. Karp, "New York Chooses," 137–38.
16. Abraham Cahan, "The Late Rabbi Joseph, Hebrew Patriarch of New York," *American Monthly Review of Reviews* 26 (September 1902): 312–13; Dr. Kimmy Caplan, email to the author, November 13, 2022.
17. Literally, a "rabbinical letter," an appointment letter setting out the terms of employment.
18. Yonah Landau, *The Rav HaKolel and His Generation*, trans. C. B. Weinfeld (self-pub., 2011), 218.
19. Landau, *Rav HaKolel*, 219.

20. "Rabbi Jacob Joseph," *Daily People*, August 4, 1902; Landau, *Rav HaKolel*, 225. A married son, Raphael, would not immigrate to America until many years later.
21. "The Chief Rabbi's Reception," *New York Herald*, July 9, 1888.

2. "An Old Fogy in Their Eyes"

1. "Domestic News," *Jewish Voice*, March 2, 1888; "A Learned Rabbi Arrives," *New York Sun*, July 8, 1888. Other sources suggest that the rabbi may have occupied only one floor of the house, which had earlier been divided into apartments, rather than the entire building.
2. "Learned Rabbi Arrives."
3. "Learned Rabbi Arrives"; "The Chief Rabbi's Reception," *New York Herald*, July 9, 1888; "A Learned Rabbi Come to Judgment," *New York Tribune*, July 15, 1888.
4. "Flocking to Rabbi Joseph," *New York Sun*, July 9, 1888; Landau, *Rav HaKolel*, 242.
5. "Will He Be an Autocrat?," *New York Herald*, July 21, 1888.
6. "Excited Hebrew Throngs," *New York Herald*, July 22, 1888.
7. "Thronging Rabbi Joseph," *New York Sun*, July 22, 1888.
8. "Thronging Rabbi Joseph."
9. "Hearing the New Rabbi," *New York Times*, July 22, 1888; "Thronging Rabbi Joseph"; "Excited Hebrew Throngs."
10. "Rabbi Joseph's First Sermon," *New York Sun*, July 23, 1888; "The American Jews," *New York Sun*, July 24, 1888.
11. "Opposed to the New Rabbi," *New York Sun*, August 12, 1888; Eugene Markovitz, "Henry Pereira Mendes: Architect of the Union of Orthodox Jewish Congregations of America," *American Jewish Historical Quarterly* 55, no. 3 (March 1966): 368, quoting Morris Weinberger, *Ha-Yehudim veha-Yahadut be-New York* (New York, 1887), 22.
12. "Rabbi Joseph's First Sermon"; "American Jews."

3. "Protect Our Holy Faith"

1. "Rabbi Joseph Preaches Again," *New York Sun*, July 29, 1888; "Still Thronging the Chief Rabbi," *New York Sun*, August 12, 1888; "The City," *American Hebrew*, July 27, 1888; "Hebrew Free School Association," *American Hebrew*, September 21, 1888; "The City," *American Hebrew*, October 19, 1888; "Local News," *Jewish Messenger*, October 26, 1888; "Hebrew Free Schools," *Jewish Messenger*, December 14, 1888.
2. "Local News," *Jewish Messenger*, August 31, 1888; "Opening a New Synagogue," *American Hebrew*, August 31, 1888; "Objectionable Emblems," *Jewish Voice*, August 10, 1888; "The City," *American Hebrew*, November 15, 1889; *Jewish Messenger*, August 10, 1888 (untitled).
3. "Hearing the New Rabbi," *New York Times*, July 22, 1888.
4. "Israel and the Centennial," *New York Herald*, April 20, 1889.
5. "A Warning to the Jews," *New York Sun*, November 6, 1888.
6. "Rabbies [*sic*] Not Politicians," *New York Herald*, October 29, 1892; "Rabbi Joseph's Denial," *New York Times*, November 1, 1892.

7. "For Sending Jews to Palestine," *New York Sun*, October 2, 1890; "The City," *American Hebrew*, August 10, 1888.
8. "Local News," *Jewish Messenger*, October 19, 1888; "To Reclaim a Cemetery," *New York Times*, November 13, 1892; "Against the Jewish Law," *New York Times*, November 28, 1892; "The City," *American Hebrew*, November 25, 1892; Landau, *Rav HaKolel*, 301–2.
9. "Wed His Uncle's Widow," *New York Sun*, December 10, 1894.
10. "An Outrage," *New York World*, February 8, 1889; "Little Tina," *New York World*, February 11, 1889. Tina Weiss was eventually returned to her parents.
11. "City," November 15, 1889; Jacob Joseph, "Letakant Harabim," *Hazefirah* 16, no. 57 (March 20, 1889): 2 [Hebrew], per Kimmy Caplan, email to the author, November 13, 2022.
12. "Rabbies [*sic*] Called Together," *New York Herald*, August 11, 1892.
13. "Gotham Gossip," *Daily Picayune*, August 15, 1892.
14. "The Conflict in the Jewish Church," *Northern Christian Advocate*, August 17, 1892; "The Conclave of Rabbis Postponed," *New York Tribune*, October 10, 1892; "Orthodox vs. Reform Rabbis," *Macon Beacon*, October 15, 1892; "The Schism in Israel," *New Orleans Item*, November 15, 1892.
15. Isaac Mayer Wise, "To the New York Herald, the Cincinnati Commercial Gazette and All Whom It May Concern," *American Israelite*, August 18, 1892; "Schism in Israel."
16. "The Chief Rabbi," *New York Sun*, November 11, 1892.

4. "A Flower Transplanted to Uncongenial Soil"

1. H. R. Rabinowitz, "Two Letters from the Chief Rabbi of New York R'Jacob Joseph Harif," *Talpiyot* 8, nos. 3–4 (1963): 569–73 [Hebrew].
2. "A Shechitah Association," *Jewish Messenger*, August 1, 1879.
3. Joseph Adler, "Twilight Years of Rabbi Jacob Joseph," *Jewish Frontier* 67, no. 1 (January–August 2000): 639; "To Indict Rabbi Joseph," *New York Sun*, January 8, 1889.
4. "Opposing Rabbi Joseph," *New York Sun*, October 1, 1888.
5. "An Anti-Tag Movement," *Jewish Messenger*, October 5, 1888.
6. "The Clean and the Unclean," *New York Herald*, October 8, 1888.
7. "Our Gossip," *Jewish Messenger*, October 12, 1888.
8. "Rabbis Carry Quarrel into a Police Court," *New York Sun*, September 20, 1888; "Rabbi Joseph on Chicken Killing," *New York Tribune*, September 25, 1888; Isaac Levitats, *The Jewish Community in Russia, 1772–1844* (New York: Octagon, 1970), 52–54.
9. "To Indict Rabbi Joseph"; "Local News," *Jewish Messenger*, December 21, 1888.
10. Editorial, *American Hebrew*, January 11, 1889.
11. Adler, "Twilight Years," 639; Oran Zweiter, "Turning a Church into a Synagogue: Jewish Law Meets Communal Politics on New York's Lower East Side," *American Jewish Archives Journal* 71, no. 1 (2019): 1–17.
12. Yitzchok Levine, "The Chief Rabbi Encounters Opposition," Jewish Press, June 4, 2008, https://www.jewishpress.com/sections/magazine/glimpses-ajh/the-chief-rabbi

-encounters-opposition/2008/06/04/; "The First Lubavitcher Rov in America," Anash.org, accessed November 29, 2023, https://anash.org/the-first-lubavitcher-rov-in-america/; Jeffrey S. Gurock, "No Place for a Chief Rabbi," Jewish Press, December 26, 2012, https://www.jewishpress.com/indepth/opinions/no-place-for-a-chief-rabbi/2012/12/26/.

13. "A Word of Complaint," *Jewish Messenger*, February 22, 1889.
14. Kimmy Caplan, "The Ever Dying Denomination: American Jewish Orthodoxy, 1824–1965," in *The Columbia History of Jews and Judaism in America*, ed. Marc Lee Raphael (New York: Columbia University Press, 2008), 173; "To the Jewish Public," *Jewish Messenger*, February 15, 1889; "Kosher Meat the Best," *New York Herald*, February 18, 1889; Advertisement, *Jewish Messenger*, March 1, 1889.
15. Harold Philip Gastwirt, "Fraud, Corruption and Holiness: Kashrut Supervision in New York City, 1881–1940" (PhD diss., Columbia University, 1971), 134.
16. "New York," *Jewish Voice*, March 20, 1981; "Rabbinical Scholarship," *Hebrew Standard*, February 8, 1901; "Word of Complaint"; Timothy D. Lytton, *Kosher: Private Regulation in the Age of Industrial Food* (Cambridge MA: Harvard University Press, 2013), 23–24; Abraham Cahan, "The Late Rabbi Joseph, Hebrew Patriarch of New York," *American Monthly Review of Reviews* 26 (September 1902): 314.

5. "One Solid Gang of Criminals"

1. James Lardner and Thomas Repetto, *NYPD: A City and Its Police* (New York: Henry Holt, 2000), 65; Bernard Whalen and David Doorey, "The Birth of the NYPD," B. J. Whalen, accessed June 18, 2022, http://www.bjwhalen.com/article.htm.
2. A. E. Costello, *Our Police Protectors* (New York: Augustine E. Costello, 1885), 266–67, 287.
3. Lardner and Repetto, *NYPD*, 65.
4. Fred A. McKenzie, "Tammany," *Eclectic Magazine* 67, no. 1 (January 1898): 128–35.
5. "Is It Cross or M'Laughlin?" *New York World*, August 10, 1894; "Cross May Be Tried Next," *New York Herald*, August 11, 1894; "Is Cross to Be the Next?" *New York Tribune*, August 11, 1894; *The Police Department of the City of New York: A Statement of Facts; Address by Police Commissioner Greene* (New York: City Club of New York, 1903), 364.
6. "Paid Money for Captain Cross," *New York Times*, August 18, 1894; "Mrs. Sanford's Many Lies," *New York Sun*, August 18, 1894; "Cross' Defense Begun," *New York Tribune*, August 22, 1894; "Defenders of Cross," *New York Tribune*, August 23, 1894; "Five More Heads Fall," *New York World*, August 31, 1894; "Stephenson Gives Bail," *New York Herald*, November 3, 1894.
7. Philip Messing, "When Cops Were Robbers: The Early Days of the NYPD," *New York Post*, April 12, 2015.
8. "Roosevelt Was Hissed," *New York Sun*, March 17, 1897.
9. Theodore Roosevelt, *An Autobiography* (New York: Macmillan, 1914), 191–92.

10. "Big Game for Mr. Roosevelt," *New York Sun,* January 15, 1892; "Mayor Strong Acts," *BJ,* April 2, 1895; "Mr. Kerwin Refuses," *New York Herald,* May 5, 1895.
11. "Gallagher, New 'Red Light' Commander, Starts Right in to Cleanse the District," *New York World,* August 2, 1902.
12. A pro-cathedral is a parish church that serves temporarily as a cathedral of a diocese.
13. "Felix Adler Plans a Crusade," *New York Tribune,* December 19, 1899.
14. "Church Resents Police Insult," *New York Times,* September 29, 1900; "Herlihy Charges Are Dismissed," *New York Times,* February 21, 1901.
15. "Paddock Would 'Kick' at Heaven," *New York World,* January 22, 1901.
16. "Read to Aid Dr. Potter," *New York Tribune,* October 1, 1900; "Paddock Testifies," *Daily People,* December 29, 1900.

6. "Disgusted with the Corrupt Methods of the Police"

1. Arthur M. Silver, "Jews in the Political Life of New York City" (PhD diss., Yeshiva University, 1954), 7.
2. "Home News," *New York Tribune,* June 27, 1883; "Jewish Seminary Dedicated," *New York Herald,* May 26, 1892; "Hard at Work for Low," *New York Tribune,* October 26, 1897; "For Hebrew Young Men," *New York Tribune,* May 31, 1900; "The New Mt. Sinai Hospital," *Jewish Messenger,* May 24, 1901; "United Hebrew Charities," *American Hebrew,* July 19, 1901.
3. "Orthodox Jews in Convention," *San Francisco Call,* December 31, 1900.
4. "Jerome Attacks Library Gift," *New York Tribune,* October 27, 1901.
5. "Policemen Not Held for Clubbing," *New York Herald,* October 14, 1894; "Riot Preceded the Parade," *New York Times,* October 12, 1894.
6. "Gompers Exhorts the Tailors," *New York Sun,* August 9, 1896; "Rioting in the Ghetto," *New York Tribune,* September 26, 1898; "Yom Kippur Riot Ended by Police," *New York Evening Journal,* September 26, 1898; "East Side Rioting Kept Up," *New York Tribune,* September 27, 1898.
7. James Lardner and Thomas Repetto, *NYPD: A City and Its Police* (New York: Henry Holt, 2000), 134.
8. Edward T. O'Donnell, "Hibernians versus Hebrews? A New Look at the 1902 Jacob Joseph Funeral Riot," *Journal of the Gilded Age and Progressive Era* 6, no. 2 (April 2007): 217–18; Leonard Dinnerstein, *Anti-Semitism in America* (New York: Oxford University Press, 1994), 69; Leonard Dinnerstein, "The Funeral of Rabbi Jacob Joseph," in *Anti-Semitism in American History,* ed. David A. Gerber (Urbana: University of Illinois Press, 1986), 278.
9. "Clubs, Not Trumps," *New York World,* October 12, 1894; "Byrnes Takes a Hand," *New York Herald,* October 13, 1894; "Byrnes Upholds the Police," *New York World,* October 13, 1894; "The Charges of Brutal Clubbing," *New York Tribune,* October 13, 1894; "Threaten to Sue Police," *New York World,* October 13, 1894; "Clubbing Not Proved," *New York Sun,* October 14, 1894.

10. "Policemen Not Held"; "Williams Denounced," *New York Tribune*, October 14, 1894; "The Rutgers Square Strikers," *New York Sun*, October 20, 1894; "Charged with Assaulting Strikers," *Rock Island Argus*, November 1, 1894; "Captain Grant and His Clubbers," *New York Tribune*, December 4, 1894; "Capt. Grant Gets Off," *New York World*, January 8, 1895.
11. Both Williams and Byrnes got their comeuppance in 1895, however, when Theodore Roosevelt engineered the former's retirement and the latter's resignation.
12. "Anti-Vice Mass Meeting," *New York Times*, April 23, 1900.
13. "Twain on the Tiger Banana," *New York Tribune*, October 30, 1901.
14. "Anti-Push Cart Crusade," *New York Times*, September 29, 1900.
15. "Jerome Attacks Library Gift."
16. "Low Outlines the Issues," *New York Tribune*, October 5, 1901; "Vote for the East Side Children," *New York Tribune*, October 15, 1901.
17. "Election Notes," *American Hebrew*, October 18, 1901; "Humors of the Campaign," *New York Tribune*, October 21, 1901; "Seth Low for Mayor," *Jewish Messenger*, October 25, 1901; "Moss Goes Guarded to Meeting," *New York Tribune*, October 30, 1901.
18. "In Memoriam," *American Hebrew*, October 18, 1901; "Tammany Intimidation," *New York Tribune*, October 1, 1901.
19. "Tammany Intimidation."
20. "In Memoriam."
21. "Col. John N. Partridge Dies," *New York Tribune*, April 9, 1920; "Col. J. N. Partridge Dies at Age of 83," *New York Herald*, April 9, 1920; "Colonel Thurston Resigns," *New York Times*, October 5, 1902.
22. "Devery Goes Out in Tears," *New York Sun*, January 2, 1902; Bernard Whalen and Jon Whalen, *The NYPD's First Fifty Years: Politicians, Police Commissioners & Patrolmen* (Lincoln NE: Potomac Books, 2014), 20.
23. Police Commissioner Francis Vinton Greene, as quoted in *The Police Department of the City of New York: A Statement of Facts; Address by Police Commissioner Greene* (New York: City Club of New York, 1903), 401.
24. *Police Department of the City*, 401; "No More 'Sensational Raids,'" *Daily People*, January 2, 1902.
25. "Deveryism Won't Down," *New York Tribune*, April 11, 1902.

7. "So Impressive a Funeral"

1. "The Case of the Chief Rabbi," *New York Sun*, October 20, 1895; "Rabbi No Longer Paid," *American Hebrew*, September 6, 1895.
2. "Rabbi Joseph and the T. T. T. O. I.," *New York Sun*, February 3, 1894.
3. Abraham Cahan, "The Late Rabbi Joseph, Hebrew Patriarch of New York," *American Monthly Review of Reviews* 26 (September 1902): 313.
4. From *Jacob Epstein's Autobiography*, as quoted in Milton Hindus, ed., *The Jewish East Side, 1881–1924* (New Brunswick NJ: Transaction, 1996), 7.
5. "Sugar for Passover," *American Hebrew*, February 21, 1902.

6. "Chief Rabbi Joseph Ill," *New York World*, January 25, 1901; "Rabbi Joseph," *Hebrew Standard*, February 1, 1901; "Congregation Zichron Ephraim," *Hebrew Standard*, January 25, 1901.
7. "Chief Rabbi Joseph Ill"; "Rabbi Jacob Joseph," *Hebrew Standard*, February 1, 1901; "Fund for Support of the Rabbi," *American Hebrew*, May 31, 1901.
8. State of New York, Official Record of Death, Certificate no. 22552, July 28, 1902.
9. "Six Injured in Riot at Rabbi's Funeral," *Brooklyn Citizen*, July 30, 1902.
10. "Death of Chief Rabbi Jacob Joseph," *New York Times*, July 29, 1902; "Reverent Throngs Kneel in Street in Front of Dead Rabbi's Home," *New York World*, July 29, 1902.
11. Cahan, "Late Rabbi Joseph," 311.
12. Arthur Aryeh Goren, "Sacred and Secular: The Place of Public Funerals in the Immigrant Life of American Jews," *Jewish History* 8, nos. 1–2 (1994): 274.
13. Goren, "Sacred and Secular," 270–72.
14. Leonard Dinnerstein, "The Funeral of Rabbi Jacob Joseph," in *Anti-Semitism in American History*, ed. David A. Gerber (Urbana: University of Illinois Press, 1986), 280; "Six Injured in Riot."
15. "Hundreds Hurt in Riot at Rabbi's Funeral and Many Arrests Made," *New York World*, July 30, 1902.
16. "Full Text of the Report," *New York Times*, September 16, 1902.
17. "Funeral Caused Riot," *Auburn Bulletin*, July 31, 1902.
18. "Six Injured in Riot"; "Hundreds Hurt in Riot of East Side Hebrews and Many Arrests Made," *New York World*, July 30, 1902; "Grief for Rabbi Turns to Rage," *New York Herald*, July 31, 1902; Goren, "Sacred and Secular," 274.
19. "Funeral and Riot," *Brooklyn Times Union*, July 31, 1902; "Riot at a Funeral," *Daily People*, July 31, 1902; "Hundreds Hurt in Riot at Rabbi's Funeral."
20. "Funeral of Ulysses S. Grant," National Park Service, accessed March 12, 2022, https://www.nps.gov/articles/000/funeral-of-ulysses-s-grant.htm; "Storm the Cathedral," *New York Tribune*, May 9, 1902; "Hundreds Hurt in Riot of East Side Hebrews."
21. "Hundreds Hurt in Riot of East Side Hebrews"; "The Testimony before the Mayor's Committee," *American Hebrew and Jewish Messenger*, August 22, 1902.

8. "Get Out, You Sheenies! We'll Soak You!"

1. Frank E. Comparato, *Chronicles of Genius and Folly: R. Hoe & Company and the Printing Press as a Service to Democracy* (Culver City CA: Labyrinthos, 1979), 165–67.
2. "An Apprentices' School," *New York Times*, June 15, 1902.
3. "Baited Jews Make Riot," *New York Sun*, July 31, 1902; "Jews Denounce the Police," *New York Times*, July 31, 1902.
4. Gregory Weinstein, *The Ardent Eighties: Reminiscences of an Interesting Decade* (New York: International Press, 1928), 23–25, 143, as quoted in Comparato, *Chronicles of Genius*, 580–81.
5. "The Testimony before the Mayor's Committee," *American Hebrew*, August 22, 1902.
6. "Baited Jews Make Riot."

7. "East Side Riots before Grand Jury," *New York Herald*, August 19, 1902; "East Side Wrath Aflame," *New York Sun*, August 1, 1902; "Hebrews Accuse Cross of Ordering Use of Clubs," *New York World*, August 1, 1902; "The Report of the Mayor's Committee," *American Hebrew*, September 19, 1902.
8. "Mayor Low Starts Riot Investigation," *New York Times*, August 1, 1902.
9. "Jews Denounce the Police."
10. "Riot at a Funeral," *Daily People*, July 31, 1902; "Baited Jews Make Riot"; "Jews Denounce the Police."
11. "Hearse Bombarded with Stale Bread," *New York World*, August 4, 1902; "Riot at a Funeral"; "Baited Jews Make Riot"; "Jews Denounce the Police."
12. "Riot Mars Funeral of Rabbi Joseph," *New York Times*, July 31, 1902; "Hundreds Hurt in Riot of East Side Hebrews and Many Arrests Made," *New York World*, July 30, 1902.
13. "Riot Mars Funeral."
14. "Reports of Riot Arouse Officials," *New York Herald*, August 1, 1902; "East Side Wrath Aflame"; "Baited Jews Make Riot."
15. "Jewish Riot Hearing," *Brooklyn Citizen*, August 21, 1902; "Tried to Bribe Riot Witness," *New York World*, August 5, 1902; "Two Hoe Employees Held," *New York Tribune*, August 6, 1902.
16. "Probing Funeral Riot," *Rome Citizen*, August 5, 1902.
17. "Baited Jews Make Riot."

9. "Club the Life Out of Them"

1. "Hundreds Hurt in Riot of East Side Hebrews and Many Arrests Made," *New York World*, July 30, 1902.
2. "Riot at Rabbi's Funeral," *New York Post*, July 30, 1902; "Police Blamed," *Syracuse Telegram*, August 1, 1902.
3. "Grief for Rabbi Turns to Rage," *New York Herald*, July 31, 1902; "Hundreds Hurt in Riot."
4. Scott D. Seligman, *The Great Kosher Meat War of 1902: Immigrant Housewives and the Riots That Shook New York City* (Lincoln NE: Potomac Books, 2020), 88.
5. "The East Side Riot," *New York Times*, September 16, 1902.
6. "Riot Mars Funeral of Rabbi Joseph," *New York Times*, July 31, 1902; "East Side Riot"; "Riot at a Funeral," *Daily People*, July 31, 1902.
7. "Hebrew Funeral Procession Mobbed," *Poughkeepsie Daily Journal*, July 31, 1902; "Hundreds Hurt in Riot of East Side Hebrews"; "A Big Row at a Funeral," *Evening Tribune* (Hornellsville NY), July 31, 1902; "Jews Denounce the Police," *New York Times*, July 31, 1902.
8. "Baited Jews Make Riot," *New York Sun*, July 31, 1902.
9. "Riot Mars Funeral"; "Six Injured in Riot at Rabbi's Funeral," *Brooklyn Citizen*, July 30, 1902; "Riot at a Funeral."
10. "Baited Jews Make Riot"; "East Side Riot"; "Riot at a Funeral."
11. "Riot at a Funeral."

12. "Riot Mars Funeral"; "Riots at Rabbi's Funeral," *New York Tribune*, July 31, 1902; "Six Injured in Riot"; "No Riot at Wurster's," *Brooklyn Times Union*, July 31, 1902; "Hebrews in Two Riots," *Brooklyn Daily Eagle*, July 30, 1902; "Mayor Low Demands Police Report on the Hebrew Riots," *Brooklyn Standard Union*, July 31, 1902.
13. "Riot Mars Funeral."
14. "Grief for Rabbi"; "The Rev. Israel Cooper Dies at 69," *New York Tribune*, January 12, 1909; "Scenes at the Burial," *Brooklyn Daily Eagle*, July 31, 1902; "Hundreds Hurt in Riot of East Side Hebrews."
15. "Scenes at the Burial."
16. "Our New York Letter," *Jewish Exponent*, August 8, 1902; "Editorial Notes," *American Hebrew*, August 9, 1902; "Resisters and Accommodators: Varieties of Orthodox Rabbis in America, 1886–1983," *American Jewish Archives* 35, no. 2 (November 1983): 110–11.

10. "Commissioner Partridge Is a Sleepy Old *Bubbie*"

1. "Justices and City Magistrates Appointed by the Mayor," *New York Journal and Advertiser*, July 2, 1899.
2. "Mr. Gottlieb Leaves Tammany," *New York Tribune*, September 19, 1895.
3. "New York's Disgrace," *American Israelite*, August 7, 1902.
4. "Baited Jews Make Riot," *New York Sun*, July 31, 1902.
5. "Denounced by Justice Ryan," *New York Times*, July 17, 1893.
6. "Denounced by Justice Ryan"; "East Side Turbulents," *New York Sun*, July 18, 1893; "Justice Ryan and the Hebrews," *New York Times*, July 18, 1893.
7. "Baited Jews Make Riot."
8. "Hebrews Accuse Cross of Ordering Use of Clubs," *New York World*, August 1, 1902; "Riots at Rabbi's Funeral," *New York Tribune*, July 31, 1902.
9. "Baited Jews Make Riot."
10. "Riot Mars Funeral of Rabbi Joseph," *New York Times*, July 31, 1902.
11. "Baited Jews Make Riot"; "Mayor Low Demands Investigation of Riot," *Brooklyn Daily Eagle*, July 31, 1902.
12. "Riot Mars Funeral"; "Grief for Rabbi Turns to Rage," *New York Herald*, July 31, 1902.
13. "Riot at a Funeral," *Daily People*, July 31, 1902; "Hundreds Hurt in Riot at Rabbi's Funeral and Many Arrests Made," *New York World*, July 30, 1902.
14. "Baited Jews Make Riot"; "Riots at Rabbi's Funeral."
15. "Partridge Don't Know Yet," *Brooklyn Daily Eagle*, July 31, 1902.
16. "Riot Mars Funeral."
17. "Mayor Low Demands Investigation."
18. "Partridge Don't Know Yet."
19. "Police Crimes," *Arbeiter Zeitung*, August 2, 1902.

11. "There Never Was Such an Outrage on Our Race"

1. "A. H. Sarasohn Dies; Lawyer 51 Years," *New York Times,* June 21, 1940; "East Side Mourns at Bier of 'Kaplanaha,' Its Beloved Doctor," *New York Tribune,* January 7, 1918; "Many Diseased Immigrants," *New York Tribune,* September 13, 1905; "United States Deceased Physician File (AMA), 1864–1968," Family Search, accessed May 7, 2022, https://www.familysearch.org/search/collection/2061540.
2. "Dr. Julius Halpern Dies," *New York Times,* March 25, 1928; "Funeral Crowd in a Fierce Riot," *Chicago Tribune,* July 31, 1902; "Jews Denounce the Police," *New York Times,* July 31, 1902.
3. "Jews Denounce the Police"; "Mayor and Aldermen to Avenge Hebrews," *New York World,* July 31, 1902.
4. Jonathan D. Sarna, *When General Grant Expelled the Jews* (New York: Schocken, 2012), 148.
5. "Number of Jews in New York," *New York Times,* August 17, 1902, quoting *Di Yidishe Velt*; "The City Congressmen," *New York Sun,* August 14, 1898.
6. "Editorial Notes," *American Hebrew,* January 10, 1902; "Julius B. Mayer Appointed," *American Hebrew,* January 17, 1902.
7. "Hebrew Clubbings Tammany's Revenge," *New York Herald,* August 13, 1902.
8. "Editorial Notes," *American Hebrew,* February 14, 1902; "Fair Play for Hebrews," *New York Tribune,* April 19, 1902; "The Patrolmen on Trial," *New York Tribune,* April 19, 1902.
9. "No Blue Law for Low," *New York Post,* April 18, 1902; "Local News," *Jewish Messenger,* May 9, 1902; "Mayor Low and the Passover," *Hebrew Standard,* April 19, 1902.
10. "Jerome's East Side Home," *New York Tribune,* January 22, 1902; "Jerome and Jewish Meat," *Forverts,* May 24, 1902; "Fierce Meat Riot on Lower East Side," *New York Times,* May 16, 1902.
11. "Hoe's Factory Under Guard," *Brooklyn Daily Eagle,* July 31, 1902.
12. "Reports of Riot Arouse Officials," *New York Herald,* August 1, 1902; "Aldermen to Confer Over P. R. R. Franchise," *Brooklyn Daily Eagle,* July 31, 1902; "Police Conduct at a Riot," *New York Post,* July 31, 1902.
13. "East Side Wrath Aflame," *New York Sun,* August 1, 1902; "Riots at Rabbi's Funeral," *New York Tribune,* July 31, 1902; "Jews Denounce the Police"; "Hebrew Vigilants Form a Committee in Self-Defense," *New York Press,* August 1, 1902.
14. "Jews Offer Reward," *New York Tribune,* August 1, 1902; "Pen Point Portrait No. 49, Mr. Benjamin F. Spellman," *Wall Street Daily News,* November 14, 1906; "Calls Jerome Names," *Daily People,* April 10, 1902; "B. F. Spellman, 76, Attorney 55 Years," *New York Times,* April 26, 1952; "Hebrew Vigilants."
15. "Jews Offer Reward."
16. "Jews Offer Reward."
17. "Hebrew Vigilants."
18. "Hebrew Vigilants."
19. "Hebrew Vigilants"; "Jewish Protection League," *New York Times,* September 17, 1902.
20. "Hebrew Vigilants."

12. "Action Is Called For! Examples Should Be Made!"

1. "Yesterday's Riot," *New York World,* July 31, 1902.
2. "Jew Baiting in New York," *Brooklyn Standard Union,* July 31, 1902; "The East Side Riots and the Police," *Brooklyn Standard Union,* August 1, 1902.
3. "Baited Jews Make Riot," *New York Sun,* July 31, 1902; "Baiting the Jews," *Brooklyn Daily Eagle,* July 31, 1902.
4. "Baiting the Jews."
5. "The Funeral Riot," *Brooklyn Citizen,* July 31, 1902.
6. "Readers' Views of the Riot," *New York Times,* August 3, 1902.
7. "A Shameful Outbreak of Bigotry," *Irish World and American Industrial Liberator,* September 13, 1902.
8. "Holocaust Encyclopedia," United States Holocaust Memorial Museum, accessed November 8, 2022, https://encyclopedia.ushmm.org/content/en/article/pogroms.
9. "Yesterday's Police Pogrom," *Forverts,* July 31, 1902.
10. "Yesterday's Police Pogrom."
11. "Tzadik's Casket Desecrated; On to the Protest!," *Di Yidishe Velt,* July 31, 1902. The *Sun* reported that "hundreds of Jews" were beaten by the police in "Baited Jews Make Riot."
12. "Tzadik's Casket Desecrated"; "Open Letter: *The Jewish World* to the Highest Officials of New York," *Di Yidishe Velt,* August 1, 1902; "A Jewish Protest," *New York Tribune,* August 2, 1902.

13. "Cross Is Cross with the Jews"

1. "Hebrew Vigilants Form a Committee in Self-Defense," *New York Press,* August 1, 1902; "Brooks to Investigate," *New York Tribune,* August 2, 1902.
2. "East Side Wrath Aflame," *New York Sun,* August 1, 1902; "Hebrew Vigilants."
3. "Escaped Puma Captured," *New York Tribune,* July 30, 1902.
4. "Mayor Low and the Police," *New York World,* August 1, 1902; "Commissioner Partridge's Former Right Hand Man Star Victim of a Sensational Shake-Up—McLaughlin and Grant Shifted," *New York World,* August 1, 1902.
5. "Hebrews Given Hearing by Police Officials," *Brooklyn Citizen,* August 1, 1902; "Hebrews Accuse Policemen," *Brooklyn Times Union,* August 1, 1902; "Hebrews Make Formal Charges," *Brooklyn Standard Union,* August 1, 1902.
6. "Hebrews Given Hearing"; "Hebrews Accuse Policemen"; "Hebrews Make Formal Charges."
7. "Hebrews Given Hearing"; "A Jewish Protest," *New York Tribune,* August 2, 1902; "The New Police Captains," *New York Times,* July 1, 1887.
8. "Partridge Rumors Again," *New York Tribune,* July 29, 1902.
9. "Hebrews Given Hearing"; "Jewish Protest"; "New Police Captains."
10. "East Side Jews Lodge Complaints with Colonel Partridge," *New York Sun,* August 1, 1902.
11. "Hebrews Given Hearing"; "Jewish Protest."

12. "Jewish Protest"; "East Side Hebrews Excoriate Police," *New York Herald*, August 2, 1902; "Testimony of Jews Beaten by Police," *New York Tribune*, August 2, 1902.
13. "Police Inspector Cross, Charged with Ordering the Beating of Jews, Hastily Transferred," *New York World*, August 1, 1902; "Jews Tell Their Story," *New York Sun*, August 2, 1902.
14. "Police Denounced by Jews in Mass Meeting," *New York Times*, August 2, 1902.
15. Allen Street was famous for its brothels.
16. "Mass Meeting at Cooper Union," *New York Tribune*, August 2, 1902; "Jews Tell Their Story."
17. "Police Denounced by Jews"; "East Side Hebrews."
18. "Capt. Thompson Retires at His Own Request," *Brooklyn Citizen*, August 2, 1902; "Captain Thompson Out," *New York Tribune*, August 3, 1902; "Riot Inquiry On; Thompson Quits Force," *New York World*, August 2, 1902.

14. "Driving Them like a Lot of Hogs"

1. Edward T. O'Donnell, "Hibernians versus Hebrews? A New Look at the 1902 Jacob Joseph Funeral Riot," *Journal of the Gilded Age and Progressive Era* 6, no. 2 (April 2007): 215–16.
2. "Police Crimes," *Arbeiter Zeitung*, August 2, 1902.
3. "Police Inspector Cross, Charged with Ordering the Beating of Jews, Hastily Transferred," *New York World*, August 1, 1902; "Jews Denounce the Police," *New York Times*, July 31, 1902.
4. "Say Riot Witness' Life Is Threatened," *New York Telegram*, August 2, 1902.
5. "Riot Inquiry On; Thompson Quits Force," *New York World*, August 2, 1902.
6. "Witnesses Fear Wrath of Police," *New York Herald*, August 3, 1902.
7. "Jews Urge Calmness," *New York Times*, August 3, 1902; "East Side Jews Demand Subpoena for John Doe," *Brooklyn Daily Eagle*, August 3, 1902; "Jews Prepare Their Case," *New York Sun*, August 3, 1902.
8. "Witnesses Fear Wrath"; "Calls Coney a Cesspool," *Brooklyn Times Union*, August 4, 1902.
9. "Riot Witness a Fakir," *New York Post*, August 4, 1902.
10. "Heard Roundsman Jackson Shout 'Club the Jews!,'" *New York World*, August 4, 1902.
11. "Evidence against Cross," *New York Tribune*, August 3, 1902.
12. "*The Jewish World* Is Pursuing a Murderous Policeman," *Di Yidishe Velt*, August 1, 1902.
13. "East Side Riot Clubbing Investigation Is Started," *Brooklyn Daily Eagle*, August 4, 1902; "Committee Asks for Riot Investigations," *New York Times*, August 5, 1902; "Heard Roundsman Jackson Shout"; "Jews Appeal Unto Caesar," *New York Sun*, August 5, 1902.
14. "Jews Appeal Unto Caesar."
15. "Grand Jury Will Investigate Riots," *New York World*, August 4, 1902; "Jews Appeal Unto Caesar"; "Police Conduct at a Riot," *New York Post*, July 31, 1902; "New Rabbi Talk Arouses Hebrews," *New York Telegram*, August 5, 1902.
16. "Jews Urge Calmness"; "Grand Jury Will Investigate."
17. "Jews Appeal Unto Caesar"; "Committee Asks."

18. "Jews Offer Reward for Evidence," *New York Tribune*, August 5, 1902; "Jews Appeal Unto Caesar."
19. "Jews Appeal Unto Caesar."

15. "The Well-Considered Opinion of a Committee of Citizens"

1. "Hoe Employees Held," *New York Post*, August 5, 1902.
2. "New Rabbi Talk Arouses Hebrews," *New York Telegram*, August 5, 1902; "Hoe Employees Held."
3. "Tried to Bribe Riot Witness," *New York World*, August 5, 1902.
4. Editorial, *American Israelite*, August 7, 1902.
5. Lucy S. Dawidowicz and Louis Marshall, "Louis Marshall's Yiddish Newspaper, *The Jewish World*: A Study in Contrasts," *Jewish Social Studies* 25, no. 2 (April 1963): 102.
6. "For Hebrew Charities," *New York Tribune*, January 1, 1899; Letter to the Editor, *American Hebrew*, November 1, 1901.
7. "Mayor Low's Committee to Investigate Riots," *Brooklyn Daily Eagle*, August 7, 1902.
8. Marilynn S. Johnson, *Street Justice: A History of Police Violence in New York City* (Boston: Beacon, 2003), 76–77.
9. "Investigating the Riots," *Brooklyn Daily Eagle*, August 8, 1902; "More Riot Witnesses," *New York Post*, August 8, 1902; "Testimony for Jews All In," *New York Tribune*, August 9, 1902.
10. "More Riot Witnesses"; "Six Policemen Are Accused," *New York World*, August 8, 1902.
11. *Richmond Dispatch*, May 1, 1900 (untitled); "Hebrew Notes," *Brooklyn Daily Eagle*, May 6, 1900.
12. "Not Wanted," *Jewish Messenger*, December 21, 1900; "Not Wanted," *Reform Advocate*, January 5, 1901; "The Jewish Regiment," *New York Tribune*, December 22, 1900; "Opposition to Jewish Regiment," *New York Tribune*, December 23, 1900.
13. "A Hebrew Regiment as a Result of Riots," *Brooklyn Daily Eagle*, August 9, 1902.
14. "Religion in the Guard," *New York Tribune*, August 13, 1902.
15. "New York Gossip," *St. Paul Globe*, August 21, 1902.

16. "The Trouble Was All Over When We Got There"

1. "Riot Facts Coming Out," *New York World*, August 11, 1902.
2. "Riot Investigation Is Resumed Today," *Brooklyn Standard Union*, August 12, 1902.
3. "Thompson a Riot Witness," *New York World*, August 12, 1902.
4. "Accused of Blackmail," *Daily People*, August 15, 1902; "The Bluecoats Make a Riot," *Forverts*, August 14, 1902.
5. "Head of Police Compared to Bashi-Bazouks," *New York Herald*, August 14, 1902.
6. "Hebrews Tell Tales of Police Oppression," *Brooklyn Standard Union*, August 14, 1902; "Stories of Clubbing at Riot Hearing," *New York Times*, August 14, 1902.

7. This is a reference to the August 1900 Manhattan race riot that stemmed from an altercation between a Black man and a white undercover policeman. Many Blacks were arrested and severely beaten while in police custody.
8. "Hearing of Jews' Charges," *New York Times*, August 13, 1902.
9. "Accused of Blackmail."
10. "Hebrews Tell Tales"; "Head of Police Compared."
11. "Head of Police Compared"; "Hearing of Jews' Charges."
12. "Head of Police Compared."
13. "Thurston Hits at East Side Hebrews," *New York Herald*, August 15, 1902.

17. "The Attack Was Deliberately Planned"

1. "Editorial Notes," *American Hebrew*, August 15, 1902.
2. "Thurston Hits at East Side Hebrews," *New York Herald*, August 15, 1902.
3. "East Side Riots before Grand Jury," *New York Herald*, August 19, 1902; "Jewish Riot Testimony," *New York Times*, August 19, 1902.
4. "Riot Planned," *Daily People*, August 19, 1902.
5. "Riot Planned."
6. "Hoe Foreman Says Riot Was Planned," *New York World*, August 18, 1902.
7. "Hoe's Men Feared a Raid," *New York Sun*, August 19, 1902; "Riot Indictments Found," *New York Sun*, August 20, 1902.
8. "Hoe Employees Give Testimony," *New York Tribune*, August 19, 1902; "Hoe's Men Feared."
9. "Hoe's Men Feared."
10. "East Side Riots"; "Hoe Employees Give Testimony"; "Jewish Riot Testimony."
11. "Indict Policemen for Funeral Riot," *New York Herald*, August 20, 1902.
12. "Two Policemen Indicted," *Brooklyn Daily Eagle*, August 19, 1902.
13. "Police Indicted," *Daily People*, August 20, 1902.
14. "Indicted Policemen Plead," *New York Post*, August 20, 1902.
15. "Partridge Transfers Alleged Jew Clubbers," *New York World*, August 21, 1902.
16. "Riot Indictments Found."
17. "Policemen Plead Not Guilty," *New York Tribune*, August 21, 1902.

18. "Because We Are Hebrews and the Police Are Irishmen"

1. "Cross Tells of Jew Clubbing," *New York World*, August 25, 1902.
2. "Cross Gives Riot Testimony," *New York Tribune*, August 26, 1902.
3. "East Side Wrath Aflame," *New York Sun*, August 1, 1902; "Hebrew Vigilants Form a Committee in Self-Defense," *New York Post*, August 1, 1902; "Officials Probe East Side Riots," *Syracuse Post-Standard*, August 1, 1902; "Committee Asks for Riot Investigations," *New York Times*, August 5, 1902; "Funeral Riot Result of Plot," *Philadelphia Inquirer*, August 5, 1902.

4. Letter from Abraham H. Sarasohn, Esq., to Police Commissioner John N. Partridge, September 5, 1902, Abraham H. Sarasohn Papers 1902–1943, call no. MS#1109, bib ID 4079299, Butler Library, Columbia University.
5. "Hebrews Tell Low of Police Insults," *New York Herald*, September 8, 1902.
6. "Hebrews Again Accuse Police," *New York Telegram*, September 8, 1902.
7. Editorial, *Jewish Messenger*, September 12, 1902.
8. "Mayor Low Waits for the Report of His Committee," *Forverts*, September 8, 1902.
9. "Our New York Letter," *Jewish Exponent*, September 26, 1902.
10. "Fixes Blame for the Riot," *New York Tribune*, September 16, 1902.
11. "Fixes Blame for the Riot"; "Full Text of the Report," *New York Times*, September 16, 1902.
12. "Comments on the Report," *New York Times*, September 16, 1902.
13. "Comments on the Report."
14. "Report on the Rabbi Joseph Riot," *New York Sun*, September 17, 1902; "Now Push Riot Indictments," *Brooklyn Standard Union*, September 16, 1903.
15. "The East Side Riot," *New York Times*, September 16, 1902.
16. "East Side Riot."
17. "The Police as Protectors," *New York Tribune*, September 17, 1902.
18. "The Report upon the Police," *New York Post*, September 16, 1902.
19. "Will Something Come of This?," *Forverts*, September 16, 1902; "Our New York Letter."

19. "A Direct Snub to the Commissioner"

1. "Mayor Puts Police on Rack of Inquiry," *New York Press*, September 16, 1902.
2. "Low Acts Sharply on Riots," *New York Tribune*, September 18, 1902.
3. "Police Astounded by Mayor's Letter," *New York Times*, September 19, 1902.
4. "Low After Police Clubbers," *New York Sun*, September 18, 1902.
5. "Low's Action Creates Panic in Police," *New York World*, September 18, 1902; "Mayor Opens War on Brutal Police, Partridge May Go," *New York Herald*, September 18, 1902; "Partridge Pensions Sergeant Whose Trial Mayor Ordered," *New York Telegram*, September 18, 1902.
6. "Police Astounded"; "Magistrate's Reply to Mr. Low," *New York Post*, September 23, 1902; "City Magistrates Reply," *New York Times*, October 1, 1902; "Reply to City Magistrates," *New York Times*, November 3, 1902.
7. "Protests Help," *Di Yidishe Velt*, October 1, 1902; "Mayor Low Does What Has to Be Done," *Forverts*, September 18, 1902.
8. "Riot Charges to the Front," *New York World*, September 30, 1902; "Riot Charges Approved," *New York Tribune*, October 1, 1902.
9. "Col. Thurston Resigns," *New York Times*, October 5, 1902; "Peggy Thurston Gets Out," *New York Sun*, October 5, 1902.
10. "Peggy Thurston Gets Out."
11. "Partridge's Man," *Waterbury Democrat*, December 27, 1901.

20. "These People Are Ignorant"

1. "Herlihy's Case Not Dismissed," *New York Telegram*, October 20, 1902; "Cross, On Trial, Says Not Guilty," *New York World*, October 20, 1902; "Inspector Cross on Trial," *New York Post*, October 20, 1902; "Inspector Cross on Trial," *New York Tribune*, October 20, 1902.
2. "Cross, On Trial."
3. "Cross, On Trial"; "Herlihy's Case Not Dismissed"; "Inspector Cross on Trial," *New York Post*; "Inspector Cross on Trial," *New York Tribune*; "Cross Scoffs at Charges," *New York World*, October 21, 1902; "Testimony for Capt. Cross," *New York Times*, October 22, 1902; "Thompson Sorry He Retired," *New York Sun*, October 22, 1902.
4. "Defense for Cross Begins," *New York World*, October 22, 1902.
5. "Captain Price on Riot Tactics," *New York Post*, October 31, 1902.
6. "Price Stirs Cross's Side," *New York World*, October 31, 1902.
7. "Cross Placed on Rack Again," *New York World*, November 28, 1902; "Cross Admits Wrong Report," *New York Press*, November 29, 1902.
8. "I'm Getting Old—Partridge," *New York Tribune*, November 29, 1902.

21. "I Don't Need This Job"

1. "Hoe's Man Not Indicted," *New York World*, October 20, 1902.
2. "Manhattan and Bronx," *Brooklyn Standard Union*, October 25, 1902; "The People vs. Henry Doupe," New York County Court of General Sessions, ACCN 2010-023, case file 39952-1902, Municipal Archives, City of New York; "The People vs. James M. Jackson," New York County Court of General Sessions, ACCN 2010-023, case file 39954-1902, Municipal Archives, City of New York.
3. "No Justice," *Forverts*, October 26, 1902; "Jackson Free!," *Di Yidishe Velt*, October 26, 1902.
4. "Riot Damage Claim Rejected," *New York Times*, December 11, 1902; "Grout Rejects Hoe & Co. Claim," *New York Tribune*, December 11, 1902; "The City," *American Hebrew*, December 12, 1902.
5. "Editorial Notes," *American Hebrew*, December 12, 1902; "Jackson Indictment Dismissed," *Brooklyn Daily Eagle*, December 10, 1902.
6. "Police Commissioner Partridge Resigns," *New York Times*, December 13, 1902.
7. "Police Commissioner Partridge Resigns."
8. "Big Bill Devery Has His Say about Partridge and Then Makes a Few Wise Philosophical Remarks," *New York World*, December 13, 1902.
9. "Accepted By the Mayor," *New York Tribune*, December 14, 1902; "Colonel Partridge Resigns," *New York Tribune*, December 13, 1902.
10. "General Greene in Police Department," *Baltimore American*, December 24, 1902.
11. "Inspector Cross Is Exonerated," *New York World*, December 14, 1902; "Complaints Growing Out of Riot at Funeral of Rabbi Joseph Dismissed by Partridge," *New York Telegram*, December 24, 1902.

12. "Police Crimes," *Arbeiter Zeitung*, August 2, 1902.
13. *The Police Department of the City of New York: A Statement of Facts; Address by Police Commissioner Greene* (New York: City Club of New York, 1903), 402.
14. "The People of the State of New York vs. Emil Adams," New York County Court of General Sessions, ACCN 2010-023, case file 40320-1902, Municipal Archives, City of New York.

22. "I Withdraw the Statements Challenged"

1. Louis Marshall and Charles Reznikoff, *Louis Marshall: Champion of Liberty: Selected Papers and Addresses*, vol. 1 (Philadelphia: Jewish Publication Society of America, 1957), 11–12.
2. Marshall and Reznikoff, *Louis Marshall*, 10–11.
3. Marilynn S. Johnson, *Street Justice: A History of Police Violence in New York City* (Boston: Beacon, 2003), 76–77.
4. Raymond W. Kelly, *The History of the New York City Police Department* (New York: Police Department of the City of New York, 1993).
5. "Rowdies Attack Jews," *New York Times*, June 6, 1904; "'Rainmakers' Attack Inoffensive Hebrews," *Brooklyn Standard Union*, June 6, 1904; "Riot in Jewish Colony," *Brooklyn Times Union*, June 6, 1904; "Rowdies Assault Many Jews," *New York Sun*, June 6, 1904; "Firebugs at Work in Big Tenement," *Brooklyn Standard Union*, July 27, 1903.
6. "English Department," *Yidishes Tageblatt*, January 15, 1905; "Huge Crowd at Funeral," *New York Tribune*, January 14, 1905; "Sarasohn's Funeral," *New York Post*, January 18, 1905; Arthur Aryeh Goren, "Sacred and Secular: The Place of Public Funerals in the Immigrant Life of American Jews," *Jewish History* 8, nos. 1–2 (1994): 276; "Domestic News," *Jewish Outlook*, January 27, 1905.
7. "Hebrew Playwright Dies," *Washington Evening Star*, June 11, 1909; "25,000 Pay Tribute to Jacob Gordin," *Augusta Chronicle*, June 14, 1909; "Thousands Honor Gordin's Memory," *Reform Advocate*, June 19, 1909; "Sholem Aleichem Buried as the East Side Mourns," *New York Sun*, May 16, 1916.
8. As quoted in "Criminals among the Jews," *New York Sun*, August 12, 1908.
9. Theodore A. Bingham, "Foreign Criminals in New York," *North American Review* 188, no. 634 (September 1908): 383, 385.
10. "Jews Confer on Bingham," *New York Tribune*, September 6, 1908; "Only 460 Jews Convicted," *Brooklyn Daily Eagle*, September 6, 1908; "The Jews and Bingham," *Brooklyn Daily Eagle*, September 14, 1908.
11. "Bingham and the Jews," *New York Times*, September 16, 1908; Bingham, "Foreign Criminals," 392–94.
12. "Wrong about Jews," *New York Times*, September 17, 1908.
13. "Rabbi Magnes Satisfied," *New York Times*, September 17, 1908.
14. Allan Tarshish, "The Board of Delegates of American Israelites, 1859–1878," *Publications of the American Jewish Historical Society* 49, no. 1 (September 1959): 16–32; "Personal and General," *Richmond Times Dispatch*, September 11, 1903.

15. Harold Philip Gastwirt, "Fraud, Corruption and Holiness: Kashrut Supervision in New York City, 1881–1940" (PhD diss., Columbia University, 1971), 34.
16. Naomi Cohen, *Not Free to Desist: A History of the American Jewish Committee, 1906–1966* (Melrose Park PA: Jewish Publication Society of America, 1972), 8, 10.
17. "Jews Again Put in Racial Conflict," *Abilene Reporter-News*, July 2, 1958; *New York City*, Jewish Virtual Library, accessed June 3, 2022, https://www.jewishvirtuallibrary.org/new-york-city.
18. "Jews Again"; *New York City*.

FURTHER READING

On Rabbi Jacob Joseph and His Funeral

Adler, Joseph. "The Twilight Years of Rabbi Jacob Joseph." *Jewish Frontier* 67, no. 1 (January–August 2000). https://www.ameinu.net/frontier/jf_1-00_adler.html.

Caplan, Kimmy. "Rabbi Jacob Joseph, New York's Chief Rabbi: New Perspectives." *Hebrew Union College Annual* 67 (1996): 1–43. In Hebrew.

Karp, Abraham J. "New York Chooses a Chief Rabbi." *Publications of the American Jewish Historical Society* 44, no. 3 (March 1955): 129–98.

Levine, Allan. "The Lower East Side Riot." *Tablet* (June 21, 2021). https://www.tabletmag.com/sections/community/articles/lower-east-side-riot.

Levine, Yitzchok. "The Chief Rabbi Encounters Opposition." *Jewish Express*, June 4, 2008, 4–67.

O'Donnell, Edward T. "Hibernians versus Hebrews? A New Look at the 1902 Jacob Joseph Funeral Riot." *Journal of the Gilded Age and Progressive Era* 6, no. 2 (April 2007): 209–25.

On the New York Police Department

Johnson, Marilynn S. *Street Justice: A History of Police Violence in New York City*. Boston: Beacon, 2003.

Lardner, James, and Thomas Reppetto. *NYPD: A City and Its Police*. New York: Henry Holt, 2000.

Richardson, James F. *The New York Police: Colonial Times to 1901*. New York: Oxford University Press, 1970.

Whalen, Bernard, and Jon Whalen. *The NYPD's First Fifty Years: Politicians, Police Commissioners & Patrolmen*. Lincoln NE: Potomac Books, 2014.

On the Lower East Side Jewish Community

Gurock, Jeffrey S. *Orthodox Jews in America*. Bloomington: Indiana University Press, 2009.

Hindus, Milton, ed. *The Jewish East Side, 1881–1924*. New Brunswick NJ: Transaction, 1996.

Moore, Deborah Dash, and Jeffrey S. Gurock. *Jewish New York: The Remarkable Story of a City and a People*. New York: New York University Press, 2020.

Polland, Annie, and Daniel Soyer. *Emerging Metropolis: New York Jews in the Age of Immigration, 1840–1920*. New York: New York University Press, 2012.

Rischin, Moses. *The Promised City: New York's Jews, 1870–1914*. Cambridge MA: Harvard University Press, 1962.

Seligman, Scott D. *The Great Kosher Meat War of 1902: Immigrant Housewives and the Riots That Shook New York City*. Lincoln NE: Potomac Books, 2020.

Weinberger, Moses. *People Walk on Their Heads: Jews and Judaism in New York*. Translated by Jonathan D. Sarna. New York: Holmes and Meier, 1982.

On R. Hoe & Company

Comparato, Frank E. *Chronicles of Genius and Folly: R. Hoe & Company and the Printing Press as a Service to Democracy*. Culver City CA: Labyrinthos, 1979.

On Antisemitism in America

Dinnerstein, Leonard. *Anti-Semitism in America*. New York: Oxford University Press, 1994.

Gerber, David A., ed. *Anti-Semitism in American History*. Urbana: University of Illinois Press, 1986.

On the New York Kehillah

Goren, Arthur A. *New York Jews and the Quest for Community: The Kehillah Experiment, 1908–1922*. New York: Columbia University Press, 1970.

Gurock, Jeffrey S. "Why Albert Lucas Did Not Serve in the New York Kehillah." *Proceedings of the American Academy for Jewish Research* 51 (1984): 55–72.

On American Jewish History

Diner, Hasia R. *A New Promised Land: A History of Jews in America*. New York: Oxford University Press, 2003.

Diner, Hasia R. *The Jews of the United States, 1654 to 2000*. Berkeley: University of California Press, 2002.

Hertzberg, Arthur. *The Jews in America: Four Centuries of an Uneasy Encounter; A History*. New York: Simon & Schuster, 1989.

Raphael, Marc Lee. *Judaism in America*. New York: Columbia University Press, 2003.

Sarna, Jonathan. *American Judaism: A History*. New Haven CT: Yale University Press, 2004.

INDEX

Page numbers in *italics* refer to figures.